THE EDIBLE
INDOOR
GARDEN

the edible indoor garden

A COMPLETE GUIDE TO GROWING OVER 60 VEGETABLES, FRUITS, AND HERBS INDOORS

PEGGY HARDIGREE

DRAWINGS BY PEGGY ELLEN REED

ST. MARTIN'S PRESS   NEW YORK

Library of Congress Cataloging in Publication Data

Hardigree, Peggy Ann, 1945-
    The edible indoor garden.

    1. Vegetable gardening. 2. Fruit-culture.
3. Indoor gardening. I. Title.
SB324.5.H37   635   80-21657
ISBN 0-312-23689-1
ISBN 0-312-23690-5 (pbk.)

Design by Mina Greenstein

Contents

Introduction

Snow is falling outside my window as I write this—the very first snowfall of the year—and for most of my friends and acquaintances, the gardening season has long been over. But for myself and many others like me, the gardening season is never over—it just becomes more rewarding when snow blankets the fields where others grew their summer crops.

Lettuce and mustard fill a window box behind me, reminding me that sometime this week they are to be cut and used in a salad, probably in combination with the leeks, green onions, and garlic growing elsewhere in the apartment. The cucumber vines are setting their first fruit, the cherry tomato vines are bright with blossoms, and the eggplant is well on its way to maturity. The citrus crop looks promising this year, but I am beginning to wish I had set aside more space for strawberries—they are especially good when the bite of winter is in the air.

Many people are surprised by the suggestion that such plants can grow to maturity indoors. Probably their surprise would be even greater if they were told that there is nothing new about the idea—people have been growing food indoors for many centuries. Only the technology has changed, making this indoor gardening far easier than ever before.

Engravings on Egyptian tombs indicate that the pharaohs attempted to grow citrus and other fruits in their indoor gardens. The degree of their success is not known, but others took up the effort and established that it could be done. Foremost among these was the Roman emperor Tiberius, who reigned from 14 to 37 A.D.

Tiberius, pretty much like myself, had a passion for cucumbers—in or out of season. How to satisfy this passion was a problem he placed in the hands—or perhaps on the heads—of his gardeners. The gardeners solved the problem by setting the young cucumber plants in beds of manure covered with sheets of mica cut so thin that sunlight could penetrate. How they solved the problem of pollination at a time when the need for it was not even suspected is a good question, but solve it they did, and Tiberius had his cucumbers throughout the long Roman winters.

Other horticulturists soon improved on this technique. They built what they called *specularia,* small sheds with roofs made of mica and equipped with ducts to carry heated air or water for temperature control. In them they grew not only cucumbers but also grapes, peaches, roses, and numerous other ornamental plants.

The fall of the Roman Empire saw a subsequent decline in horticulture. Yet potted herbs and fruits played important roles in many a medieval monastery. This was not indoor gardening in the strictest meaning of the term, for the plants were frequently given an early start indoors and then moved to the outdoor garden as the weather grew warm—container gardening. A few herbs, however, were grown indoors, providing seasoning for winter meals as well as plant materials for mystic rites.

The Italian Renaissance brought about a real revival of the ancient skills that had been lost with the decline of Rome. The first recorded account of the revival appears in the tales of the great entertainments held in 1295 in the heated garden of Albert Magnus, a leading citizen of the time.

By the seventeenth century growing orange trees had become the fashion, in structures called orangeries that were set up to protect them from the frost. Early in that century Solomon the Caus invented a system of shutters that were placed over and around 340 orange trees in the municipal garden of Heidelberg each fall, then removed in the spring. English gardeners quickly improved on this method. At Beddington, where the first orange trees in England were grown, an amateur horticulturist named John Evelyn added a heating system and called his structure a greenhouse—the first known use of the word.

Orangeries proliferated among the landed gentry of England. But it was at the magnificent palace of Versailles that gardening in orangeries reached its peak. The palace was heated by sunlight coming through enormously tall windows with a southern exposure. The main section of the orangerie built there was 508 feet long, 42 feet wide, and 45 feet high. The royal gardener, one M. LaQuintinya, later added stoves for additional heat during the colder months—and from this vast garden he provided ripe cherries and figs for the royal table in winter.

The fumes from the stoves that heated those early greenhouses killed many plants. But early in the eighteenth century, horticulturists returned to the old Roman method of heating with flues through which hot air flowed. The orangerie was now truly a greenhouse, and many more foods could be enjoyed throughout the winter months. By 1714 George I, then the King of England, was able—like Tiberius who started it all—to satisfy a craving for cucumbers at Christmastime.

Glass was the real key to it all, at least in those days. By the middle of the nineteenth century, when glass became commonly available to the wealthy, a real madness for greenhouse gardening took hold. The aristocracy undertook breathtaking ventures such as the glass house built for the duke of Devonshire, which was so large that a carriage pulled by a team of horses could tour it.

By this time most of the techniques for successful greenhouse gardening had been worked out, but the costs of construction and maintenance were such that greenhouses remained luxuries for the elite. However, the elite were not the only ones interested in having out-of-season fruits and vegetables.

The common people in Europe had always wintered a few perennials indoors, returning them to the outdoor garden with the advent of spring. Just about every gardener kept a few plants in the house during forbidding weather. As the miracle called glass became available to the average family, beautiful and useful greenery began to appear in at least one window in nearly every home.

Indoor gardening moved a stride closer to the present during the Victorian era, a time of parlor windows bright with sun and filled with terra-cotta pots holding herbs, geraniums, and perhaps a few tomato plants vining out toward the early spring sunshine.

Then came Edison's invention of the electric lightbulb. Scientists and amateurs alike began to experiment with this new means of providing illumination for indoor plants, but without a great deal of success, because these bulbs alone did not provide the quality of light needed for plant development. However, by 1921 one scientist had succeeded in bringing squash plants to the blossom stage using only incandescent light—an amazing achievement considering what we now know about the light requirements of such plants.

That same year two scientists with the United States Department of Agriculture, Allard and Garner, while working with a species of tobacco, established the existence of the phenomenon of *photoperiodism* in plants. For the first time scientists realized that plants not only require light of sufficient intensity, but that if they are to produce blossoms, fruit, and seed, they need that light for a certain number of hours each day. Horticulturists then divided plants into groups known as long-day and short-day plants. We know a great deal more about photoperiodism at the present, but it still is not entirely understood and remains one of the most puzzling aspects of plant growth.

With the invention of fluorescent lights in the 1930s, indoor gardening was truly on its way to new heights. While scientists were using these tubes to study the effects of light on various plants, amateur gardeners had already discovered that many favorite plants absolutely flourished beneath them. A few plants began to appear in offices and business places, where fluorescent lighting was most commonly seen in the early days of its existence.

The introduction of fluorescent lighting and its sudden popularity among indoor gardeners set off a great search by the seed and plant companies for more plants that could be grown in the cool light of these tubes. Thousands and thousands of plants were made available, most of them exotics from jungle floors in the tropics and subtropics, with relatively low light requirements. Most of these were purely ornamental plants, but a few among them were edible or capable of producing edible fruits and berries.

Plant lovers placed these alongside plants they had discovered for themselves—beside the chives and parsley, next to a tiny pot of radishes, or close up against the creeping fig that they had found capable of producing tiny fruit indoors. Ornamental plants were the ones most popular for growing beneath these lights, but more and more kitchens became fragrant with herbs. Those with a patch of garden used the lights to start seedlings and extend the growing season, but there were also those eccentric souls who insisted on growing lettuce and other salad greens to maturity inside the home, often in the dead of winter. A few were even playing at being royalty, attempting to grow cucumbers and similar crops long after the season was over.

Many of these gardeners were successful—or unsuccessful—without knowing why. They knew only that some plants thrived under artificial lights or in a sunny window, while others wilted and died. They had no real understanding of why a plant might produce only foliage year after year and then, for no obvious reason, burst into bloom and bear fruit; or why a neighbor had a coffee tree that produced coffee while their own apparently healthier tree produced none. They knew almost nothing about the type or amount of light needed by plants.

Without having it explained to them, a few of the more successful gardeners found that some plants did better when they received light from a mixture of incandescent bulbs and fluorescent tubes, but it is likely that not one in a thousand could have told you that this was because such a mixture provided light energy from the right parts of the spectrum. Scientists were just learning that.

By the early 1950s scientists were conducting studies of the effects of light on plant growth in complex light chambers known as phytotrons—a name coined by plant scientist F. W. Went because he felt the complexity of the first such structure was similar to that of a large cyclotron or synchrotron.

The first phytotron was built at the once-famous Earhart Research Laboratory at the California Institute of Technology in Pasadena. It remained in operation until 1968 and served as a model for at least a dozen phytotrons that are now in use at universities and research laboratories in this country and around the world.

In this phytotron the environment was so carefully controlled that every person entering was required to wear special clothing. Everything entering the building was decontaminated. Even the air was filtered through special ducts as it entered.

Light was provided by row upon row of fluorescent tubes, reaching intensities equal to the brightest sunlight. Even at floor level several thousand foot-candles of light could be provided for plants growing in scientifically prepared soils or other mediums. That each plant would receive equal lighting was assured by the use of plant tables that slowly rotated.

Under such conditions scientists have been able to solve many—but not all—of the mysteries of plant growth. Much of what they have learned has been reported in the scientific and popular literature, but in the latter a great deal of the reporting has been inaccurate, especially that dealing with the effects of various types of lighting.

One writer after another has dismissed the light provided by incandescent bulbs as useless, or nearly so, in providing illumination for plant growth. This is far from the case. Each type of light has value, and the development of special plant growth lamps could be fairly described as an attempt to bring together that which is best in each of these two basic types of lighting.

Fluorescent plant growth lamps, which first appeared late in the 1950s, became available at a time when the public was eager to receive them. By providing a type of light that was workable for many purposes, they touched off the greatest craze for indoor gardening in history, along with a flood of books on gardening under lights.

As each new plant growth lamp appeared on the market, someone, somewhere touted it as the absolute solution to every light problem the gardener might encounter. Seldom were these exaggerated claims made by the manufacturers, who knew better, but more often by someone with a book to sell.

Most of these books have been devoted to growing ornamental plants with relatively low light requirements. Disappointment came when the growers experimented with more difficult plants.

The truth is that no artificial light is perfect. Some are better than others, but for growing plants no artificial light is as effective as sunlight. Success comes to those who recognize this and act accordingly by making the wisest use of every resource that is available, natural as well as artificial.

Now, both the artificial and natural resources are more available than at any time in history. Glass windows, once reserved for the wealthy, are now so common that we seldom give them a thought, and they provide the average home or apartment with brightness that would have been envied by royal gardeners of the past. And as the energy crisis worsens, even more glass is being incorporated into new homes and apartments.

Even greenhouses, which first made it possible to grow plants out of season, have undergone a remarkable transformation. Once costly beyond imagination, greenhouses are now available prefabricated, in all sizes—some are so small they can be fitted to an apartment window and tended from inside the home. Most are within the financial reach of the average person, or you can build your own at very low cost from simple plans that I have included in this book. Inexpensive prefabricated skylights offer another way to take full advantage of the sunlight that is available free to everyone.

Despite the urbanization of our society, nearly every home or apartment has at least some outdoor space available. It may be a patch of lawn, a patio, a balcony or a porch, or it may be only a few outer window ledges. The wise use of such space allows the apartment gardener to combine artificial and natural light in ways that make it possible to grow a surprising number of attractive and delicious food plants—which is what this book is all about.

Such outdoor spaces allow you to grow many plants that are not really suited for growing inside your apartment. And the wise use of artificial light vastly increases the number of outdoor plants that you can grow.

A major use for artificial light is to extend the seasons. Outdoor gardeners have commonly gotten a jump on the seasons by starting seedlings indoors, then transplanting them outside after the danger of frost is past. By using portable containers that allow you to move the plants, you can extend the season at both ends, starting plants inside before spring arrives, letting them flourish during the summer in a sunny outside area, and then placing them under indoor lights for continued production during autumn and on into the winter. The combination of natural and artificial light allows you to grow plants that require a longer growing season than is available under natural conditions. Given a healthy start in this fashion, many food plants can be made to produce almost indefinitely.

People often overlook the fact that many of our most desirable food plants are grown as annuals only because they are so easily killed by frost. For example, the eggplant is extremely difficult to grow to maturity in the outdoor gardens of our northern states, where seasons are short; and even in more moderate areas it is treated as an annual because it is so easily killed by frost. Yet eggplant is not an annual at all. If it is moved inside when the weather grows cold—or if it is grown indoors, which is relatively easy to do—this beautiful plant can live and produce for years.

A second major use for artificial light is to extend day length. No matter how bright your brightest window, the sunlight there is not likely to last long enough to allow you to grow all the plants you want to grow. Even commercial growers who use greenhouses find it necessary to extend the day length by using artificial lighting, especially during the winter when days are short. No matter how much natural sunlight you are normally able to provide your indoor plants, there will be cloudy days and other periods when you will want to use artificial light.

Artificial light is also used to increase the intensity of available sunlight. Because most natural light enters the home at an angle, it frequently fails to provide the brightness plants need for the processes of growth. By forming a partnership between artificial and natural light, you can control both the intensity and the duration of the light energy received by your plants.

And artificial light can be used alone. Even if your house or apartment has absolutely no direct sunlight available—which is seldom the case—you can use artificial light to grow an amazing variety of plants that are both decorative and delicious, fragrant as well as fun to grow. As a matter of fact, it is entirely possible to grow any plant to maturity using only artificial light.

A very large number of food plants are quite easy to grow using only artificial light. Many are only slightly more difficult. But a small number of plants are so demanding in their requirements that you would not want to grow them entirely under artificial lights, and it is with these plants that you will want to utilize all the other resources available to you.

Where space is limited, you might want to add hydroponic gardening to these resources. This method of growing plants without soil has been used for centuries. In the last year, however, hydroponic gardening kits have become available at relatively low cost, and they open new vistas for the apartment gardener. This method encourages top growth while allowing only very limited root growth, so space that was once needed for soil is no longer a requirement, and many more varieties become viable as indoor, greenhouse, or patio plants. Plants with sprawling root structures, such as watermelon, require so much space when they are grown by ordinary methods that growing them in limited space has always been out of the question. Hydroponic gardening allows you to use your space for plants instead of soil.

New plant varieties are another resource you will want to utilize. Almost any fruit tree can be had in dwarf form these days, and some of these can be grown with relative ease under artificial light alone, while almost all of them can be grown by using the combination of resources I have mentioned. In addition to the standard-size vegetables you will probably want to grow, you might also wish to delight your guests with midget carrots the size of your little finger, head lettuce the size of tennis balls (used for individual salads at the Waldorf-Astoria Hotel), tomatoes no larger than marbles, or even cantaloupe only a few inches in diameter. For beauty as well as utility, your garden might include brightly flowering kale or the magnificently beautiful flowering plants that produce okra or passion fruit.

Knowledge is the most important single resource available to you. Even though people have been tending plants for thousands of years, they have been doing so with very little understanding of how plants grow. Today, while many of the processes of plant growth are far from understood, we do know a great deal more about them, and this knowledge is the key that unlocks the door to successful gardening.

The knowledge is there, but it is difficult to come by. Since the appearance of fluorescent lighting in the home touched off the great wave of books on indoor-light gardening, most of the literature has been devoted to growing ornamental plants. Many authors have mentioned a few food-producing plants that can be grown in windows or under artificial light. The plants they mention are almost always the same: radishes, leaf lettuce, cherry tomatoes, and, almost without fail, chives and parsley. Most of the books give not even the slightest hint of how these can be grown.

There are simple reasons why this is so. Because growing food plants to maturity is not often profitable in a greenhouse or under artificial light, commercial growers and plant scientists have not directed the bulk of their research toward that goal. Most of the research has been devoted to the more profitable growing of seedlings and ornamentals—which means that information on bringing food plants to maturity under these conditions has not been so readily available. This applies not only to the plants' lighting needs, but also to such matters as pollination and nutrition. It may also be that these writers have overlooked the fact that many of the plants which produce our food are among the most attractive.

In providing this information and attempting to fill what I believe to be a gaping void in gardening literature, I have relied on the latest scientific data and on help from leading plant scientists, photobiologists, and other researchers and growers, as well as from leading manufacturers in the field of lighting. I have balanced this with my own knowledge of plants and gardening, and because of that, the ultimate responsibility for the information in this book must be my own.

As I have said, some plants are more difficult to grow than others. Some will thrive under almost any conditions; others are very exacting in their needs. In selecting plants for inclusion in this book, I have chosen some plants that can almost always be grown without failure, some that are moderately demanding in their needs, and a few that will require all your resources and gardening skills as well as a great deal of care and attention. All, however, can be grown indoors.

How much food will you be able to grow? That depends on how much space you have as well as on what facilities you are willing and able to provide, and it depends on how much care and attention you give your plants. With careful planning and equally careful plant selection, an amazing amount of food can be grown in and around the tiniest apartment—but food production for its own sake should not be the only goal in this kind of gardening.

Like Tiberius and George I, you can have cucumbers in the middle of winter; or like the royal family of France, you can snack on fruit fresh from your own trees; but it is not likely that you will meet all the food requirements of your family, greatly reduce your food budget, or even quickly recover the cost of your gardening equipment. Then why do it?

Because, as every gardener before and since the days of Tiberius has known, there is a great reward in planting a seed or cutting and watching it sprout from the earth, send forth its leaves, its blossoms, and finally, its fruit. There is something joyous about a partnership with Mother Nature, in assisting her with the nurture of her children—and no fruit or vegetable tastes quite like those you grow yourself.

Especially in the month of December.

the basics of apartment gardening

This book is about plants in the house, not about houseplants—and there is a very real difference. Even though many of the plants that I describe in this book are as beautiful as any of the tropical plants commonly described in other gardening books, the home grower must recognize that the popular ornamental plants are generally better suited for growing in an artificial environment. As a matter of fact, many of the ornamentals are so popular *only* because they are so easy to grow.

While the average indoor environment provides many of the conditions needed for good plant growth, it also differs in many ways from the plants' native habitat in the outdoors. Few living rooms have the tropical climate in which pineapples thrive, the intense light most citrus trees need, or the high humidity most other plants need.

Plants in the house must tolerate the conditions you provide, which often means relatively constant temperatures, low humidity, light that comes from only one direction and is generally less intense than sunlight in the garden, and soil in which the amount of moisture and nutrients almost always fluctuates. No gardener truly grows a plant—the plants grow themselves, making the best of what is provided. This means it is your responsibility as the gardener to provide conditions—miniclimates—in which the plants can flourish.

The text in this part of the book is intended to help you do just that. Please read each chapter carefully, for each is critical to success. While paying careful attention to the lighting needs of indoor plants—because light is the most obvious element that must be artificially provided—it is all too easy to overlook the fact that proper soil, feeding, and watering are equally important. At least as many plant failures are caused by inattention to these factors as by inadequate light.

The information on pollination is essential if you wish to grow some, but not all, of the fruiting plants, and the chapter on natural sunlight will help you make the most of the free energy that is already available. The chapter on hydroponic gardening will be of special interest to those with limited space. In short, this part of the book provides the information you will need to follow the gardening techniques described later in the book.

1. The Facts of Light

Before even attempting to grow any plant under artificial light, it is absolutely essential that you have a basic understanding of light itself and how it affects plant growth. You need not become fluent in the language of the photobiologist, but there are certain facts and terms with which you should become familiar in order to provide a situation in which your plants will flourish.

Light is radiant energy. To be a little more technical about it, light is the visible part of the electromagnetic wavelength spectrum. This spectrum is composed of rays that vary in length and frequency. In addition to visible light, the spectrum includes invisible solar radiations such as X-rays and short waves.

As you were taught in school, visible "white" sunlight is really a blend of red, orange, yellow, green, blue, and violet rays—the rainbow hues that you see when light beams through a glass prism. At one end of the spectrum, just beyond the visible blue and violet rays, are invisible rays of ultraviolet; at the other end of the spectrum, invisible infrared or far-red rays lie just beyond the visible red rays. The various colored rays, which, in combination, form white light have differing effects on plant growth. Let's look at the known effects of each.

ULTRAVIOLET RAYS

These rays appear as black in the spectrum and are therefore invisible. The human eye perceives them only on fluorescent materials. Only part of this range—known as near ultraviolet—penetrates our atmosphere from the sun. These rays have generally been considered harmful to all organic life, including plants, and they are not known to play a critical role in any of the processes of plant growth.

BLUE LIGHT

Scientists know that the light rays in this part of the spectrum are critically important to *photosynthesis*—which, simply put, is the means by which plants convert light into food for their own use—and that these rays induce phototropism, which is the natural tendency of plants to grow toward the source of light. Scientists also suspect that, under certain conditions, blue light rays may assume the functions of other parts of the spectrum, especially those ordinarily performed by light in the red range. Little is known about the effects of blue light, but it plays a vital role in plant growth, and that is the most important thing one needs to know about it.

GREEN AND YELLOW-ORANGE LIGHT

Rays from the yellow and orange part of the spectrum are generally regarded as neutral, that is, as playing no major role in the important processes of plant growth. Since the chlorophyl in leaves, due to its own greenness, filters out the green light from the sun, this color too is considered unessential to plant growth—though many scientists are coming to believe that these parts of the spectrum may serve as much-needed supplements to the others.

RED AND FAR-RED LIGHT

In the various light chambers at research centers around the country, light from this part of the spectrum has been receiving the greatest amount of attention. This is where the most significant discoveries have been made regarding the effects of specific parts of the spectrum on plant growth and flowering.

While red light is within the visible part of the spectrum, far-red light is only partially visible. One major effect of this kind of light is on a plant pigment known as phytochrome. This pigment acts as an enzyme that triggers growth changes in plants, and it occurs in two forms. The enzyme reacts to red light by triggering growth; it responds to far-red light by causing growth to cease. In ways that are far from understood, the two kinds of light and the two forms of enzyme work together to control the growth habits of individual plants.

When scientists at the United States Department of Agriculture's research center at Beltsville, Maryland, isolated the phytochrome pigment a few years ago and made public their discoveries about its interaction with red and far-red light rays, this triggered a great rush by the lighting industry toward the development of light sources that provided higher and higher emissions in the red and far-red part of the spectrum. As each new tube or bulb was introduced, the public was confronted with new claims of superiority, especially with regard to the effects of that bulb on flowering. A proper amount of red and far-red light is desirable for plant growth and flowering, but one should not take manufacturers' claims too seriously without considering this excerpt from a letter written to me by R. J. Downs, Director of the Phytotron at the Southeastern Plant Environment Laboratory of North Carolina State University:

> Use of red and far-red is not recommended because the response is difficult to predict. For example, using far-red to extend the day and get day-lengths long enough to induce long-day plants to flower will, in some cases, fail to provide the long-day effect and the plants will not flower. Other long-day species will flower more slowly in long days obtained with red light than they will under ordinary unfiltered incandescent light. I know this sounds contrary to what you've read about red and far-red light. . .

It was contrary to what I had read in the popular books on indoor gardening, but it is a statement that is strongly supported by the most recent scientific material.

Remember, always, that the color of the tube or bulb has little to do with the parts of the spectrum in the light it emits. Probably you have seen those red-coated incandescent bulbs that appear to give off a very dark red light. Actually there is very little of this light being emitted. Likewise, a fluorescent tube that appears to be white is probably emitting light that contains a great deal of blue and a lesser amount of red. Light becomes visible only when it strikes an object, making it very difficult for the human eye to measure its intensity or judge what parts of the spectrum are being emitted. For that reason you need to know not only how to provide the parts of the spectrum that are needed for good plant growth, but also how intense the light must be and how that intensity is measured.

Measurement of Light

Plant scientists use several expensive and complicated devices for measuring light. These devices reveal not only how much light reaches a plant, but also how much of the light comes from each part of the spectrum, allowing them to study more closely the effects of each type of light. Such devices, however, are not only too expensive for the home gardener but are not really needed, for even if you know the spectral composition of your lighting, there is very little you can do to alter it.

Manufacturers, in their catalogs, list the output of their lamps in *lumens,* a term of measurement which allows one to compare the relative "strength" of two lamps; but this is an altogether unsatisfactory measurement for practical purposes. It is a way of measuring the amount of light at its source, which will certainly be quite different from the amount of light striking an object some distance away. You are interested only in how much light actually reaches the plants you are growing—and for that purpose the foot-candle measurement is the only practical one.

The foot-candle measurement is archaic, and far less than perfect, but it is the only way we have of measuring and describing the amount of light that reaches a given surface. Your light source emits so many lumens. Your plant receives so many foot-candles.

One foot-candle of light is the amount of light produced in a totally dark space by one candle shining on a white surface that is one square foot in size, one foot from the candle. As the distance between candle and surface increases, the light received by the surface decreases. This obviously means that in order to determine how far away from the light source your plants may be, you must have an accurate way of measuring light in foot-candles.

Several companies manufacture light meters specifically designed for this purpose. Most cost about twenty-five dollars, and they can be found at lighting-appliance stores, large gardening centers, and some camera shops. To use one, hold the meter parallel to the surface you are measuring for light, throw a switch, and the needle on the meter tells you how many foot-candles of light are present.

You can also use a camera with a light meter for this purpose. The procedure sounds complicated but is really quite easy. To start, set the film-speed dial to ASA 25 and the shutter speed to 1/60 of a second. Put a sheet of opaque white paper where the plant will stand. Aim the camera at the paper, making sure that the camera is no further from the paper than the paper's narrowest dimension. (If, for example, the paper measures 15 inches by 20 inches, the camera should be no further from the paper than 15 inches.) Adjust the f-stop until the meter indicates the correct exposure. If the f-stop is f/2, the illumination is about 100 foot-candles; f/2.8 is about 200 foot-candles; f/4 is about 375 foot-candles; f/5.6 is about 750, and f/8 reveals about 1500 foot-candles of illumination.

Remember that these meters measure only visible light, and that some of the light produced by the special plant growth lights is in the far-red range and thus invisible to the meter as well as to the human eye. When you are measuring the light from these bulbs or tubes, increasing the reading by 25 percent will provide you with a fairly accurate measurement, though it will not be—and does not really need to be—exact.

As I have mentioned, the human eye is a very poor judge of the intensity of light, and for that reason it is a good idea to use one of the instruments I just described for measuring light. But if such an instrument is unavailable, there are a few common situations that may help you arrive at an approximation of how much light your plants are receiving. Remember that these figures are for comparison only, and trying to calculate the intensity of your own light this way is far less desirable than using a light meter.

Try holding a plant about 3 inches below a single white 40-watt fluorescent tube of the type commonly found in bathrooms and kitchens. Remember that the amount of light such a tube emits will vary according to its manufacturer, its shielding, and most of all, its age. But you are probably looking at about 450 to 550 foot-candles of light.

Try placing the plant the same distance below the center of a two-tube 40-watt fluorescent fixture of the type commonly suspended from ceilings or used for growing houseplants. The light now striking the plant should be in the area of 1000 foot-candles of light—once again depending on the age, shielding, and manufacturer of the tubes. In the discussion of natural sunlight, you will find more examples that may help you visually calculate the intensity of light.

Light Sources and the Quality of Light

In seeking to provide artificial light for plants, you must not only concern yourself with providing light that is intense enough to support the processes of growth, but also with providing light of the right kind. This means giving plants light with the best spectral quality possible. While it is not possible to provide all the qualities of natural sunlight, using the lights that are now available from manufacturers—mainly because scientists do not fully understand how each plant utilizes what parts of the spectrum for which purposes—it is possible to give plants light under which they will grow quite well.

Plants make the best of what they have. This can often be observed in nature. On a woodland floor, for example, you may often come across plants that ordinarily grow only in the brightest situations.

These plants may not be as lush as their relatives in the open fields, but they will be making the best of what they have—which is precisely what the home gardener must do.

These are the light sources that are available:

FLUORESCENT LIGHTS

These are the lights indoor gardeners most commonly use. Each fluorescent lamp is a glass tube or bulb coated on the inside by fluorescent material called *phosphor.* Sealed within the tube are a gas—argon or argon mixed with neon—and a small amount of mercury, which vaporizes during operation. Extending from the seals at each end of the tube are single or double pins, which serve as electrical contacts.

The phosphors within the tube can be any of a number of chemicals. When it is properly excited by radiant energy, each phosphor will glow with a specific color. The phosphors produce the light; by careful selection of the right mix of phosphors, lighting scientists and engineers can control which parts of the spectrum the light will contain.

Fluorescent tubes have two advantages that have made them popular not only for home gardening but also for residential and commercial lighting. They are extremely efficient at converting electricity into light, and they do it while producing only very small amounts of heat. This last feature makes them extremely attractive to home gardeners, where placing the plants as close to the light as possible is frequently a necessity.

Standard tube lengths are 24-inch, 48-inch, 72-inch, and 96-inch, with those of less than 48 inches commonly using 40 watts of electricity and requiring no special fixtures, while the longer lengths need special fixtures and use 75, 110 or even 215 watts of electricity. In tubes 48 inches or longer, one can also obtain very high and superhigh output tubes, which produce light that is almost blinding in its intensity and which can be very useful to obtain a greater distance between lamp and plant.

Shorter lengths fluorescents—usually about 24 inches—are new on the market. They come with tube and fixture in a single unit. With these, one simply mounts the single fluorescent tube where it is wanted—a job requiring just seconds—and plugs it in. The tubes have a life expectancy of five to seven years, at the end of which the entire unit is discarded. The output of a single tube is too low to be of much real use in growing plants, but these can be extremely useful when several are banked side by side, as in a cabinet, or when a small supplement is needed to other lighting. These tubes are made by Sylvania and General Electric, who market them as Sun Sticks, Sun Stix, and Gro-Sticks.

Fluorescent tubes produce almost no light over an area of about 3 inches at each end of the tube, a fact you should keep in mind when buying fixtures and tubes. In a 24-inch tube this means that about 6 inches of it—or 25 percent of the surface area—is virtually useless. In a 72-inch tube the unlighted area remains at 6 inches, or roughly 8 percent of the tube's length. This means that if you want to spread light over a greater area, one long tube generally serves better than two tubes of half the length.

Manufacturers label fluorescent lamps according to color designations. These designations have little relation to true color but are simply a convenient way of telling them apart. As taken from the manufacturers' catalogs, these designations are: White, Sign White, Cool White, Deluxe Cool White, Soft White, Natural, Daylight, Warm White, and Deluxe Warm White. The term "Deluxe" means that the phosphors of the tube include a special fluorescent chemical emitting more light from the red part of the spectrum.

Cool White quickly became the standard for indoor light gardening, though many early growers preferred a mix of light such as one Cool White tube and one Natural or Daylight tube, which, as you will see, was a step in the right direction. However, while the white fluorescent tubes produce light that is adequate for some of the growth processes, they are weak in the red and far-red parts of the spectrum and do not provide the ideal spectral mix found in natural sunlight.

Early light gardeners and researchers attempted to correct this deficiency by providing supplemental light from incandescent bulbs, which do emit higher amounts of red and far-red light. The usual mix was 80 percent fluorescent to 20 percent incandescent lighting. The mixture solved some growing problems but it also created others. Most of the problems were caused by the heat given off by the incandescent bulbs, but others were due to too much far-red light, the effects of which were only slightly understood at the time and which, as scientist Downs has stated, remain highly unpredictable.

To avoid the problems caused by these incandescent bulbs, manufacturers tried to develop alternative fluorescent lamps with emissions higher in the blue, red, and far-red parts of the spectrum. As you may recall, the first growth lamps were vivid purple, with very little output of green, yellow, or orange light. They provided plenty of blue light, with some red and far-red added, but the mix was far less than perfect. These lamps have been improved somewhat over the years, but their emission of red light remains low, and their far-red emissions still leave much to be desired.

The fluorescent tubes, then, are quite adequate for growing many plants. Most plants can be brought to maturity using no other source. But all fluorescents, including the special plant growth lights, lack the ideal mixture of red, blue, green, yellow, and far-red light that is needed for optimum results. That is why growth will always be better if fluorescents are used in combination with natural sunlight, which does provide the ideal spectral makeup.

INCANDESCENT LIGHTS

Incandescent bulbs are the most common light source in the home. Most common of all is the type which produces radiant energy by heating a tungsten filament, and which is screwed into a socket by means of a thread at its base.

Incandescent bulbs do a very poor job of converting electricity into radiant energy, or light. About 85 percent of the energy becomes heat, while only about 15 percent becomes the radiant energy needed for plant growth. Because of the amount of heat given off by the bulbs, ordinary incandescents are not as widely used in light gardening now as they were in earlier days. However, there are times when raising the temperature around a plant may be highly desirable, and incandescent lighting offers a fairly convenient way of doing this.

Even unwanted heat need not pose a problem. On the market now are several types of incandescent plant lights which reflect the heat back toward the socket and thus away from the direction taken by the light. These are generally available only in the sizes using higher energy—150 watts of electricity or more—and are designed for use in porcelain sockets, which can tolerate the heat being directed back from the bulb.

If you want to raise the temperature slightly around a plant, it is better to use several low-wattage incandescents than a single bulb of higher wattage. The former will distribute heat and light more evenly, while a single large bulb may burn the plant. Since these bulbs will fit all your standard lamps and sockets such arrangements are fairly easy to achieve.

Incandescent bulbs produce what scientists call a point source of light—a beam of light which is relatively narrow but which can easily be aimed in the desired direction. It is also a diffuse light, quickly losing its effectiveness over a distance.

Ordinary incandescent bulbs produce light that is noticeably lacking in the blue and green parts of the spectrum, which are critically important to plant growth. Much of the light produced is yellow to yellow-orange, the value of which is unknown. But as I have previously noted, their emissions are extremely high in red and far-red, and it is the valuable red light that makes them useful as a supplement to fluorescent lighting, while the unpredictable far-red can cause problems.

But those are the ordinary incandescent lamps. The incandescent growth lamps not only reflect heat away from your plants, but also use special filters that cause them to transmit light in the blue and green range as well as in the red. The filter also reduces the amount of far-red emissions. They are available in low or high wattage, with the higher wattage bulbs, of course, producing more light, and all major manufacturers supply special fixtures for using them.

Two types of incandescent bulbs designed for commercial use may be of interest for certain situations. These are the reflector and parabolic reflector lamps, which are generally used as outside spotlights and floodlights. Since they require special fixtures and, in some instances, special wiring, they must always be installed by an electrician. The first type uses a dichroic filter lens that causes it to transmit in the blue, green, and red parts of the spectrum, while the second uses both a filter and a reflector to achieve the same result. These are expensive and tremendously powerful lamps, typically using 650 or more watts of electricity, but they provide light of fair quality, and a single lamp may provide enough to illuminate an entire shrub or small tree.

MERCURY LAMPS

Like incandescent reflector lamps, mercury lamps—or mercury vapor lamps, as they are also known—are intended for commercial and industrial use and require special installation for home use. However, they have shown fair results in experiments by plant scientists, and the indoor gardener who is remodeling or adding a room may decide they are worth the expense. Leading manufacturers may also be about to introduce mercury lamps requiring no special installation.

Light from a mercury lamp is produced by an electric current passing through mercury vapor. The type of light can be changed by changing the pressure placed on the mercury in the bulb. Generally, the pressure is very high, applied inside a bulb of double glass that also holds the cathodes that emit the electrons which excite the mercury and create light.

Mercury lamps are available in size ranging as high as 1500 watts. They come with or without reflectors. All require ballasts and other special components that must be precisely matched to the type of lamp to be used.

Although these lamps are coated with phosphors similar to those used in fluorescent lamps, they have less spectral flexibility, because the light is created by the mercury, not by the excitation of the phosphors. Like fluorescents, they produce a great deal of light in the lower part of the spectrum—blue and green—but are weak in red emissions. Where a very intense spotlighting effect is needed, however, they can be useful, and the missing parts of the spectrum could be added by using supplementary incandescent lighting.

METAL HALIDE LAMPS

The construction of these lamps is quite similar to that of mercury lamps, but in addition to being much more efficient in converting energy to light, their spectral emissions are also more easily manipulated, and they are only slightly more expensive. Wattages are generally the same as for mercury-vapor lamps, and the metal halide bulbs can often be used in the same fixtures. The type of emission is changed by adding thorium, thallium, and sodium—the metal halides—to the mercury in the lamp.

Like mercury lamps and fluorescents, these lamps provide a great deal of blue and green light, but unlike the others, they are also very rich in the red part of the spectrum—the only vapor lamps of which this can be said. As with mercury lamps, there are unconfirmed reports that manufacturers are developing these for residental use.

Light Fixtures and Arrangements

One real problem in choosing indoor-garden fixtures is that manufacturers have not kept pace with the demand for light fixtures that are both attractive and workable. Garden stores sell small tabletop light gardens, already assembled and small enough to fit on a coffee table, but most are designed to accept only two 24-inch, 40-watt fluorescent

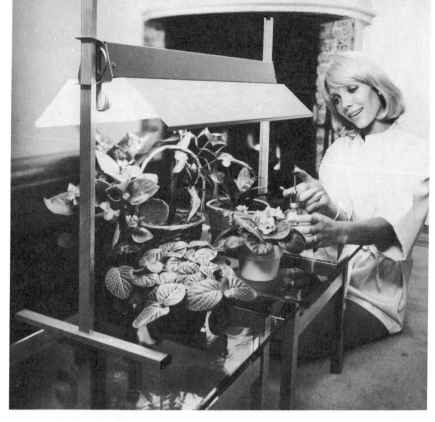

An adjustable light fixture can be put on a coffee table or other flat surface.

tubes—which will provide enough light for growing a few plants with low light requirements, but not enough for serious gardening.

Other dealers, including some of those listed in the back of this book, offer shelved light gardens that make it possible to give the plants light of greater intensity. These generally are free-standing, with either four or six 40-watt tubes on the underside of each shelf. The light thus beams on the plants on the shelf beneath the tubes. The larger number of fluorescent tubes produces light of a greater intensity (though it is still not enough for a *few* of the plants in this book), and the shelved arrangement is convenient where floor space is limited.

You can also buy window valances that are fairly attractive; they conceal the fluorescent tubes, but the tubes they hold produce only a limited amount of light and thus are good only when they are used in partnership with natural sunlight.

Some other fixtures are so elaborate that they are actually pieces of furniture. They are spacious and handsome, with the lights hidden away in the piece itself, but they're also very expensive—and they have two serious drawbacks. They will accept only a certain number

This large lighting étagère allows the home gardener to grow many plants simultaneously.

of fluorescent tubes of a certain wattage, which means there is little you can do to increase the intensity of the light as needed; and the distance between the shelves and light is fixed, which means you must place the plants on some kind of support when you wish to move them closer to the lights.

With fluorescent lighting, the distance between plant and tube is of utmost importance. The intensity of this light diminishes so rapidly as the distance between tubes and light is increased that at a distance of just 36 inches, the light from two 40-watt tubes would have almost no effect on your plants.

The ability to move your lights as needed, then, can be an enormous advantage. Since fluorescent tubes produce too little heat to damage your plants easily, a movable fixture allows you to increase the intensity of the light your plants receive by placing the tubes as close as you like to the plants.

The most common type of fluorescent fixture accepts two tubes, which are set into place in front of a reflector shield. This is the fixture commonly seen on ceilings. Its greatest disadvantage is that it is singularly unattractive, although manufacturers have begun to improve the situation somewhat by offering the units in a variety of colors other than the standard white.

Such a two-tube arrangement, if the tubes are only 40 watts each, will allow you to grow a few plants as long as the lights and plants are kept very close together; but if you wish to grow many plants or plants requiring stronger light, you will need either more tubes or higher wattage tubes.

When fluorescent tubes are banked side by side, the light not only covers a larger surface area, thus allowing you to provide light for a large number of plants, but it also overlaps and becomes more intense, thus allowing you to grow plants with higher light requirements. If you already have two fixtures which accept two tubes each, you can, of course, arrange them side by side. But if you are buying fluorescent fixtures, it is far wiser to choose ones that will accept four or even six tubes—and a fixture that accepts four tubes costs far less than two fixtures that will take two tubes each.

The fluorescent fixtures that accept higher wattage tubes are nearly identical to those that use 40-watt or smaller tubes, but they are not available in the shorter lengths. When you are buying the initial fixtures, then, it is important to remember that fluorescent tubes are not interchangable between these fixtures; if you buy fixtures designed for the 40-watt tubes, you will not be able to achieve brighter light by using stronger tubes but only by buying additional fixtures and adding more tubes.

Fluorescent fixtures are most commonly suspended directly over plants. The best arrangement of this type is one in which the plants can be raised and lowered as needed. By using hooks fixed to the ceiling and chains or cable to suspend the lights—perhaps with pulleys for ease of operation—you can let the lights down until they are only inches above the plants; then, when company comes or you want to display the plants for a while, the lights can be raised up and out of the way.

Probably because we are accustomed to seeing fluorescents fixed to

Here a Vita-Lite Power-Twist general purpose fluorescent bulb is used with a free-standing light fixture.

the ceiling or horizontally inside display cases, we often overlook the fact that these lights can be used vertically as well, and vertical arrangements can sometimes be very useful.

Providing light to the lower leaves of a tall plant can sometimes be difficult. The lower leaves are not only further from lights suspended above the plants, but much of the light is blocked by the upper leaves, thus the lower ones receive little or no illumination.

By placing a fluorescent tube vertically close alongside a small tree, shrub, or vining plant, you can assure that the light is evenly distributed from top to bottom, though the light will be coming from only one direction, and you will have to turn the plant often to compensate for this. You can use such vertical arrangements in combination with overhead lighting, or as a way of converting an upright cabinet into a small light chamber.

Incandescent bulbs provide a continuous spectrum of light and can be installed in any medium-base light fixture.

Incandescent bulbs, simply because they will fit nearly all the lamps and fixtures already in your home, generally do not pose the problem of being fixed into position. Even the incandescent growth lights now available are usually self-contained and easy to place where you want them. For lighting a small tree or shrub with them, for instance, you can beam a pair of lamps down from above while beaming two more upward and providing light to the lower leaves.

Reflector, mercury vapor, and metal halide lamps, all of which require special installation, share the problem of being fixed light sources, though it is not so severe as with fluorescents. Once the light is installed, it is fixed in place, and the distance between plant and lamp can only be changed by moving the plant, though many of the lamps do swivel and allow you to direct light exactly where it is needed. You can usually achieve brighter light simply by using a lamp of higher wattage, thus compensating for changes in distance between lamp and plant. Another advantage of these lamps is that since they are frequently used for commercial displays, the fixtures are generally more attractive than those used for fluorescent lighting.

You may also want to consider adding timers to your fixtures. Several types are available. Some will turn off all the lights in a room at a set time; others are designed for turning a single lamp or set of lamps

In this nursery, high-pressure sodium lamps are used in fixtures specially designed to withstand the high humidity of a greenhouse.

on and off according to a predetermined schedule. They are especially useful for those who are frequently away from home or who have trouble remembering when the lights should go on and off. Most are inexpensive and so simple that anyone can put them into service—but there is one kind of which this cannot be said.

These are the atmospheric timers, and several authors have suggested their use. These, as you may know, are timers which will turn your lights on when the sun rises each morning in your area and turn them off as the sun goes down. That sounds fine—until you remember that you probably do not want your lights to go off when the sun sets during the short days of winter. I asked plant scientist R. J. Downs, Director of the Phytotron at the Southeastern Plant Environment Laboratories, if these served any useful purpose for the home gardener. His response was: "An astronomical (or atmospheric) timer that works is expensive and in my opinion unnecessary." So I'd suggest you go to this expense only if you are interested in duplicating exactly the outdoor lighting conditions that exist in your own region.

Intensity of Light—How Much Is Needed and How to Achieve It

In talking about intensity of light, we are addressing the question of how bright the light should be that is provided to plants, and it is a question that cannot be answered by any scientifically verifiable means. We must make certain assumptions, but the assumptions can be based on facts and arrived at in ways that will provide workable guidelines for indoor gardeners.

Plants in the outdoor environment are exposed to a nearly infinite number of lighting situations. Light does not remain at a constant level of brightness. It is constantly changing, not only with the season and with the time of day, but also as the sunlight is blocked by clouds, trees, or buildings. It may be made brighter by reflections from nearby water or white sand, and it can be diluted by smog. A low-lying area may be almost always in the shade, but a shady area in Florida may receive light as intense as that shining on an open field in New York.

Indoors, it is nearly impossible to provide food-producing plants with light that is too bright. Try to imagine the lighting at noon on the brightest day you have ever seen—perhaps a summer day at the beach with the sunlight reflecting off the sand. In such a situation the light may meter as high as 10,000 foot-candles—far too high for many plants, but also far higher than you are likely to achieve in an indoor situation. Compare this in your mind to a day that is gloomy and overcast, when the lighting at ground level may drop to 1000 foot-candles or even less, and you will begin to realize how varied natural lighting can be and why it becomes nearly impossible to establish the *exact* lighting requirements of any plant.

The only way to establish such requirements is to compare what is known about the natural conditions under which the plant grows, to what is known about other plants that grow alongside it under the same conditions, and to use actual experience in growing the plants, including not only one's own experience but the experience of others as well. But in relying on the experience of others, one must move with extreme caution.

In response to a query about how one might establish minimum lighting requirements for various plants, scientist R. J. Downs warns that

> About the only information on light requirements of plants deals primarily with foliage and house plants. Moreover, these data seem to concern maintenance of the plants, often at survival levels, rather than the light necessary for good growth and production. . . . However, there are several papers in the scientific literature that refer to the amount of light necessary. . . .

Most popular books on the subject of light gardening agree that our common vegetables need between 1000 and 2000 foot-candles of light, and our own experiments with plants have confirmed this, but they have also shown that these figures are frequently misleading. Many vegetables *can* be grown with only 1000 foot-candles of light, or in some instances even less, but this does not mean they will do as well as when they are grown under brighter light.

Lettuce, carrots, radishes, and leeks are among the plants that most books state will grow under 1000 foot-candles of light, but when I tested that theory by growing the plants under light that weak, the lettuce sent up stems that were white and spindly, far too thin to support good top growth; the carrots produced roots that were too thin to be of use; the leeks were no thicker than wire; and the radishes produced only top growth and no bulbs at all. When I planted seed from the same packages under lights producing about 1500 foot-candles, the plants grew almost as well as in the outside garden.

Another book told me that cucumbers could be grown under light as weak as 750 foot-candles. Attempting to test this, I took a cucumber plant that had already bloomed and started to produce its first crop under stronger light, and moved it back until the light meter showed it was receiving about 750 foot-candles of light. Within three days it was showing obvious signs of light deficiency—its leaves were yellowing, withering, and falling, its blossoms dropping away, and the trio of tiny cucumbers that had been developing under brighter light quickly shriveled to nothing and fell from the vine. Other experiments along these lines convince me that authors give the lower figures for lighting needs because they know that these conditions are easier to achieve and they will thus attract more readers, not because they are adequate for good plant growth.

As R. J. Downs notes:

> It is sometimes claimed that pineapple can be grown to produce fruit at 1000 foot-candles; some say more than 1000 is necessary but fail to say how much more. This may be possible, but the leaves will be abnormally narrow and the fruit small. At 4000 foot-candles, however, the plants are normal and the fruit equal in size to those produced in Hawaii fields.

The 4000 foot-candles of brightness needed to grow a pineapple to the size it would reach in a field in Hawaii probably represents the strongest light needed to grow any common plant. In few areas is the natural sunlight brighter than in Hawaii, and 4000 foot-candles of light at floor level is the intensity plant scientists seek in their phytotrons—a level of lighting that allows them to grow virtually any plant to maturity. For example, Downs informs me that in the phytotron he directs, "We routinely grow soybean, milo, corn, peanut, tobacco and other field crops to maturity." All these are plants of the open field, where natural sunlight would obviously be at its strongest.

But what of those plants not requiring light of such great intensity? Certainly there are many, and a study of the scientific literature allows one to draw certain reasonable assumptions about their needs.

Generally speaking, plants that are grown only for their foliage—such as herbs and salad greens—have the lowest lighting needs, and these needs are the easiest to meet. Since these plants are not being grown to produce blossoms and fruit and will thus accept any number of hours of light you wish to provide, you can stimulate growth by leaving the lights on for longer periods of time, assuming that the light is bright enough in the first place to start the growth process. As a matter of fact, scientists say that long periods at a given light level generally produce more vegetative growth than half the time at twice the illumination.

With most of these foliage plants, 1000 foot-candles of light will stimulate the process of photosynthesis, and most growers use twelve to fourteen hours of lighting. As I have said, however, we find that our plants are healthier when the level of lighting is increased and applied over longer periods of time—as long as eighteen hours out of each day. Root crops such as radishes will also grow with only 1000 foot-candles of light, but these under-the-soil crops also appear to be stimulated by brighter light.

Generally, the vining and foliage plants which produce blossoms followed by fruits, drupes, or berries require more intense light than that needed by the foliage plants. This group includes plants such as strawberry, tomato, and cucumber, which are among the plants that have been most thoroughly studied by scientists.

As early as 1957 plant scientist F. W. Went published in the *Chronica Botanica* his findings that dry-weight production in tomato plants levels off at 1500 foot-candles. But this was a study of dry weight—or foliage—increase, and other studies have since shown that *fruit production* increases under lighting of up to 2000 foot-candles. Other plants in this group have similar requirements.

At the very highest level in terms of their lighting needs are the woody plants—trees. Less is known about the ways in which they utilize lights, but in general, simply because of their size and woody growth, brighter light is needed to stimulate the processes of growth. Only a few trees can grow in light weaker than 1500 foot-candles, and many require the intense light of a special light chamber or phytotron—as many as 4000 foot-candles.

There are exceptions in every group. A tree native to the tropical forest—where light is blocked and filtered by the branches and leaves of taller trees—will probably not require light as intense as a flowering plant that is native to the open fields of North America. And perhaps this explains why the coffee tree is so popular as a window plant.

Unlike the foliage and root plants in the first group, the plants in these last two groups are likely to be grown for the fruits that follow their blossoms, and this means that, in many instances, it is not possible to help growth along simply by giving them more hours of light. Many will blossom only when the light is of the right duration, thus their needs can be met only by increasing the intensity.

It becomes obvious, then, that the greater the intensity of the light you provide, the wider the variety of plants you will be able to grow. There are a few plants described later in the book that will thrive in less than 1000 foot-candles of light, but I believe the bare minimum of lighting you should plan for is 1000 foot-candles, and preferably half again that much. With a light intensity of 1500 to 2000 foot-candles, you will at least double the variety of plants that you can grow in your garden, and you will find that many of the plants that you can grow under weaker light will improve noticeably at this higher level. If you decide to make special arrangements to achieve the very highest level of lighting—2000 to 4000 foot-candles—you will be able to grow almost any plant you choose, including many that are not mentioned in this book.

How, then, can you obtain these levels of light?

The first step consists in knowing how much light you already have. Unless you intend to grow all your plants in cabinets, closets, the basement, or other enclosed areas where darkness is nearly total, you will have a fair amount of natural light available to you. Unless this light is a great deal brighter and of much longer duration than that in the average home, it will not be adequate by itself for growing very many plants—but only by first knowing how much natural light is available will you know how much artificial light you must add.

Artificial light, you should remember, can be used in three ways. It can be used as the sole source of radiant energy for plant growth. It can be used in partnership with natural sunlight as a means of achieving greater intensity of light. Or it can be used in partnership with natural sunlight as a means of providing light that is longer in duration. Most indoor gardeners use it in all three ways.

This is why you will find more light gardens placed near windows than in other parts of the home. But natural light does not exist only near the windows; a certain amount will be available even at the far side of the room, and it is up to you to determine how much.

Select a bright spot in your brightest, most sunlit room. Measure the light with a light meter, taking at least three readings at intervals throughout the day and then averaging them out. The readings will change throughout the day, from day to day, and with the seasons, but that need cause you no great concern. You are not trying to determine exactly, to the very foot-candle, how much light is there, but merely to arrive at a good estimate. Remember, also, that plants outside are exposed to light that is almost constantly changing in intensity.

The amount of light you find with the meter will depend on many things—the number and size of your windows, their cleanliness, their distance from the spot you are metering, even the color of your walls—but you may be surprised at how much you find.

Unless you are metering the light on a bright sun porch or directly in front of a south-facing window, however, your light readings will probably reveal an average of just a few hundred foot-candles. But when you add this to the artificial light that you can provide, it becomes far easier for you to achieve the lighting level at which your plants will grow, not just survive.

Because of the way fluorescents are made and because even the manufacturers admit that their quality control is very poor, it is difficult to say exactly how much light will be produced by any setup of fluorescent tubes; even two tubes of the same wattage from the same manufacturer may produce light of different intensity. The tubes also weaken during use, which means they should be changed after about six months, or half their rated life. Light also varies according to the type of reflector shield behind them.

With almost all reflectors, the light goes out in a cone that widens as it moves away from the tubes. The light will be brightest directly under the center of the tubes, weaker as the edges of the cone are approached. It loses strength quickly with distance.

Directly under the center of two 40-watt, 48-inch tubes, at a distance of 3 inches, the light should meter at about 1000 foot-candles; but when the distance increases to just 18 inches, the light will be only about half that much (and even less near the edges of the cone).

Rowing fluorescent tubes alongside one another causes a light gain not only very close to the tubes but also where the widening cones of light overlap; thus with more tubes, the distance between lights and plants can be increased, with the amount of the increase depending on the number of tubes, their individual strength, and, of course, the needs of the plant.

Four 40-watt, 48-inch fluorescent tubes, kept close to the plants, should easily provide the 1500 foot-candles of light that a wide variety of plants need, and six tubes of the same size and wattage will provide 2000 foot-candles or more. The same intensities can also be achieved by using a smaller number of higher-output tubes, which use higher wattage. For example, two 75-watt tubes (a total of 150 watts) should produce light almost as bright as four 40-watt tubes (a total of 160 watts), but the light would be spread over a smaller area.

The very high intensities of up to 4000 foot-candles can only be reached artificially by setting up a special light room. The number of fluorescent tubes needed for such an arrangement depends, of course, on the size of the room, but for a 10-by-12-foot room, there should be no less than twenty 72-inch fixtures using forty tubes, covering the ceiling of the room. In some of the phytotrons, or light laboratories, 40-watt Cool White tubes are alternated with tubes using 110 watts, a mix under which plants do well and which provides 4000 foot-candles right down to the floor.

Such a light room should at the very least be painted white on all possible surfaces, but you might want to do as they do in phytotrons and cover virtually every surface with mirrors, an expensive addition but one that will allow you to reach light levels under which even the most demanding plants will grow.

Mirrors can increase the available light by as much as 25 percent. Nearly every popular book on gardening says that mirrors should be avoided, the theory being that they produce a "hot" light that is damaging to plants. But in a recent booklet, *Lighting for Style and Staying Power,* scientists from the U.S. Department of Agriculture's Agricultural Research Center at Beltsville, Maryland, strongly urge commercial growers to use them.

Mirrors are expensive, and you would not, in any case want to turn your home into a "hall of mirrors." But just a few mirrors spread around a room can increase its natural brightness somewhat as well as make the room more attractive; and displaying small trees or shrubs before a mirror creates a tropical effect while the plants enjoy the advantages of higher light.

Perhaps the most effective way of using mirrors is placing them under the plants. Since your plants are most likely to be lighted from above or from a high angle, this arrangement will bounce some light back up to the lower leaves, which is always a problem area. A mirror-topped table is ideal for this purpose.

Aluminum foil is less attractive than mirrors, but it is also less expensive and can be used much like mirrors, though its reflective quality is lower and it will not do the job as efficiently. Especially if you are growing plants in a cabinet, closet, or some other out-of-sight location, you might want to line the shelves and perhaps even the walls around the plants with foil. In doing some experiments with plants at low lighting levels, I added foil in this fashion, and they almost immediately perked up and showed new signs of life.

Aluminum foil, shredded and used as mulch, will also bounce light back up to your plants. This idea was developed by Henry M. Cathay, perhaps the nation's leading plant scientist, and has been thoroughly tested at the Beltsville research center. Just cut foil into thin strips and place the strips over the soil in the planter. They will not only reflect light but will also help keep the plants' roots cool and slow down moisture loss through evaporation.

Remember, too, that the surrounding color will affect the level of your lighting. Dark colors absorb light, while bright colors bounce it back. White is the best color for reflecting light, followed by the pastels. While you will probably not want to repaint a room just to accommodate your plants, those color values should be kept in mind when you are choosing a location for your lights and plants. Consider, too, that green foliage is far more attractive against a bright background, especially white.

These methods allow you to make small increases in the intensity of light. Probably the easiest and least expensive way to achieve larger increases is to use a combination of fluorescent and incandescent plant-growth lighting.

Assume that you have a standard fluorescent fixture using two 40-watt tubes and providing only about 1000 foot-candles of light, but you want to start a plant that requires twice that intensity. A 150-watt incandescent plant-growth spotlight, which will provide an additional 900 to 1000 foot-candles, can be beamed across the planter under the fluorescents, thus giving the needed increase. Adding the incandescent plant-growth lighting is far less expensive than buying new fluorescent fixtures that will accept tubes with greater output. Also, you can merely clamp the incandescent fixtures to the plant table or to the planter itself, and thus the increase can be quickly, easily, and inexpensively achieved.

Probably the single most important thing to remember about light intensity is that you should always aim high. It is far easier to reduce the level of lighting than to increase it. It can be increased only by using more or stronger lights—which can be troublesome and expensive after the initial fixtures are in—or, to a lesser extent, by using mirrors, foil, and so forth. To lower the level of lighting, which you may infrequently wish to do, you need only increase the distance between lamps and plants.

Which Light Is Most Effective?

While providing light of the right intensity is a big step in the right direction, it is also essential that you provide light of the right quality. As you have probably realized by now, no single type of artificial light provides light energy that is ideal for every plant in every situation—despite many claims to the contrary. Some plants thrive under the light provided by the plant-growth fluorescents, others do better un-

At Pittsburgh Plantworks, standard Grow-Lux lights were mounted
in clusters of four-lamp fixtures recessed on the underside of shelves.
A total of 102 grow lights were used in the store.

der ordinary fluorescent lighting, and still others require at least some sunlight if they are to grow at all.

Plants grown under artificial light alone will not develop exactly as they would if they were grown under sunlight, and each type of light causes different plant responses. Scientists at the U.S. Department of Agriculture have studied these plant responses; here are some of the major differences:

Plants grown under Warm White and Cool White fluorescent lights develop green foliage, which tends to expand parallel to the surface of the lamp. Stems elongate slowly, developing multiple side shoots, and flowering occurs over a long period of time.

Plants grown under standard plant-growth fluorescents develop a darker green foliage than plants under ordinary fluorescent light, extrathick stems develop and elongate very slowly, and flowering occurs late on flower stalks that do not elongate.

Substituting so-called wide-spectrum plant-growth lamps for standard plant-growth fluorescents causes the plants to develop light green foliage which ascends toward the lamp. The stems elongate rapidly, with longer distances between the leaves. Flowering occurs soon, but the plants mature and age more rapidly than is normal.

Plants grown under mercury or metal halide lamps develop almost exactly like those grown under the Warm White and Cool White fluorescents.

Incandescent plant-growth lights cause foliage that is thinner, longer, and lighter in color than on plants grown in sunlight. Stems may be spindly, excessively long, and easily broken. Flowering occurs rapidly, with the plants maturing faster than normal.

Since no artificial light source provides exactly the kind of energy found in sunlight, one must seek the best from among that which is available, relying on the carefully developed opinion of the experts.

In the Department of Agriculture publication *Lighting Plants for Style and Staying Power,* H. M. Cathey, L. E. Campbell, and R. W. Thimijan, three leading plant and lighting scientists from the Agricultural Research Center at Beltsville, Maryland, advise,

> For growing, we suggest you use one Cool White or Warm White and one grow-fluorescent lamp, or one Cool White and one Warm White in an alternating pattern. We find that most plants grow well and are attractive in appearance. . . . Of the energy required to generate the light, only twenty percent is produced as visible light; the remaining energy must be gotten rid of to avoid over-heating the plants. The grow-lamps are all less

efficient in generating visible light and produce more waste energy than Cool White fluorescent and Warm White fluorescent.

The suggestion that this combination is more effective than growth lamps is contrary to nearly everything that has been published in recent years, yet commercial growers and plant scientists around the country typically use this Warm White and Cool White combination, and it is the standard I have used in establishing minimum light requirements for most plants in this book.

There are reasons why the combination is effective: The Cool White tube provides light that is strong in the critical blue rays, while the Warm White tube adds much-needed light from the red part of the spectrum. Growth lights attempt to combine both in one tube. If you already own such growth fluorescents, use them—but when the time for replacing the tubes arrives, I urge you to switch to the combination just described.

Incandescent plant-growth bulbs do not provide an ideal spectral mix, but they do make it easier to direct light where it is needed, and for that reason they are sometimes suggested as the best means of providing light for certain plants. And as with fluorescents, they can be more effective if you use them in wise combination with the most effective light of all: natural sunlight.

The Processes of Growth—And the Importance of Darkness

Light strongly regulates three major plant processes: phototropism, photosynthesis, and photoperiodism. Some understanding of each is necessary for successful indoor gardening.

Phototropism is controlled by a growth hormone in plants that occurs near the stem tips and in the youngest plant leaves. This hormone—or auxin, as it is known to scientists—is highly reactive to light and causes the plant to adjust itself continuously to the light source. This is why a sunflower turns to face the sun and why some plants, when they are grown under fluorescent lights, spread their foliage parallel to the light source. In most plants the reaction is positive tropism, a condition where the plant moves toward the light source, but in a few species the reaction is negative, with the plant moving away from the source.

Indoor light too frequently comes from only one direction. Most plants, then, exhibit stronger growth in one direction. To avoid growing misshapen plants you must occasionally rotate them to compensate for the unequal lighting, though the problem is greatly alleviated by using overhead lighting or mirrors. There are also many times when phototropism can be used to advantage—for instance, to train a vine up a trellis toward the light source.

Photosynthesis is the most important chemical process in the world. Life could not exist anywhere without plants—if bacteria are included as plants. Green plants are not only the basic source for the sugars, proteins, and fats that are the material of life, but they are also the primary source of oxygen for animal respiration, creating an estimated 400 billion tons of it each year during the process known as photosynthesis.

Primarily, photosynthesis supplies the plant itself with food compounds and energy for growth. After the young seedling exhausts the reserve foods that were present in the seed, it is absolutely dependent on daily photosynthesis to supply its current needs. Certainly not everything about the process is understood, but some facts have long been established.

The raw materials for this process are carbon dioxide and water. These combine chemically in the leaves and other green parts of the plant, forming such carbohydrates as sugar and starch. These combinations form through a series of complex reactions requiring the presence of the green pigment chlorophyll—and light. Radiant energy is stored during the process and released later, usually through respiration.

With the carbohydrates generated by this process, the plant produces new foliage, roots, stems, and flowers. If the light provided is enough to reach what the scientists call the saturation level, the foliage will be luxuriant, the roots and stems thick and healthy, all growth normal. If the light is less, growth will be slow and weak, or the plant will soon die.

Photosynthesis occurs as long as light is present. It stops in the absence of light. This is why luxuriant foliage and healthy root growth can easily be achieved by providing long hours of light, even though the light might not be as intense as it would be in nature. If a foliage plant shows the yellow, widely spaced leaves, elongated stems, and skinny roots and stalks that are the symptoms of light deficiency, the situation can be corrected by providing light that is of longer duration. But with some of the blooming plants that is not possible—because such an increase might interfere with the process of photoperiodism.

The discovery of *photoperiodism* gave us the short-day, long-day, and day-neutral definitions that we commonly use to describe the duration of light needed by groups of plants, definitions that are now familiar to most gardeners. Later research into the phenomenon of photoperiodism reveals those definitions to be scientifically incorrect. Plants do not calculate the hours of light in the process that leads to blooming; they keep track of the hours of darkness.

Photoperiodism refers to the response of plants to the relative lengths of day and night, or, put another way, it is a time-dependent response to the absence of light. Most gardening books have dismissed the process all too quickly—perhaps because people have understood so little about it until recently—but according to photobiologist Stuart Dunn of the University of New Hampshire:

> The researches leading to basic facts about light and plant growth relationships have far-reaching importance for farmers, florists, gardeners, and in fact, plant growers everywhere. Nowhere is this more strikingly shown than in the discovery of photoperiodism and the developments that have come from it.

The discovery of photoperiodism in plants came about because two scientists observed that a variety of tobacco, called Maryland Mammoth, flowered so late in the summer season near Washington, D.C., that its seeds had no time to mature. They tried numerous experiments without being able to change the habit of growth. Then they tried altering the day length, finally providing seven hours of light and seventeen hours of darkness per day. After a few days of such treatment, the plants bloomed and produced seed. Further experiments with other plants showed that plants differ in the proportion of day and night they need to produce seeds—and thus plants came to be divided into four groups according to the duration of light they need to induce bloom.

Plants that normally flower in late spring or summer were found to respond to long hours of light and came to be known as long-day plants. Plants in this group remain vegetative when days are short.

On the other hand, plants that normally flower in the short days of autumn or winter came to be known as short-day plants. Such plants remain vegetative when days are too long.

Fortunately for the gardeners who must artificially meet their lighting needs, a third group comprises the largest number of plants, called day-neutral or indeterminate-day plants. These can flower and fruit under a wide range of day lengths. The tomato is a notable example of this group.

A few plants are so close to requiring an even division of day and night into twelve hours each that they were assigned to a group known as intermediate. Members of this group are likely to be native to areas on or near the equator, where night falls abruptly and the hours of light and darkness are about equal.

More recent studies have shown that photoperiodism in plants is far more complex than scientists originally thought. They now know that the response can be affected by other factors, such as temperature and humidity, and that with some plants it may vary according to latitude. They also know that plants do not necessarily respond in an all-or-nothing way to day length. Some plants will flower with any day length but will flower earlier with short days and long nights. Conversely, others may flower on any day length but will flower earlier on long days. When flowering is promoted by long or short days, the response is known as quantitative. But where plants will not flower without a specific day length, such a response is called qualitative.

Probably the most important discoveries about photoperiodism were those which revealed the importance of darkness. Up to 1937 it was assumed that plants had some way of measuring daylight. In that year experiments with soybeans showed that plants measure the dark period in a twenty-four-hour cycle, not the period of light. Those experiments showed that light applied for just a single minute at midnight would prevent flowering in the soybean, a very sensitive plant often used in experiments. Scientists learned that when the darkness was interrupted in this fashion, the plants' dark timer disregarded all the previous darkness and began calculating the hours of darkness all over again. Not all plants are this sensitive to interruption of the dark period, but serious interruptions can prevent many plants from blooming.

For example, look at the flowering plants on display in shopping malls, where security lights are left on overnight. Because these security lights may interfere with the blooming process, the plants must generally be covered in a way that prevents the light from reaching them. Many indoor gardeners have also encountered the phenomenon when spillage from streetlights or other sources interferes with the photoperiod and prevents a favorite plant from blooming.

Deliberate disruption of the dark period can sometimes be used to advantage. Sometimes a plant grown under lights may attempt to blossom before the plant is large enough and strong enough to support fruit. Giving light at night may prevent blossoming until the plant has added enough vegetative growth. The same result can be achieved—unless the plant is from the day-neutral group—by providing light with duration that is in direct contrast to its requirements; providing a short-day plant with long hours of lighting, for example, until such time as you are ready to promote blooming.

Light applied at night to disrupt the dark period may also be used to promote blooming, but only when it is the right kind of light applied for just the right length of time and in the proper amount.

Barley is one long-day plant that has been induced to bloom during winter by applying light at midnight to keep its dark periods short. With many other plants, however, the disruption fails to promote blooming, for reasons that are not clearly understood. In more recent years scientists have learned that red and far-red light are the parts of the spectrum that control photoperiodism and thus flowering. Breaking the dark period of the short-day plants with such light is more likely to inhibit blooming, while blooming is more likely to be promoted when such treatment is given to long-day plants. Incandescent lighting is ordinarily used to break the dark period, but only in a few instances will the home gardener want to attempt this.

The leaves are the sensing organs that control photoperiodism, causing a complicated series of reactions involving a hormone known as phythochrome, about which less is known than almost any other plant process. The most important thing we know is that the influence of darkness prevails in all plants, and that for good blooming followed by equally good fruit production, your plants need not only adequate light of the right duration but the proper amount of darkness as well.

This means that plants with relatively precise photoperiods are best kept apart from plants of other groups. It also means that they should not be grown in areas where the dark period will be disrupted at random. Not every plant is extremely sensitive to disruption of the dark period, but some can be thrown out of cycle by the light coming through a window from an outside source or by the spillover from a reading lamp in the same room. You should place flowering plants in an area that will allow you to maintain complete control of the amounts of light and darkness they receive.

Plants with precise photoperiods have what has been referred to as a photocritical point—a point when exactly the right mix of light and darkness causes optimum bloom and fruit and seed production. If this photocritical point is achieved—all others factors being equal—a plant grown indoors will produce just as well as one raised in the outdoor environment.

Precise photoperiods have not been established for every plant, for less is understood about photoperiodism than any of the other processes of growth. But scientists, through their experiments, have established the requirements of many of the more popular plants, and several lists have been published in the scientific literature, most notably in the *Handbook of Biological Data*. I have established the requirements for others through direct contact with researchers and growers. These lighting periods are, I feel, critically important to growing plants that bloom, and I hope you will follow them as carefully as I have sought them out.

2. Natural Sunlight and the Partnership of Light

As you saw in the last chapter, no artificial light source provides *exactly* the right spectral quality for growing plants. Some lamps come closer than others to achieving spectral perfection, yet all are lacking in one way or another. There is only one light that contains all the right parts of the spectrum in exactly the right proportions, and that is natural sunlight.

Yet you obviously cannot depend solely on daylight for growing plants. There are too many cloudy days, short days, and naturally shady spots in and around the average home. Even when unshaded outdoor areas are available, the length of time they are available is limited by the seasons. Attempting to use sunlight as the sole source for growing plants inside the home is even more complicated, for there the natural light is not only more limited but is also constantly changing, much as it does outdoors. A spot that receives full sun during one part of the day is likely to be in shadow at other times, and vice versa. These fluid conditions have an enormous impact on our plants.

Most gardeners are only vaguely aware of the changing intensity and direction of sunlight at various times of the day, yet there are many ways in which this free natural resource can be used in combination with artificial light to make your home gardening more successful. By forming a sensible partnership between artificial and natural light, you can more easily achieve the high intensities that are needed for growing some plants, you can control the duration of light, and you can extend the growing season throughout the year. But in order to do this, you must fully understand the individual quirks of each member of the partnership.

Between the time when the sun rises and the time it sets, its rays cause ever-changing light patterns in the home, providing light to just three of the four exposures. It begins in the morning, when light comes from the east.

The eastern exposure receives direct sunlight from sunrise to near mid-day. As the morning progresses, the direct sunlight fades from the room, a departure that is hastened if there are eaves or other outside overhangs. Eastern rooms remain cooler because the house has had less time to absorb radiant heat, and thus this exposure has long been a favorite of gardeners.

Because eastern sunlight is cooler than light from the south or west, it is therefore less dehydrating to plants. The early rays of the sun awaken the plants and set them to the daily work of photosynthesis. Few and far between are the plants that do not welcome at least a few hours of eastern sunshine.

Around mid-day, the sun swings to the south. The light is far brighter now, even though direct sunlight is likely to have retreated from the far corners of the room, except in that most desirable of all gardening rooms, the one with a southern exposure.

The seasonal variation for southern light is greater than that for any other exposure. During the winter, when the sun is low in the sky, sunlight streams across such a room for most of the daylight hours. During this season, the room will be much like a greenhouse, a spot where you can grow almost any plant. During the summer months, when the sun is further north than in the winter, the south-facing window receives sunlight only briefly around mid-day.

After mid-day, when the sun has passed its zenith, the downward arc begins, and sunlight comes from the west, which it will continue to do until the sun falls below the horizon and the day is ended. Like the east-facing window, a window with a western exposure will receive four or five hours of direct sunlight each day, depending on the season.

The United States, being in the Northern Hemisphere, always receives its sunlight from the south. Even at summer solstice (June 21), when the sun is as far north in the sky as it ever comes, it is just far enough north to give only brief sunlight to a north-facing window. Consequently, of the four exposures the northern one receives the least light and heat throughout the year. Gardeners with only this exposure available must rely almost entirely on artificial lighting for their plants.

How intense will the light be at your window? That is the question with which you are concerned, yet it is a question to which there is no precise answer. Any situation involving natural sunlight raises an infinite number of possibilities. Not only is the intensity of light constantly changing as the sun moves across the sky, and not only does it vary with the seasons, it is also affected by latitude and altitude. Light intensity is higher in the mountains than at sea level—not simply because the higher elevations are closer to the sun, but also because the atmosphere is thinner there and less light is filtered out before striking the earth.

Several years ago, in a guide for commercial greenhouse growers, the United States Department of Agriculture (USDA) published some examples of light intensities. The measurements were taken at noon on winter days, under clear skies, in a 38–42-degree belt of latitude across the United States. This belt of latitude includes New York, Philadelphia, Boston, Detroit, Chicago, St. Louis, Denver, Salt Lake City, and San Francisco. The USDA found that unobstructed outside light averaged about 4000 foot-candles but sometimes ranged as much as 25 percent higher.

Those light levels would be higher in other seasons and in areas south of latitude 38, as they would at very high elevations. They would be lower at any other time of day, or north of latitude 42. These levels of lighting would be sufficient for growing most plants, but the number of cloudy days during winter is such that the bright days are more than offset; and even if they were not, winter temperatures would kill off most of the plants you might want to grow.

Remember, too, that those readings were taken in unobstructed areas, which is not likely to be your own situation. If you live in a city, it is much more likely that the obstruction of nearby buildings will prevent your patio, balcony, or porch from receiving full sunlight. Even in the country outside spaces may be shaded by trees and probably will be shaded by the building to which they are attached. Much of the light the plants receive will be indirect.

That is perfectly all right. Relatively few plants need direct sunlight. Even those which reach optimum growth under the extreme brightness of direct summer sun can usually adapt to the lower intensities of indirect light. Using outdoor areas, however small they may be, will greatly broaden your gardening horizons—and artificial light can help you make the most of them.

The most obvious and best known way to use artificial light is to get a jump on the season. Your artificial lights can be used to start plants indoors well before the last frost of spring. Mobile containers allow you to move them outside after the danger of frost is past. The plants can grow there, and then you can return them to the artificial environment when cold weather once again threatens. In numerous instances the plants will then continue to produce right on into the winter months.

Extending the seasons is an obvious advantage of this mobile gardening. The other reasons are not quite so obvious. The first has to do with the effectiveness of light.

Sunlight is by far the most effective energy for growing plants. How much more effective is a matter of debate, but there is absolutely no doubt that plants grow faster under sunlight, develop stronger root systems, and are generally more healthy than plants grown under artificial light alone. Even a plant that has been grown from seed indoors will show signs of improvement when transferred to the proper outdoor environment. Using the summer sun to give your plants a good grip on life will, in return, give you healthier plants for growing under artificial lights, in most instances.

Outdoor spaces also allow you to grow plants that, for one reason or another, you might not want to grow in your living quarters. Most members of the cabbage family make delicious eating, for example, but they are frequently odorous and capable of permeating your furniture and draperies with their odor if they grow to maturity in your home.

The least obvious advantage of using outdoor spaces is that it frees your artificial lights for other uses. This is the most important advantage, I think, because the average gardener is going to have a fairly small number of light fixtures and an equally small space beneath them. For example, if you have been growing a citrus tree under your artificial lights, there is no good reason why it should not be moved outside during the warm summer months. As a matter of fact, it will probably show definite signs of improvement after a few weeks of summer sunshine. The space under your artificial lights can then be used for other crops.

The outdoor space also has other uses. Not only do some plants need very intense light, which can be difficult to provide inside the home as well as difficult for humans to tolerate, but many plants require periods of cold temperatures that you would not want to provide inside your home. Wise use of your outdoor areas will allow you to provide these conditions.

This is, of course, no more than the highly popular container gardening. However, there is an even better way to utilize your limited outdoor space—one that allows you to use it throughout the year, that allows you to overcome the problems caused by short hours of sunlight and cloudy days, and that allows you to greatly increase the number and variety of plants you can grow.

Home Greenhouses

It all began in the greenhouse, this idea of growing plants after the season was at an end. By enclosing an outdoor area with glass and providing it with heat, it has long been possible to capture the radiant energy from the sun while protecting plants from the low temperatures that would kill them. Until fluorescent lighting came along, however, the greenhouse environment was not quite ideal; especially during the winter months, there were simply too many short and cloudy days to allow the gardener the long hours of light needed for certain plants.

The modern greenhouse allows you to give your plants nearly perfect lighting. Its walls and ceiling of glass or other transparent material allow your plants to enjoy the full benefit of natural sun on bright days, and supplementary fluorescent lighting takes over when days are too short or too cloudy. Inexpensive heating elements protect the plants from cold, and the naturally humid greenhouse environment is one in which most plants thrive.

Not only that, but the modern greenhouse, at least in the variations I discuss here, allows the plants to be seen, enjoyed, and, in some instances, tended from inside the home. They place year-round greenery of any kind within easy reach of gardeners who live in the north as well as those in warmer climes.

Once reserved only for the very wealthy, greenhouses are now well within the financial reach of most; they are likely to become less and less expensive as time goes by and this type of gardening becomes increasingly popular. And while it is true that the initial cost of the greenhouse is higher than the cost of most light arrangements, you should remember that in buying or building a greenhouse, you are obtaining a passive solar system that costs little or nothing to operate and which is fully capable of producing, in a very short time, enough food to justify your investment.

The amount of that investment depends on the size, type and construction of the greenhouse you choose. There are many fine professionally constructed greenhouses on the market, available already assembled or as do-it-yourself kits or dealer-installed models. Prefabricated units cost about half as much as assembled or dealer-installed units, and building your greenhouse from components can reduce your costs even more. In the appendix I have listed several suppliers of prefabricated units and greenhouse components, and on pages 283-288 I have provided plans which, if you are handy with tools, will show you how to construct your own small greenhouse from locally available materials.

The least expensive type of greenhouse is the window extension. These units extend out from your windows to capture the sun while providing you with more space for growing plants. They can be tended from inside or outside the home, and they utilize heat escaping from inside the home, so little supplementary heat is needed. By following the plans on pages 289 and 290, you can build a window greenhouse for about $75, not counting the cost of lights.

The lean-to type greenhouse is more expensive by far, and also more appropriate for homeowners than for apartment dwellers. Such a unit creates a walk-in nook against one side of the home and is large enough to allow the growing of dwarf fruit trees and other large plants. These usually have an outside entrance, and the plants are tended from the inside.

Also really more suitable for the homeowner are the extension greenhouses. These are glass rooms appended to the house. Most are large and designed to cover a patio to fit close against the wall of the house. The entrance is through the sliding glass doors leading to the patio. Most have vents for moisture control.

For renters and city people, a deck greenhouse or a window extension greenhouse are nearly ideal and may, indeed, be the only possibilities. Otherwise wasted space on a porch, balcony, or patio or outside window can often be transformed into a small year-round garden right off the living room. These can very easily be taken apart, transported, and reassembled elsewhere.

Many of the prefabricated greenhouses come ready to accept supplementary artificial lighting. If, however, you must add your own, remember that there is no need to attempt to match the intensity of the sun—which is impossible in any case. Just add enough light to keep the process of photosynthesis going on dim days or to extend day length when you want to extend it. A few hundred foot-candles should do. Place the lights beneath the framework of the greenhouse or on the side facing the house, so the fixtures do not block the natural light. Depending on the exposure and the plants you want to grow, you may be able to get by without any artificial light at all, but having it will make the unit more worthwhile and give you almost complete freedom in selecting the plants you want to grow.

In choosing a site for a home greenhouse, select the exposure that gets the most direct sunlight. Your first choice would be on the south or southeast side of the home. If you have no spot with this exposure, consider, in order, the east side, the southwest side, and the west side. If a northern exposure is the only one available to you, then you probably should not invest in a greenhouse, for the northern light is too limited and too weak to justify the investment.

Once the greenhouse is in and you are ready to start planting, you might want to consider adding a hydroponic gardening unit, as described elsewhere in the book. With such a unit it is possible to grow several plants in the space ordinarily needed for one, and so your greenhouse space can be used for plants rather than for planters and soil.

The home greenhouse is not for everyone. It is just one way that natural sunlight can be used. But some natural sunlight enters every home, and you can do much to increase the amount and use it in partnership with the artificial light you provide.

Indoor Sunlight

As you have seen in the chapter on artificial light, many food plants can grow at relatively low light levels, but many of these same plants do far better when the intensity of light is raised. As you have also seen, it is far more difficult to increase the intensity of lighting than to lower it, for an increase requires that you use more or brighter lights, while a decrease can be achieved simply by increasing the distance between plant and lamp. Natural sunlight makes it easier to achieve the higher levels.

Assume for a moment that you want to grow radishes, and that you have fixtures capable of providing 1000 foot-candles of light. They will grow at this level, as I have said, but the plants will be spindly and the edible roots undersized. At 1500 foot-candles growth will be normal.

Adding new fixtures would not be worthwhile. But you almost certainly have those extra foot-candles available in the form of natural sunlight. You may have them available for only a few hours each day, but even so, the extra light during those hours will help your radishes grow faster, better, and more normally than they would under artificial light alone.

Remember that the level of lighting does not have to be constant as long as it remains high enough to keep the process of photosynthesis going. Remember also that the spectral quality of natural sunlight is far superior to that of artificial light, so your plants will welcome all the sunlight they can get.

Distribution of light is another problem that can be at least partially solved by using natural sunlight. Providing light for the lower leaves of taller plants that you grow under artificial light is a problem for many growers, because most people place the light fixtures overhead. But if you place those same fixtures and plants near a sunny window, sunlight slanting through the glass will do much to solve the problem.

Sunlight enters your home through glass. Its intensity and duration depend on many things, but it always has the proper spectrum for plant growth; a major goal of the gardener should be to use it as efficiently as possible, especially with low-cost energy rapidly becoming a thing of the past.

The size and type of your windows has a great deal to do with how much light they admit. The most common windows are the classic double-hung and the aluminum frame crank-out type, generally located about three feet off the floor and covering twenty to thirty percent of a vertical wall. The sunlight they admit will cover a comparable twenty to thirty percent of the floor space in a room. At the other extreme are window walls, which allow sunlight to brighten an entire room and which are becoming increasingly popular as a means of adding light without using energy, and bay windows, which protrude beyond the plane of the wall to admit light from three directions and which may, therefore, admit light for as long as fourteen hours each day.

The glass in your windows may decrease the intensity of the light by as little as 10 percent or as much as 50 percent, depending on the angle at which the light enters. The more obliquely the light strikes the glass, the more the intensity is decreased; therefore, the high overhead light at midday in summer coming through a south window may be cut in half, while the early morning and late afternoon sun coming through east and west windows will be reduced by only 20 percent or even less.

Because of the infinite number of possibilities where natural light is involved, you should use a light meter to measure the light in the room where you will grow your plants. This is not absolutely essential, but it will give you a far better idea of how much artificial light you will need.

The light will be brightest near the windows and directly in front of them, and less bright on either side and further away. The following readings were taken in the 38-to-42-degree belt of latitude at noon on a cloudless December day. Many factors will cause your light readings to be different, but these will give you some idea of what you may find.

Directly in front of a south window, with no trees or buildings blocking the sky, the light measured 1400 foot-candles. Five feet from the window the available light dropped to 750 foot-candles. Ten feet from the window the meter registered only 450 foot-candles, as it also did at a distance of 2 feet on either side.

Directly in front of an east-facing window, the meter reading was 500 foot-candles. Five feet away the light dropped to half that amount, and at a distance of 10 feet, only 200 foot-candles were present, about the same as 3 feet to either side of the window.

Readings for a west window were only slightly lower than for the one facing east. But remember that these were mid-day light intensities. Eastern levels would be far higher in the morning; western levels would climb as the sun moved toward that horizon.

Directly in front of a north-facing window the meter revealed a mere 200 foot-candles of light, clearly demonstrating why this exposure is the gardener's last choice. On either side of the window, as well as at a distance of 6 feet, the light dropped to only 150 foot-candles, barely enough to register on the meter and nearly worthless for growing purposes.

With the possible exception of a south-facing bay window, which might receive 1000 or more-foot-candles of light for twelve or fourteen hours each day, these light levels are not high enough or long enough to grow many plants by themselves. But there are many simple and relatively inexpensive things you can do to increase both the intensity and the duration of inside sunlight. When you bring natural light to its optimum level, not only will your plants be healthier and more beautiful, but your home will also be a cheerful and more enjoyable place in which to live. It is not by coincidence that the most successful gardeners have bright and cheerful homes.

Increasing Natural Light

If some of the techniques I suggest here seem self-evident, take them as friendly reminders; simple as they seem, they may make the literal difference between night and day for a room full of plants. Most require less cost than care.

The most obvious but certainly not the least important step is to keep both your windows and the plants as clean as possible. Dirty windows reduce the amount of light reaching your plants by 30 percent or more. But even keeping your windows crystal clear will do no good if the foliage is covered with dust. About once a week the leaves should be misted or lightly bathed with a wet paintbrush. Use water that is slightly warmer than room temperature.

You may also be able to increase the light entering your home by pruning outdoor plants. Large outdoor shrubs or trees too frequently block sunlight for all or part of the day. Mature oaks, lindens, avocados, and certain evergreens can steal all the precious light if they are allowed to do so. Thinning and pruning can admit the light your indoor plants need and will improve the outdoor tree's health, too. Sometimes the problem may be solved by tying branches back to let light pass. You might also want to consider removing tall plants that are beyond their prime and replacing them with smaller specimens that will not block the entry of light.

Another obvious piece of advice is to open the curtains or shutters and raise the shades early each morning. Or even better, open all but the bedroom curtains upon retiring so that plants can take advantage of the sun's earliest rays. Heavy curtains, as well as ordinary window shades, can bar all effective light as far as plant growth is concerned. A common mistake is to adjust the movable louvers of window shutters to one position, ignoring the fact that the sun changes angles throughout the day. It is better to open the shutters completely.

It is better still to do away with shutters and curtains completely. Since natural light is brighter directly in front of the windows, that is where you are likely to be growing most of your plants. Why not let plants replace your curtains? Place artificial light fixtures above or around the glass, let some plants grow upward from inside window boxes while others vine down from hanging planters, or place your indoor trees directly in front of the window. Not only will this help solve many of your lighting problems, but it is one of the most attractive ways to display your plants.

As you have seen, the intensity of light decreases rapidly as you move away from the window. If you decide you want to grow some plants on the far side of the room, there are several tactics you can employ to guard against this loss of light intensity. Oddly enough, one of the best of these tactics calls for using curtains instead of doing away with them—but only sheer curtains will work.

Sheer curtains act as thousands of tiny reflectors, dispersing light into areas further away from the windows than it would ordinarily reach. While they will decrease the intensity of light in the window area, they will increase the amount of light further back into the room because of their reflective quality. A white nylon net curtain can decrease direct sunlight by as much as 75 percent in the area immediately in front of the window, but double the brightness of the light at a distance of five or six feet away.

As I mentioned, wall colors are important, with white being the best. Matte white paint reflects 75 percent or more of the light that strikes it and can easily increase your light by 250 foot-candles, depending on the angle and the intensity of the light itself. (Oddly enough, semi-gloss white reflects less light than matte does.)

Remember that mirrors and mirrorized walls can be powerful allies in directing and distributing light, but that the amount of light a mirror reflects can be no larger than the surface of the mirror itself. This means that mirrors must cover a fairly large surface area if they are to have any real effect. Mirrors placed behind your plants will visually expand the size of your garden, and mirrors below can serve to bounce light back up to lower leaves. Mirrorized tiles make the job easier. A plant surrounded on three sides by mirrors should, according to the United States Department of Agriculture, enjoy at least a 25 percent increase in brightness.

Less expensive than mirrors and only slightly less reflective is aluminized Mylar, one of the newer products on the market. It is a thin plastic sheet to which a thinner coat of aluminum is applied by a vacuum process. Mylar is applied much like wallpaper, and you can use it to create a large reflective area at reasonably low cost.

A related product is metalized wallpaper, which has only recently become available through decorators. This reflects less light than aluminized Mylar but more than any painted surface. It comes in a number of patterns and tints and so may be more compatible with your interior design.

These are all methods of admitting and increasing the light that comes at an angle through your windows, and several of the techniques will also increase the effectiveness of your artificial lights, but they do nothing to capture the brightest light of all—that given off by the sun when it is high in the sky.

Throughout most of the hours close around noon, when the sun is at its brightest, sunlight is blocked by walls, roofs, and overhangs. The only way this light can be brought into the home is through a window in the ceiling—a skylight.

These have been around for some time, primarily in industrial buildings. Recently, however, they have become available in low-cost prefabricated form, and they are becoming increasingly popular as a means of bringing direct sunlight into rooms that would otherwise have access to only limited amounts of sunlight. Like greenhouses, they are not for everyone, but many will welcome them as an energy-efficient means of providing quality light of high intensity.

Skylights are available in both glass and acrylic plastic, in various tints and translucencies. The most common forms are flat panels, pyramids, and bubbles. Prices start at about $125 for a 48-by-48-inch kit and go up from there. Some homes require custom designs, but most do not. (Skylights are available from the dealers listed in the Appendix.)

The design possibilities of skylights are nearly unlimited. The flat panels or bubble type can be installed singly or in tandem. A whole ceiling could be made into skylights, turning any room into a veritable greenhouse and almost, but not quite, doing away with the need for any artificial light at all. Plants that hang under the skylight can serve as a garden in the sky.

Before rushing out to buy a skylight, however, there are several things you should consider. The first is installation.

If you are very good with tools, you can probably do the installation yourself, no matter what the construction of your home. But if you have any doubts about your skills, you should take a look at the construction of your home. If there is a crawl space between the ceiling and the roof, it will be necessary to box in the skylight and form a light well, a job not everyone is capable of doing. If no crawl space is present, prefabricated kits make the installation so simple that anyone capable of handling basic tools can perform the work. Enclosed sun porches seldom have crawl spaces, so if you have such a porch, you can almost certainly add a skylight there without building a light well.

You should also give consideration to the amount of light you want to admit. The larger the surface area of the glass, the greater the duration of the light. The more translucent the glass, the higher the light intensity.

You should also consider where the light will fall when the skylight is in place. In North America skylights will light the north sides of rooms—where light is most likely to be needed by plants—and the sunlight will move from the west side of the room in the morning to the east side in the afternoon. In combination with existing wall windows, then, a skylight can keep many rooms brilliantly lit throughout the daylight hours.

These are some of the best ways to brighten your home and make your garden greener, prettier, and more productive. You may not be able to employ them all, at least not initially. But as time goes by and you see how effective the partnership between natural and artificial light can be, you may want to try to use more of the available gardening resources.

Because light is the most obvious element that you must provide for plants in the hostile home environment, it is all too easy to overlook the fact that no amount of light will grow healthy plants without proper attention to soil, water, nutrition, temperature, and humidity. These important factors for a healthy environment are explained in the chapter that follows.

3. The Garden Environment

Over many thousands of years plants have adapted to certain environmental conditions. They are accustomed to having nearly unlimited soil in which to spread their roots, free movement of air, higher humidity than is found in most homes, temperatures that are often much higher than indoors, and water that nature provides at irregular intervals but in fairly predictable amounts. Every seed and seedling inherits the need for these conditions, and plants are always healthier when the outdoor environment is duplicated, or nearly so.

The average indoor environment is naturally hostile to most plants. Conditions in a greenhouse are better, but far from perfect. Even when plants grow in containers on an outside porch, balcony, or patio, not all the conditions found in nature are likely to be present—unless the grower provides them.

But plants are remarkably adaptable and hardy. Even in a totally hostile environment, they struggle to remain alive and to grow. When conditions are reasonably close to those found in nature, plants quickly respond by providing us with fragrance, beauty, and food throughout the year.

Plants also are individuals, with individual needs. The conditions needed by one are not always the same as those needed by others. This means that the grower must provide those conditions not by creating one environment but many miniature climates suited to the plants that are to be grown.

Once you provide adequate light, drastic changes, in most instances, are not really needed. A very large number of plants will do quite well in the surroundings of the average home. Many others demand only slight differences that are easy to provide. A few plants are so demanding that you would not want to live with the conditions they need, but these plants can be reserved for your outdoor spaces or for growing in a greenhouse.

Planters

No matter what part of the home you select for your plants, planters and containers will become part of their environment, and in selecting these you are making a decision that will affect the health of your plants; so containers should be chosen with an eye toward the needs of the plant, not just your decor.

How well the planter suits the needs of the plant should be your first consideration. This refers to how well the container will function in helping provide the proper plant-growing environment, especially the conditions needed by the plants' roots.

The container itself can and does influence the growth effects of any of its contents—soil, organic matter, microbiological life, nutrients, air, and water. Choosing the proper container insures that this influence is positive and contributes to the healthy growth of the plants.

All containers should have a hole or holes so that drainage of water occurs and the proper balance of air is restored to the soil after each watering. A good supply of air is essential to root function and growth. Containers made of porous materials are best for this reason. As moisture evaporates from the outer surface of such pots, the soil and the roots remain cool and the air near the plants remains humid. Porous pots tend to dry out more rapidly at warmer temperatures, but this can easily be prevented by burying the pots in a bed of moist sphagnum, peat moss, vermiculite, or even sawdust inside a larger container.

Nonporous containers, such as those of glazed terra-cotta, stoneware, glass, or plastic, allow no evaporation through the planter and do not keep the contents as cool nor the air above them as humid as do porous containers. Plants in nonporous containers will need water less frequently, but this is not really an advantage, and these planters are less desirable.

A container's ability to retard heat is relatively important, especially when the plants are in a very warm room, in a greenhouse, or in direct sunlight. Roots generally function better at a temperature several degrees cooler than the above-ground portion of the plant. Wooden containers—which resist heat penetration and do a good job of keeping the roots cool—are best for plants that are to be grown at high temperatures.

Like all other pots and planters, wooden containers should have slots or holes in the bottom for drainage. The bottom of a wooden container should be raised an inch or so on cleats, bricks, or blocks of wood to prevent its standing in moisture that accumulates through drainage.

Container shape can be an important consideration in making the most of limited space. Planters come in nearly every shape one could imagine, many of them extremely wasteful of your gardening space. The space directly beneath your artificial lights is most likely to be rectangular. Your window ledges also consist of oblong areas. Using round or irregularly shaped planters in such areas wastes a great deal of space. Square, oblong, or rectangular planters, which can be placed side by side or end to end, allow you to make better use of your lighted space.

But container size is by far the most important consideration. The size a plant needs is roughly dependent on the size of the root mass that you wish the planter ultimately to accommodate. A container that is too small will cause restricted root masses and will slow down development of the upper part of the plant. Crowding several plants will result in none growing well. Some restrictions on the roots can be useful in keeping shrubs and trees small enough for indoor purposes, but too much restriction leads to root-bound conditions and unhealthy plants. Containers that are too large, on the other hand, may favor root growth over top growth or just be wasteful of space and soil, giving you unnecessarily heavy containers that are difficult to move— and mobility is a desirable feature in containers.

There will be many times when, for a variety of reasons, you will want to move your plants. Most pots are small enough and light enough to make this easy. Plant carts and plant perambulators make the job even faster and easier. For holding very large plants, wooden containers are good, because their lighter weight makes them easier to move, especially when they are mounted on casters. Because wooden planters are becoming so expensive, the Appendix lists the addresses of two organizations that will send you, without charge, plans for building wooden planters of all types.

Soil

Proper soil is essential to most plants as a reservoir of water and nutrients and as a place in which the roots may grow and function. Each potted plant is limited to a certain amount of soil, and the necessary watering tends to compact this and leach out the natural nutrients. This compacting of the soil is one problem that plagues all who grow plants in containers, but you can overcome it by providing soil that contains a good proportion of organic material for nourishment and moisture retention, and some inorganic material, such as sand, for drainage.

Nearly every gardening book derides "ordinary garden soil" as a growing medium, yet the simple truth is that there is no such thing as ordinary garden soil. Scientists have classified well over fifty thousand types of soil, with more being classified almost daily. No single type is ideal for growing every plant.

Scientists also divide soil into three major groups: sandy soils, loamy soils, and clayey soils. Within the major groups there are many minor groupings, such as fine sands, clay loams, and gravelly clays. By far the largest number of soils are in the loam classification, which is fortunate for those who wish to mix their own growing mediums. If you do wish to mix your own, then you should know how to perform the simple test that will give you a good idea of your soil's class and texture.

Rub a sample between your thumb and forefinger. Sand particles are gritty. Loam has a floury or talcum-powder feel when dry and is only moderately plastic when wet. Clay material is harsh when dry and very sticky and plastic when wet, and will harden and cause many problems if used in pots. Simple as this test sounds, it is the one soil scientists use in all field surveys.

The ideal soil structure is a granular one in which the rounded aggregates, or clusters of soil, lie loosely and readily shake apart. Such "crumbs" of soil are what you should look for if you intend to dig your own growing medium.

For those who live in the city, this is not always possible, and for some it is simply too troublesome. For these gardeners, commercial potting soil is a workable substitute. Its texture is akin to the best granular loam, and it has the added advantage of being sterile.

If you do dig and mix your own soil, you must sterilize it to rid it of weed and grass seeds, insect eggs, and infectious organisms. Place it in a 160-degree oven for an hour, or have the soil steamed at a nursery or garden center.

Whether you dig your soil or use a commercial mix, you should know both its pH and its nutrient content. Testing kits available for about $10 in gardening stores will tell you all you need to know about each.

The pH rating of soil refers to its acidity or alkalinity. The scale ranges from 1 (acid) to 14 (alkaline), with 7.0 as neutral. Most commercial potting soils are neutral or only slightly acid, but some are highly acidic. Generally speaking, a neutral soil has more gardening uses than any other, but there are many plants that prefer highly acid soils, while some will grow best in soil that is alkaline.

To find the pH rating of your soil with a testing kit, you simply place a soil sample in a test tube and introduce a chemical known as a reagent. The reaction is then compared to a chart which provides the pH rating of the soil. To adjust this rating toward alkalinity, you need only add ground limestone; for more acidity you can add peat moss, moss, ground sulfur, or iron sulfate. How much to use to cause the desired change is specified in the pH testing kits.

Most of the herbs and vegetables in this book are fast-growing annuals and will need no repotting. However, to grow trees and shrubs in large tubs or planters and maintain them over long periods of time, it is best to replace the soil completely at least every other year, and preferably once a year; otherwise fertilizer residues may build up, and killing fungus diseases may develop.

Nutrients

While knowing the pH rating of your soil is important, knowing its nutrient level is doubly so. Plants that grow in pots are isolated from their natural means of obtaining food and are entirely dependent on what you provide. In order to know how much of what to provide, you must first know which nutrients are adequately present and which are lacking. A soil-testing kit allows you to determine this.

The three main plant nutrients are nitrogen, phosphorus, and potassium (also known as potash). While other trace elements play lesser roles in plant growth, these three are the ones to which you must give the most attention, and they are the ones which you can most readily provide.

Nitrogen makes foliage lush and green. This element also helps give plants a longer period of active growth and thus increases fruit production. Nitrogen deficiency causes yellowing of leaves and stunted growth; but too much nitrogen, on the other hand, causes stems that are too long and weak, fruit that fails to develop, and plants that are highly susceptible to disease.

All growing plants need *phosphorus*, which is especially important for a strong root system, for flowering and fruit development, and for resistance to disease. A deficiency causes plants that are stunted and unusually thin, with purplish foliage, and fruit that fails to mature as it normally would.

Potassium carries needed carbohydrates through the plant system and is extremely important to the overall strength of the plant. It is needed if a plant is to develop its stems properly, and helps fight diseases. Potassium also decreases the water requirements of plants, promotes better color in fruit, aids plants in utilizing nitrogen, and helps plants in the production of starches and sugars. If plants are slow-growing and stunted, with browning leaves and fruit that drops prematurely from the branches, it is probably due to a deficiency of potassium.

A soil-testing kit will let you know exactly how much of each of the three major nutrients you need to add. The kits consist of glass vials in which you mix soil samples with one or the other of several liquids; the liquid changes color, and you match the color to a chart to find the content of the element causing the change.

To check for nitrogen with a typical kit, you fill the test tube one quarter full of soil, add the solution marked Nitrogen until the tube is half-full, then shake and allow the soil to settle. If the liquid turns a reddish-brown, reference to the kit's color chart indicates that a low-nitrogen fertilizer—one containing only 2 percent nitrogen compounds—is called for. At the other end of the scale, a bright green hue would indicate the need for much more nitrogen, supplied by a fertilizer containing 8 percent nitrogen compounds. In this same fashion you can determine the need for phosphorus or potassium.

The simplest way to adjust the chemical balance of the soil is to add a fertilizer that is suitably proportioned. A wide variety, high in one element, low in the others, is available. Whether liquid or solid, these mixes contain standard proportions of the three major elements—nitrogen, phosphorus, and potassium. The percentage of each is indicated by a series of numbers: a common liquid fertilizer is labeled 10-15-10, meaning that, undiluted, it contains 10 percent nitrogen compounds, 15 percent phosphorus, and 10 percent potassium. Such liquid fertilizers are well suited to home gardening, because you can give them as you water the plants, but be careful about applying them often—overfeeding is a leading cause of casualties among indoor plants.

Capsules and time-release fertilizers are also available, but I do not recommend them. These automatically spread the application over a long period of time, which can be a disadvantage. Most food plants are fast-growing. Those that are not, such as fruit trees, are likely to require a period of dormancy, most likely during the winter months. The time-release fertilizers are all too likely to be stimulating growth at a time when the plants need rest, and such stimulation can result in the death of the plant.

Using prepared fertilizer mixes will suffice in most instances, but there will be times when it is preferable to add one major nutrient without adding the other two. This is the means by which you provide the subtle variations in feeding that make the difference between ordinary plants and plants that are spectacular.

Various compounds are available for this purpose. You mix them with the soil, usually before planting, to provide the desired nutrient level. If, for example, you want to raise only the nitrogen level, sodium nitrate or ammonium sulphate is called for. To add phosphorus use superphosphate; and for potash mix in potassium sulfate or potassium chloride. There are other means, often using common household waste such as coffee grounds or readily available garden nutrients such as bone meal; you will find a few of the better ways in the text dealing with the individual plants.

Water

Water, which is essential to all life, carries minerals from the soil to the leaves of the plant and serves as raw material in the manufacture of plant food in the leaves. Probably more potted plants are lost due to improper watering than any other single reason, yet it is impossible to set absolute guidelines for meeting the water requirements of plants; there are simply too many variables.

The amount of water a plant needs will vary not only according to its species, size, and age but will also be affected by the type and amount of soil in which it is grown, the room temperature and humidity, the type of container, and even by the intensity of light. Plants need more water when setting fruit, far less when they are in dormancy.

It is for these reasons that no one knowledgeable in gardening will tell you to give a plant one or two cups of water, or any other specific amount. The best general rule is to water when the soil feels dry to the touch about an inch below the surface, adding tepid water until it drains through the hole at the bottom of the planter.

Submerging a porous pot in water to its rim, a procedure known as bottom watering, takes more time, but many gardeners do this. But whether you add moisture from above or below, pot saucers need to have excess water poured off within an hour after watering. Never allow your planters to stand in water.

Plants in nature are able to withstand relatively long periods without water, but are subject to quick decline or death when their roots are surrounded by water. Too frequent watering also encourages shallow root growth, and shallow roots are more susceptible to disease and do a poor job of feeding the upper plants. Water given too frequently from above also results in the upper soil becoming saturated with water while the bottom soil in the planter dries out and never receives water or nutrients. For these reasons it is better to allow the pot soil to become nearly dry and then provide adequate water in a single, liberal application. The few plants that do need constant moisture have been singled out in the text.

There is a very good reason why so many house plants die from overwatering: the symptoms are very much like those of dehydration, oddly enough, or of light deficiency. When the leaves and stems of a plant turn yellow, wilt, and fall, there is a natural inclination to attempt to cure the problem by feeding or watering the plant. Should your plants show these symptoms, check the moisture of the soil carefully before taking any action. If the soil seems overly damp, you may be able to save the plant by giving it a chance to dry out or by transplanting it and providing a fresh start.

Most drinking water is safe for your plants. You should, however, avoid using softened water, which is high in sodium; this is seldom a problem because most water softeners work only on the hot tap.

Several inexpensive automatic watering devices are on the market, and these help care for the needs of plants when you are away from home. Water wicks provide a constant water supply by drawing water from an adjacent container as the plant needs it. Also available are pots with built-in reservoirs for the plants to draw from whenever the soil is dry. The major gardening suppliers listed in the Appendix also sell a new potting soil called Viterra, which uses special ingredients to increase the water retention of the growing medium. It allows the plants to go longer between waterings and helps eliminate many of the watering problems. According to the manufacturers and suppliers, Viterra has been successfully used to grow a wide variety of plants and should be an acceptable medium for any plant that can be grown in commercial potting soil.

If you are one of those incurables who simply cannot pass a plant without wanting to water it, then why not give hydroponic gardening a try? In hydroponic gardening the plants grow in vermiculite through which water and nutrients constantly circulate, and the kits that have only recently appeared on the market make this the easiest gardening of all. Hydroponic gardening is more completely described in a later chapter, and while it has numerous advantages, the greatest of those may be the way in which it solves all the problems related to watering plants.

Humidity

Humidity refers to the amount of water in the air in vapor form. The warmer the air, the more moisture it is capable of holding. During the summer months, when plants are most actively growing, the outside environment is not only warmer than the interior of most homes, it is also far more humid; and the humidity is created, to a large extent, by the vast number of plants growing outside.

Plants do better in high humidity. This is one reason why the kitchen—where the humidity is raised by the steam given off during cooking and from the hot-water tap—has long been the favorite room of the indoor gardener. It is a major reason why the greenhouse environment is so favorable to plants.

Even without a greenhouse, there are many steps you can take to provide higher humidity for your plants. The simplest technique is to allow them to provide their own. Through respiration, plants release some moisture into the air. More moisture evaporates from the growing medium. It is for these reasons that plants generally do better when grown in close proximity to other plants, a situation that raises the level of humidity in the immediate vicinity.

Grouping your smaller plants together and placing them on trays filled with pebbles allows you to do even more to raise the humidity. Water you pour over the pebbles will not come into contact with the bottoms of the pots, and the trays also serve to catch the excess after watering. Evaporation adds moisture to the air, a result that can also be achieved by placing small containers of fresh water among your plant collection.

In very dry rooms, spray the leaves now and then with fresh water from a mister, which also helps keep them clean. Reserve this treatment for plants with shiny leaves or foliage, however, as it can damage those leaves that appear to be covered with tiny hairs.

Portable humidifiers are also available, as well as relatively inexpensive humidifiers that can be added to most heating systems. But humidity created through natural evaporation and respiration uses no energy and is therefore the wisest to use. When the humidity is high, humans are far more comfortable in the cooler winter temperatures now being suggested for homes because of the energy crisis, so a large number of plants may prove functional as well as beautiful.

Temperature

Most plants will grow quite well in the temperature range in the average home—in the sixties during the day and the fifties at night. Most plants prefer cooler temperatures at night, as a matter of fact, but a few tropical and semitropical plants may suffer when temperatures drop below 60 degrees, and these may need to be kept in an especially warm room.

Within any room of the house, you will find surprising variations in temperature. Even though the thermostat in a room may be set at 68 degrees, not every part of that room will maintain exactly that temperature; areas exposed to direct sunlight may be several degrees warmer, while those near a door may be several degrees cooler. In selecting the site or sites for growing your plants, you should carefully check the temperature with a thermometer and keep a fairly constant check on it thereafter. A special greenhouse thermometer, which will reveal at a glance the highest and the lowest temperature recorded during the previous 24-hour period, is the ideal instrument for this purpose.

While most plants will grow quite well at ordinary room temperatures, many can be harmed by constantly fluctuating conditions. For that reason your garden should be protected from prolonged blasts of hot or cold air from opened doors or windows or from heating or cooling sources. Remember, too, that many plants will not tolerate air blowing directly on them, although they do require enough ventilation to keep water vapor from forming on their leaves.

The processes of growth normally become slower or stop altogether in extreme temperatures—either too hot or too cold. Inside plants are protected from these extremes. On the other hand, there are times when some of your plants may require temperatures much higher or much lower than you can provide in your home. For example, a few plants may need higher temperatures when setting fruit and some others may not set fruit unless they have been exposed to near-freezing temperatures during the previous winter. These temperature conditions are best provided by growing the plants in an outdoor container or in a home greenhouse, where the temperature can be raised and lowered at will.

There are also times when increasing the temperature only a few degrees will help. The easiest way to do this, without increasing the temperature of the entire room, is to place ordinary incandescent light bulbs, which produce heat, over or around the plants. Be sure to use low wattage bulbs, adding only 20 watts of incandescent for each 80 watts of fluorescent light, and be careful not to increase the temperature too much and burn the plants. Incandescent plant-growth bulbs, even the supposedly cool ones that require porcelain fixtures, produce more heat than fluorescents and can be highly useful for this purpose, providing more light even as they warm your plants.

The problems caused by extreme temperatures outnumber the benefits. Bear in mind that the higher the temperature, the more humidity plants need to compensate for loss of moisture through evaporation. Plants in a greenhouse or under a skylight may also need to be protected from the effects of the hottest sun.

On the other end of the thermal scale, even indoor plants close to windows may freeze when the temperature drops during a severe winter. These plants must be protected by moving them to a warmer spot, or by placing a piece of cardboard between the plants and the window.

4. The Miracle of Pollination

Pollination, an early step in the process by which plants produce fruit and seeds and thereby reproduce themselves, is truly one of the great miracles of nature, akin to the miracle of human birth. In assisting your plants with the pollination that is necessary for the production of many types of fruit, you work more closely with nature than at almost any other time, and you will surely find it one of the most enjoyable tasks in home gardening.

Pollination refers to the transfer of pollen from the anthers to the stigma of a flower. In nature pollen is moved about by one of two means: carried by insects or carried by wind.

Most wind-pollinated plants are small and insignificant, with their stigma and anthers freely exposed to the wind. The pollen they produce is very fine and light, for otherwise the wind could not carry it far. But they produce pollen in great abundance (as it must be if pollination must be achieved by such haphazard means), and a small shower of pollen may result when a wind-pollinated plant is accidentally jostled.

Ragweed, grasses, corn, and several types of grain as well as many of our trees are pollinated by the wind. These are important plants, to be sure, but few are suited to home gardening, and members of the group are not included in this book.

Early gardeners were vaguely aware of the need for pollination in fruit-bearing plants, but they had little idea that it was a form of sexual generation or that bees and other insects played an important role in carrying the pollen from blossom to blossom. Greek and Roman authors as early as 373 B.C. described the hand pollination of date palms, and Aristotle described the habits of honey bees in his history of animals, but the action of the honey bees was not linked with pollination until much later.

An awareness of sexual fusion in plants seems to have developed in the seventeenth century. In a paper he read before the royal society in

1682, Cehemiah Drew, an English botanist, said, "The attire [sta-mens] doth serve as the male, for the generation of the seed."

By 1694 experiments in Germany established that a sexual genera-tion does occur, but it was not until 1780 that a botanist named Christian Conrad Sprengel carried out experiments that established the relationship between insects and flowers. Nearly a century later Darwin published his studies of pollination, and for the first time people realized how critically important to food production the lowly insects are.

The insects do not, of course, realize that they are pollinating the plants. They visit the plants for other reasons. But pollination does not occur purely by accident: it is one of the most carefully constructed scenarios in all of nature.

Most often insects visit blossoms in search of nectar; they are drawn to the plant by the large and showy blossoms that are typical of plants pollinated in this way. But the nectar that they seek is hidden in such a manner that, to reach it, the bee or other insect must brush against the reproductive organs of the plant. But even this is not left to chance. Most nectar-producing flowers have color patterns, called nectar guides, that surround or point to the opening that the insect must enter in order to reach the nectar. The face of a pansy is its nectar guide. In irises and violets, the guides are lines leading to the nectar. A star-shaped pattern surrounds the nectar opening in morn-ing glories and petunias. These nectar guides take various colors and forms, but they are always placed so that, when they are followed by a bee or other insect, pollination or a part of the pollinating process is almost certain to occur.

Exactly what occurs next depends on the type of flower the bee or insect enters. Flowers have four main parts. These are the sepals, petals, stamens, and pistils. The sepals on most flowers are green and look like leaves, and are the lowermost part of the flower, usually surrounding the other flower parts. Above these are the petals, usually shaped like leaves but some color other than green.

The stamens of the flower play the male role in pollination. Usually, but not always, the stamens rise above the other parts of the flower. A flower may have several stamens or, where only female blossoms are borne on the plant, it will have none. Each stamen consists of two parts: a filament and an anther. The filament is merely a stalk. The anther extends from the top of this stalk, and it is here that pollen is produced.

Pollen usually looks like a yellow dust. But when they are placed under a microscope, the pollen grains of each species of flowering plant will reveal its own peculiar shape and markings. No matter what its shape and markings, though, each pollen grain consists of two living cells; one is called a tube cell, the other a generative cell, and each plays an important part in the reproduction of the plant, which begins when pollen reaches the female parts of the plant.

These are the pistils, These, too, come in different numbers, sizes, and shapes. The pistil has three parts: ovary, styles, and stigmas. The ovary is the lowermost, swollen part of the pistil. Above the ovary are one or several stalks, the styles. At the top of each style is a feathery stigma, which serves to collect any pollen that comes its way.

The ovary holds several minute white objects known as ovules. Inside each ovule is an embryosac, a young plant that will develop if it is pollinated. Each embryosac holds two cells: the egg cell and the generative cell. These are activated by contact with the two cells in any pollen grain from the right stamen that is transferred to the ovary of the flower.

When the ovules inside the ovary are pollinated and ripen, they become the seeds that will start the new plant, while the ovary itself ripens into fruit. Most ovaries will not ripen into fruit unless their ovules are ripening into seed, although bananas, pineapples, and a few other seedless fruits are exceptions.

The vast majority of plants have both stamens and pistils in the same flower. Such flowers are known as hermaphroditic, a term that is derived from the names of the Greek god Hermes and the goddess Aphrodite, and which means having both male and female parts. In such flowers pollination occurs very readily in most instances, for the male and female parts are usually arranged in a fashion that makes the transfer of pollen very easy to accomplish. Generally the male stamens are above the female pistils, and both are above the nectar well. This means that a bee seeking nectar must first pass the stamens, picking up a bit of pollen on a body that nature has made ideal for this purpose, and then go beyond the pistils, where a few grains of pollen will be deposited to continue the cycle of life.

Most plants with hermaphroditic flowers are easily pollinated by the home gardener, because all the necessary elements are present. Just by gently easing a tiny cotton swab or the tip of a watercolor brush into the center of each blossom, the gardener can transfer enough pollen from stamens to pistils to be sure of the development of fruit.

A small number of plants with hermaphroditic flowers cannot easily be pollinated in this manner, because their stamens produce pollen at a time when the pistils are not receptive or the pistils are receptive only when the stamens are not producing pollen. For example, some avocado plants have flowers in which the anthers shed pollen only in the afternoon, while the stigmas are receptive only in the morning. Other trees of the same species reverse the cycle. This means that two or more plants must be present before pollination can occur, thus making it possible for each plant to pollinate, and be pollinated by, the other. For the oudoor gardener with unlimited space, this usually poses no problem. But for the indoor gardener with limited space at his or her disposal, such plants are clearly unacceptable, and so those species which require more than one plant for pollination have been excluded from this book.

Which brings us to the matter of self-pollination. To be horticulturally correct about it, *self-pollination* refers to the transfer of pollen from the anthers of a flower of one variety to the stigma of a flower of the same variety. It does *not* mean that a plant will produce seed and fruit without this transfer taking place. When a plant will not produce fruit with viable seed following the transfer of pollen from the stigma of its own flowers or the flowers of a plant of the same species, that plant is said to be self-unfruitful. Self-unfruitful plants require pollination from other plants with which they are compatible. They cannot be pollinated without the presence of the pollinator species, and so they are unacceptable for most home gardening.

Orchardists were long plagued by the problems of pollination, especially those who grew apples, plums, figs, pears, and most sweet cherry varieties. To grow these and make them bear fruit, it was also necessary to grow pollinating trees of a compatible variety.

The introduction of self-pollinating fruit trees has changed all that. All of our most popular fruit trees are now available in self-pollinating dwarf varieties, making them suitable for growers with limited space. But remember that *self-pollinating,* as used here and as used in the suppliers' catalogs, does not mean that these trees will bear fruit without the transfer of pollen; it means, instead, that they need no cross-pollinating species. They must be grown outside, where they can be pollinated by insects, or they must be pollinated by gently inserting a cotton swab into each blossom, as previously described. Even when growing these plants outside, city gardeners may find it necessary to assist the process of pollination by using the cotton swab or watercolor brush, because honeybees, nature's finest assistants, may not be present. Other insects will transfer some pollen, it is true, but not as much as the honeybee or the gentle touch of the gardener.

But what of those plants which appear to produce fruit with no help from the gardener and without the presence of insects? Probably you know some gardener who has a plant or two that has produced fruit with absolutely no assistance, even though that plant has absolutely no contact with insects. Many plants are capable of producing fruit under such circumstances, but the fact remains that pollination does occur.

These are the plants that could more rightfully be called self-pollinating, for they all have hermaphroditic flowers, will accept their own pollen, and will produce fruit and seed with no *obvious* help from any source. The tomato is a notable member of this group.

In tomato flowers the pistil is shorter than the stamen and its anther, and the two are so near to one another that no pollen escapes from the conical part of the blossom. When the flower is shaken for any reason, as by a breeze or the slightest touch of an insect, some of the pollen falls onto the stigma of the pistil, and pollination occurs. Thus an indoor tomato plant can be pollinated by giving it a gentle shaking.

Beans, peas, peanuts, lentils, and their relatives form a large class of plants known as legumes. Their flowers differ somewhat in color, but each flower has one large petal called a standard, two petals called wings, and two more petals united into a keel. The stamens and pistils are inside this keel, so near to one another that some flowers will always manage pollination, though fruiting will be increased by gently moving the vines when they are in flower.

In many of the citrus plants, the stamens and pistils are so arranged that fruiting does occur without pollination, by means of a process known as autonomic parthenocarpy. As long ago as 1928, scientists found that this phenomenon could occur even when the trees were experimentally isolated from any possible means of pollination. Some trees capable of doing this are the ordinary varieties of navel orange, the satsuma mandarin, the Marsh grapefruit, the Tahiti lime, and nearly all the lemon varieties. The fruit produced by this phenomenon is likely to be seedless and will always be much less abundant than on a tree that has been pollinated. It is advisable, therefore, to pollinate the blossoms by gently touching the center of each with a cotton swab of a suitable size. Several plants produce fruit by processes similar to autonomic parthenocarpy, and while artificially pollinating these plants may not always help, it can never hurt.

At the other extreme are the species in which some plants have only male (staminate) flowers, while the female (pistillate) flowers are borne on other plants of the same species. Such plants are called dioecious, and are obviously incapable of pollinating themselves. Since there is no way the home gardener can assure pollination with these, plants from this group have been excluded from this book. The Capri Fig, for example, is a plant you will not be able to grow for this reason.

Between the two extremes are the monoecious plants—plants that have separate male and female flowers but have them on the same plant. In many species from this group, the male and female flowers are produced at different times, making self-pollination unlikely but not altogether impossible. With such plants pollination is easier to achieve if you grow two or more plants, thus increasing the chances of having male and female blossoms present at the same time and overcoming the plant's natural resistance to self-pollination.

The reasons for this resistance are unknown, but they certainly have to do with the viability of the pollen. Fruit production is far higher when pollen can be transferred from the male flower of one plant to a female flower of another plant of the same species. Yet when a second plant of the same species is not present, most plants in this group will discontinue their resistance, produce male and female flowers at the same time, accept the transfer of pollen, and develop fruit and seed. It is as if the plant becomes desperate to reproduce.

The cucumber is a typical member of this group. Like most other monoecious plants, the male flowers of the cucumber appear well in advance of the female, and the former will far outnumber the latter, as if to assure a plenitude of pollen. Also like other members of the group, the female blossoms are easily recognized by the miniature fruit that can be seen behind them even before pollination occurs. If the female blossom does not receive pollen from a male blossom of the same species within reasonable time, the flower will fall away and the miniature fruit will shrivel and fail to develop. But if the transfer of pollen is successfully accomplished, the egg cells of the ovary will be fertilized and you will be able to witness one of the most miraculous events in nature, the growth of fruit and the final steps in the reproductive process.

Using a magnifying glass will make it possible for you to distinguish between the stamens and pistils of the flowers, but this is not really necessary unless you are interested in studying the flowers. Nor is it always necessary that you be able to distinguish between the types of flowers and their various parts. All you really need is a cotton swab or a watercolor brush small enough to easily enter the center of the blossom—and a very delicate touch. In the text dealing with the plants, I have briefly described the blossoms of the plants that require pollination. Most of these plants have hermaphroditic flowers, which means that by gently touching the swab to the center of each flower and very delicately moving it about, pollen will be transferred from the stamens to the pistils, and from flower to flower. Repeating the process several times will assure that some of the pistils will be fertilized.

Where the male and female flowers are separate, you must collect the pollen from the male flower, then deposit it in the female. This usually means getting well down inside the female flower, so just a tiny bit of cotton on the tip of a toothpick is the tool to use. With your first few attempts you will easily learn to distinguish between male and female flowers, not only because of the tiny fruit that can be seen developing behind the females, but also because you will be able to see tiny bits of pollen clinging to the cotton after it has been in contact with a male flower. If any doubts remain, just moving the swab from blossom to blossom, touching the inner parts of each several times, will assure that a few of the pistillate flowers are pollinated.

The gentle touch is the key. Most blossoms are extremely delicate, and only tenuously attached to the plant. To get inside them without knocking them from the stem and thus losing the fruit that would be produced requires caution, practice, and a steady hand. But it is well worth the time and trouble, for it greatly increases the number and variety of fruiting plants you can grow.

If you are cursed with an unsteady hand, or if for other reasons you are unable or unwilling to do the work of pollination, you will still find many fruits and vegetables described in this book that you can grow. Plants will produce fruit with no help from you. (Where the need for pollination is *not* mentioned in the text describing any fruit or fruitlike vegetable, these are plants that will pollinate themselves.)

Hormone Compounds

Two hormone compounds on the market can be useful in the production of fruits and berries. Called Blossom-set and Berry-set, both are products of Science Products Company of Chicago, Illinois.

Several authors have mistakenly assumed that these compounds actually pollinate the blossoms or that they make the pistils more receptive to pollen that is transferred from the stamens. They do neither, although in some respects they give the appearance of doing so; but they are useful in other ways.

In both these products the active ingredient is beto-napthoxyacetic acid. Nearly forty years ago, while doing research for his master's degree at the University of Chicago, a young scientist named Gene Olshansky found that this acid had certain beneficial effects on tomatoes he was growing in his own garden. Foremost among those effects was the way the treatment prevented early blossoms from dropping off the tomato plants, which is always a problem when tomatoes are grown in cool weather. By preventing the loss of blossoms, the acid enabled each plant to produce more tomatoes as well as to set its fruit earlier, thus providing a longer growing season, which allowed the tomatoes to achieve larger size. Some of the tomatoes produced in these early experiments were seedless and received attention in Ripley's "Believe It or Not" column. That publicity led to Olshansky's founding of Science Products Company.

Blossom-set gives the appearance of pollinating largely because of the way it is applied, but also because of the plants on which most people use it. Tomatoes, for example, can be pollinated by the slightest movement of the blossoms. The hormone compound is usually applied as a spray, and it is probable that the force of the spray itself causes the transfer of pollen, but the compound does not act as a pollinator of *any* plant.

It does, however, have its worthwhile effects. Not only does it help prevent the loss of blossoms before they can be pollinated and set fruit, but there is some evidence to indicate that it stimulates the naturally occurring hormones in certain fruits and vegetables, causing them to grow faster, longer, and to a larger size.

While the active ingredient in the two compounds is the same, the Berry-set action is not exactly the same as the action of Blossom-set, due at least in part to the fact that the two sprays are applied in different ways and to different types of plants. Gene Olshansky described for me the reaction of Berry-set on strawberries.

> As a strawberry grows on the plant, the growth of the berry is promoted by naturally occurring hormones in the achenes, or drupelets, of the fruit. These achenes are the site of all hormones which occur naturally in the strawberry. As the berries attain half their size, they begin to turn in color from green to white. At this period of growth the naturally occurring hormones have been used up and the size to which the berry will grow is fairly well predetermined. By spraying with the synthetic plant hormone in Berry-set, additional growth promotion is provided similar to that which was provided by the naturally occurring hormone. Thus the berries grow to a larger size than they would have without the spray. Research at Michigan State University, many years ago, proved an increase in size of as much as 57 percent.

So the Blossom-set compound prevents the open blossoms from dropping and increases the setting and possibly the size of fruit, while the Berry-set compound increases the size of fruit that is already set. Both are available at garden centers in powdered form that you can dilute in water, or already prepared in aerosol cans. They have been tested on several types of fruits and vegetables; they can help increase production in some, but don't expect them to pollinate the blossoms.

5. Hydroponic Gardening

Hydroponic gardening has been practiced for thousands of years. Marco Polo told of his discovery of floating gardens in China, similar to the floating gardens that were also being tended along the Nile; and centuries later the Spanish found Aztec lakes where rafts supported plants whose roots pulled their nutrition directly out of the water. The famous Hanging Gardens of Babylon probably worked on the same system of hydroponics—growing plants without soil.

Like many other forms of plant culture, people forgot the science of hydroponics with the passage of time. Scientists experimented with it briefly in the 1920s, then once again allowed it to slip back into obscurity. Not until the 1970s was the ancient art revived, but this time it came back with a passion, and hydroponic gardening is certainly here to stay.

In hydroponic gardening, plants are grown in sand and gravel or some sterile medium such as vermiculite. Their roots are bathed in a water-and-fertilizer solution that provides maximum nutrition, sometimes at timed intervals, sometimes continuously. The results, when compared to traditional soil gardening, can be astounding.

A typical hydroponic garden uses only about one twentieth of the water needed for a regular garden. It requires only about one eighth the space needed for gardening in soil. Since the roots are being regularly bathed with nutrients, there is no competition among the plants for food. And since there is no need for roots to spread out and struggle for food and water, the plants use most of their energy for upward growth—producing top growth three to ten times faster than plants that are grown in soil.

Because of these obvious advantages, there has been a great outburst of commercial interest in hydroponic gardening. One firm is building a fifty-thousand-square-foot facility near DeKalb, Illinois, to produce salad greens that by 1980 will be marketed throughout several midwestern states, and another firm has already established six facilities across the United States for the hydroponic production of mushrooms. Even NASA is said to be designing hydroponic systems that will be used to provide colonists in outer space with their own supply of fresh fruits and vegetables.

Since 1978 award-winning executive chef Arno Schmidt of the famed Waldorf-Astoria has been using modern hydroponics to keep his kitchen supplied with the fresh out-of-season herbs he needs to prepare the gourmet dishes served there. Although he changes the herb varieties from time to time, the kitchen hydroponic garden almost always holds the standard herbs—dill, rosemary, tarragon, marjoram, basil, chervil, sage, thyme, and oregano.

Commercial hydroponic installations have been available for several years, and all of them work along the same principles. A nutrient solution is delivered to the roots by means of electric pumps. These submersible pumps push the solution from a reservoir below to the growing space above, where the plants are rooted in vermiculite or another sterile medium. Until recently even the smallest of these units cost at least $250, and larger ones could easily set the buyer back $1000 or more.

Now, however, new hydroponic units are just coming on the market that bring the cost of this type of gardening within reach of the average home gardener. At least two firms, one in Canada and one in the United States, presently manufacture such kits, and probably more firms will enter the market in the very near future. Sales are expected to top one million units in 1980 alone, as the kits are being sold through major chains such as Sears Roebuck, Montgomery-Ward, and J. C. Penney, as well as at garden supply centers and major supermarkets. The kits are designed to retail for less than $45.

Hydrogarden, marketed by the B & C West Company of San Francisco, is the hydroponic gardening unit most readily available at the present ime. The unit comes assembled and is small enough to fit on almost any table or window ledge, yet it is said to be capable of producing as many vegetables as you could grow in ten square feet of garden space.

Like most other hydroponic gardening units, the Hydrogarden uses vermiculite as the growing medium. Water and nutrients are placed in the reservoir beneath the vermiculite, and an air pump keeps them circulating continuously. The unit is said to cost only 6¢ per day to operate, and it makes a gentle gurgling noise no louder than a coffee percolator. The unit holds 2 gallons of water.

Putting the hydroponic unit into operation could hardly be simpler.

The HydroGarden, an electrically-powered hydroponic planter.

It comes with a supply of nutrient concentrate, which dissolves in the water that is poured over the vermiculite. A fill line on the reservoir tells you when you have added enough water and indicates when more water is needed. The unit is then plugged in and allowed to run for at least ten hours daily.

The nutrient concentrate that is provided with the Hydrogarden is a 10-8-22 formula, a good all-purpose nutrient. However, if you wish to grow any plant with different nutritional requirements, such as the cucumber, which feeds heavily on nitrogen, you can dissolve another formula in the water and pour it over the vermiculite. Just remember that all the plants in the hydroponic gardening unit will be receiving the same food, and select ones that are reasonably compatible.

After the pump has run for a few minutes and saturated the vermiculite with water and nutrients, it is time to plant the seeds—and here you enjoy one of the first advantages of hydroponic gardening. The seeds need only be half the distance apart that would be required in soil, because they will develop a far smaller root structure than plants grown by ordinary methods.

Not only can you grow the plants much closer together, but you can grow plants that are not ordinarily grown in the home because they have sprawling root systems requiring too much soil. Most melon plants grown in soil, for example, have sprawling root systems that may go several feet deep. The Hydrogarden growing tank is only about eight inches deep, yet, according to its manufacturers, it has been successfully used for the cultivation of watermelon, cantaloupe, honeydew melon, zucchini, and summer squash—all of which send out extremely deep roots in soil. The cantaloupe plant that is thriving in the hydroponic unit the company sent to me for testing seems to confirm this.

Doing away with the need for a fully developed root structure opens up many gardening possibilities. The tomato provides a good example of what this means. Many favorite varieties of tomato—especially those which bear the largest fruit—are towering plants, with roots that usually penetrate to a depth almost exactly equal to the height of the plant. This has meant that the gardener using soil must either provide an extremely deep planter or select a smaller variety of tomato, such as the Tiny Tim, whose roots require only a few inches of soil. Hydroponic gardening allows you to choose the variety without worrying about its root structure. As a matter of fact, according to the manufacturers of Hydrogarden, a single unit is capable of producing 40 pounds of the largest tomatoes in just six months—nearly enough to justify the cost of the unit.

Asparagus, because its roots can penetrate the soil to a depth of 8 feet or more, is another plant that has been impossible to grow in containers. Because these hydroponic units are so new, I have not yet had the time to test asparagus in them, but I see no reason why that plant could not be hydroponically grown if it receives the right light and nutrition.

If your gardening space is extremely limited, the space-saving feature can be the biggest advantage of the hydroponic garden. Just as you want the limited space in a small home greenhouse filled with plants, not with soil, so will you want to use the limited space beneath your artificial lights as economically as possible. To grow even a dwarf cantaloupe plant would require at least 5 gallons of soil, preferably twice that much—yet three such plants could be grown in the small Hydrogarden.

Another great advantage of hydroponic gardening is that seed germination seems far more dependable in the hydroponic unit, probably because of the manner in which the vermiculite is kept constantly moist and rich in nutrients. A good use for it, then, is to start seeds in it that you want to grow later in soil.

Vermiculite, the hydroponic growth medium, is, as you probably know, heat-expanded mica, a form of rock. During the heating process it becomes sterile, which, combined with its good aeration and its ability to hold water, makes it an ideal medium for the germination of seeds. Gardeners commonly use vermiculite for this purpose.

Because plants undergo a certain amount of shock when they are transplanted, I prefer whenever possible to start them where they are to grow. However, plants started in the loose and moist vermiculite of the hydroponic unit are so easily lifted out—mainly because of their small but sturdy root systems—that they can easily be set into soil, and the survival rate is high. The edges of the planter can be used for starting seedlings even while other plants near the center are growing to maturity, so this might be considered a fringe benefit that comes with these units.

Probably the biggest single advantage of hydroponic gardening, however, is that you know that the plants in it are being properly fed and watered. With these units you need only check the water level at regular intervals, replacing it as needed and diluting the nutrient concentrate according to the manufacturer's instructions. Thus it becomes nearly impossible to kill your plants by overwatering, and their proper feeding requires only that you take a few seconds to read the label of the plant food you are using.

You will notice that I have stressed the fact that hydroponic gardening holds down the development of the plants' root structure while favoring the top growth. This means that you will not want to grow hydroponically any plant that is wanted for its roots, such as carrots, beets, radishes, or onions.

On the off-chance that I might be wrong about this, I tested several root vegetables—carrots, radishes, and beets—in a hydroponic unit. In all instances, even long after the top growth had reached full size, the roots remained almost nonexistent. But other than for growing root crops, the hydroponic gardening possibilities appear to be almost unlimited.

The kits available at this time are, of course, too small for growing trees, though it might be possible to start one in the unit and later set it in soil. If larger units become available at reasonable cost, they would probably be ideal for some of the dwarf trees now sold at most garden centers.

The small hydroponic units presently available are ideally suited for maintaining a supply of fresh herbs in the kitchen. Among those the manufacturers say can be grown in a single unit are dill, basil, tarragon, oregano, sage, thyme, parsley, and chives. The last two are notoriously difficult to start from seed, yet we found that they germinated quite readily in the Hydrogarden unit.

The manufacturers claim to have grown cherry tomatoes, lettuce, lemon cucumber, and watercress in a single unit, with a border of parsley and chives. Our own experiments indicate that the unit would easily accommodate such a mix, and probably more.

For a simple vegetable garden the firm suggests using the unit to grow sweet peas, green beans, spinach, artichokes, and cauliflower; or your assortment might include full-size tomatoes, sweet peas, spinach, and strawberries, with a garnish of parsley and watercress. All of these can grow in these small hydroponic units.

As a miniature fruit garden, the manufacturers suggest using the unit to grow watermelon, honeydew melon, and a few strawberry plants. A simple flower garden could include daisies, marigolds, pansies, primroses, geraniums, violets, and lavender—perhaps with enough room left over for a cherry tomato vine.

All these things are possible with a small hydroponic unit—assuming that you can provide the additional elements that the plants need. For while the units do provide for the water and nutritional needs of the plants, and while the manufacturer's claims of much faster growth seem supported by the tests I have conducted, the units come without any means of providing the light that is essential to growth, blossoming, and fruit production.

You must be able to provide this light. The makers of the unit suggest using two 40-watt fluorescent tubes or two 150-watt incandescent growth bulbs, coupled with as much natural sunlight as possible. With this lighting arrangement it would be possible to grow many plants, but for some of those plants requiring long days of intense light, such as the melons, the amount of natural sunlight would have to be far more than is available in most homes. The strawberries, too, would do far better under brighter light than that given off by only two 40-watt fluorescent tubes, as would watermelon and honeydew.

The manufacturers also suggest providing ten hours of natural sunlight, or fourteen hours of artificial light, but this also fails to take into consideration the individual needs of the plants, especially with regard to photoperiodism, as well as the difficulty, in the average home, of providing natural light of such long duration.

Whether they are grown hydroponically or not, the light requirements of plants do not change, except as they might be marginally
influenced by factors of temperature or humidity. Therefore, if you do
choose to grow some plants hydroponically, you should provide light
according to the suggestions made for plants grown in soil.

PART TWO

the herbs

Botanically speaking, an herb is any plant that dies back to the root each year. But by horticultural or culinary definition, an herb is an edible plant which is used for its perfume, its health-giving properties, or its flavor. They are seldom eaten alone but are more likely to be used in conjunction with other foods.

Almost every plant which is not poisonous has been used at some time as an herb, and many flowers can be used for fragrance—far more than you will find listed here. This section devotes itself primarily to herbs that are used as food, usually in small quantities for just a subtle touch of flavor.

The sweetest of the herbs are useful in fresh fruit desserts and drinks, where several can be used to take the place of sugar. In many herb-flavored meat and vegetable dishes, salt may be unnecessary; thus the herbs are especially useful for those on restricted diets. Herb teas have been used since Colonial times and are extremely popular these days; they are never better than when you blend them from herbs from your own kitchen garden.

Colonial housewives also scented their linen drawers and closets with sachets of dried herbs, which not only gave the cloth a pleasant perfume, but was also thought to chase away moths. The usual sachet contained sweet marjoram, rosemary, lemon verbena, rose geranium, and a bit of lavender.

The rich fragrance of herbs is produced by the same aromatic oils which produce their flavor. These volatile oils may occur in leaves, seeds, flowers, or roots; sometimes in all of them in the same plant, sometimes in only one or two. When herbs are dried, the oils are concentrated, so that much less of the dried product than of the fresh herb is needed for cooking. Therefore, you do not use the fresh herbs from your home garden exactly the same as the dried herbs you purchase from the grocery—but the taste of the fresh is always superior.

Fresh or dried, herbs should always be used with discretion. Properly used, herbs should impart a very slight flavor that is almost, but not quite, unidentifiable. Dried herbs are about four times stronger than the fresh, so recipe amounts should be adjusted accordingly. Dried herbs are usually added no more than thirty minutes before the dish is ready to serve, while fresh herbs are added during the last few minutes of cooking, about ten minutes before the dish is removed from the stove.

Most herbs are easily dried and stored for later use. Just cut and wash the leaves, tie them in small bunches, and hang them in a warm place where the air circulates freely; leave them there for several days. If they do not seem entirely dry at the end of a week, place them on a tray in the oven at its lowest setting, let the door stand ajar, and keep them there until the leaves crumble to dust when rubbed between the palms of your hands. Flowers are dried in the same way. Store all dried herbs in glass containers, never in cardboard or paper, which robs them of flavor and aroma.

The fine herb flavors can also be captured and preserved in vinegar. Fennel, dill, tarragon, basil, and garlic are most often preserved this way, but many others make excellent vinegars for use in salad dressings. To make any of these gourmet flavorings, just place the herbs in a bottle and pour in wine vinegar to the brim. Shake the bottle every day for three weeks, then strain off the vinegar and bottle it again.

Herbs may also be preserved by freezing. Wash the leaves or blossoms, pat them dry, and wrap them in small squares of freezer paper, putting as many as you will use in one dish in each packet. Label the packets, and freeze them as quickly as possible.

Herbs and their Culture

Most herbs belong to four great plant families, with a sprinkling of members of other groups. The major families are: *Labiatae,* the mint family; *Compositae,* the daisy family; *Umbelliferae,* the carrot family; and *Cruciferae,* the mustard family.

Those family names are fairly descriptive of the plants. The mints, *Labiatae,* have blossoms that are lipped, giving them the appearance of open mouths. The flowers are usually tiny, as in the mints themselves and in lavender and thyme, but are somewhat larger in a few of the sages. Stems are usually square.

The *Compositae* have blossoms which are actually a composite of two types of flowers—the disk flowers, at the center of the blossoms, and the ray flowers, which appear to be petals, Notable members of the family include chamomile, costmary, tansy, and pot marigold.

The largest number of herbs come from the *Umbelliferae*, or carrot family. Flowers are typically small and borne in flat clusters, or umbels, often on hollow stems. Familiar herbs from this family are dill, caraway, chervil, coriander, fennel, and parsley.

Flowers of the mustard family, *Cruciferae*, are shaped like a Maltese cross. The familiar cresses are part of this family.

Not every herb is suitable for home culture. Allspice, for example, is the dried fruit of a tropical evergreen tree that commonly grows to a height of 40 feet. Bay leaves come from a tree of similar size. A few other herbs require extreme temperatures that the home gardener cannot readily provide, and they have been excluded here.

But few things could be easier than growing herbs from the four major families. Herbs were probably the very first plants to be cultivated indoors, and modern artificial lighting makes growing them easier than ever before.

Their light requirements are in all but a few instances relatively low, and extremely flexible. A very large number of them can be grown in any window that receives six hours or so of sunlight daily, and some require even less. Just the few hundred foot-candles of light coming through such a window will keep the processes of growth going and will free your lights for other purposes.

Even if you have no natural sunlight available, you can grow a large number of herbs with even the most basic setup of artificial light. Just the 1000 or so foot-candles of light provided by a pair of 40-watt fluorescent lamps is enough to trigger and maintain the photosynthetic process in many of these plants, though growth will be slower than under the bright sun of an outdoor garden. But since most herbs are grown for their foliage alone, you can compensate for the lack of intensity simply by providing light of longer duration.

Even if you desire blossoming, you can often increase the hours of light. The greatest number of herbs blossom in the summer; thus flowering still occurs when the days are long. Many others are day-neutral plants, which means they will flower no matter how many hours of light they receive.

Seldom is it viable to grow herbs indoors for their seed, though a few plants may produce small quantities of seed with no help from you. Most herbs have blossoms that are far too tiny to be hand-pollinated, and the number of seeds produced by an individual plant is frequently too small to be of any real value. If you want seed production, the best method is to place the flowering plant outside where it can be pollinated by insects. Few plants hold greater attraction for bees and other pollinators.

Herb gardening employs more of the techniques of flower gardening than of vegetable growing. Some of the herbs are biennials or perennials, but most are annuals that are easily started from seed.

Many of the perennials and biennials may also be started from seed. A few, however, are propagated by cuttings, layerings, or root divisions, which means a parent plant must be available or young plants must be purchased. The herbs I describe in the text are likely to be available from commercial suppliers.

Herbs, perhaps even more than most other plants, prefer a humid atmosphere, but they also do much to create their own humidity. A single plant may quickly dry out in the typically arid atmosphere of the home, but a deep windowsill or a tabletop covered with plants will become a miniature jungle when a dozen or more herbs are grouped together and allowed to create their own humid atmosphere. The atmospheric moisture in their neighborhood may be increased even more by placing the pots on 3-inch-deep trays full of gravel, and keeping them flooded with water. Remember to keep the bottoms of the pots out of contact with the water, unless each pot has at least an inch-thick layer of gravel inside.

Nearly all the herbs do well at ordinary room temperature—60 to 65 degrees during the day and 55 to 60 degrees at night. The few exceptions are noted in the text on growing the individual herbs.

With only a few exceptions noted in the following text, herbs are very adaptable to different types of soil. According to the United States Department of Agriculture, most prefer an alkaline soil with a pH of 6.5 to 7.5. If only an acid soil is at hand, this pH can be achieved by working in a bit of ground limestone, the amount depending on the acidity of the soil. Commercial potting soil, which is commonly neutral, will do quite well for a number of herb varieties; however, a few potting soils are highly acid, so check the pH as noted on the outside of the bag, before buying.

Herbs also need good drainage and aeration; a superior growing medium will provide these qualities. A mix that will work well for a large number of varieties consists of two parts loam or potting soil, one part sand, and one part vermiculite, which is obtainable at all garden centers.

As a general rule, herbs should be fed sparingly. Many of the fast-growing annuals will reach maturity before exhausting the nutrients naturally contained in a planter full of rich loam or commercial potting soil. Where more nutrition is needed, a 10-8-22 formula fits the needs of most plants. This formula or a similar one should be used where plants of more than one species are grown together in a single planter, as in a window box.

Many herbs are quite capable of developing into small shrubs. You can maintain such shrubs under your artificial lights, but you may decide that it is more convenient to move them outdoors and let nature provide for their needs. If this is the case, choose an open spot that receives the most hours of sunlight possible, and provide containers large enough to accommodate the developing root structure. Of the herbs, only a few members of the *Umbelliferae*, or carrot family, are difficult to transplant successfully; with these the root system should be moved with all the soil, thus leaving the long tap roots undisturbed.

Basil
(Ocimum basilicum)

A familiar member of the *Labiatae* family, also known as sweet basil, the plant originated in western and tropical Asia. The ancient Greeks feared basil as "an enemy of sight and robber of the wits," according to their herbals, but the Romans cursed it for an entirely different reason—to get a better crop. Brahmins have long regarded the plant as holy, and Brahmin women were once expected to pray to it daily. In Italy there is a tradition that, if a young girl leaves a pot of basil on her windowsill, she does so in the hope of receiving a visit from her lover. Basil seeds are eaten in some parts of the Orient, but elsewhere the plant is grown entirely for its leaves, which are fragrant and flavorful.

Basil is available in several varieties, all of which are easy to start from seed and to grow indoors or out. For beauty as well as utility, select one of the purple varieties such as Dark Opal. A 6-inch pot will support a single plant, but you can start more and use the thinnings like mature herbs, although the flavor of the young shoots will be extremely mild. The seeds, which germinate in five to seven days, should be started ½ inch deep in loam, potting soil, or a soil mix.

Basil grows 18 to 24 inches tall. If it is left unattended, the plant grows thin and leggy. However, if the main stalks are pinched back early, the plant produces a thick crop of succulent foliage that spreads out to make an exquisitely beautiful pot plant.

Basil thrives at average room temperature. It is easily damaged by frost, however, and should not be placed outside too early or too late in the year.

Water should be given infrequently, not more often than once a week. Allow the soil to become moderately dry, then give the plants' roots a good soaking.

Basil can grow in any sunny window, as long as it receives six or more hours of sunlight each day. The plant will grow in light as low as 500 foot-candles, but growth will be extremely slow and the plants will be spindly. Plants grown in light closer to 1000 foot-candles, however, grow almost as well as in the outdoor garden—especially when the light is provided for twelve or more hours each day.

About forty days after planting, depending on conditions, you can cut a few of the scented leaves for use in the kitchen. About ninety days after planting the plant will produce purple flower buds that should be pinched off before they have a chance to open. The rest of the plant should then be harvested by cutting the main stem 6 to 8 inches above the soil. If the base of the plant is left undisturbed and provided with adequate light, food, and water, it will send up new branches and leaves, providing subsequent cuttings for use in the kitchen.

Basil leaves are good either fresh or dried. They are most commonly used to flavor dishes containing eggs, cheese, or rice, or in spaghetti sauces. In Italy the fine flavor of basil is considered so essential to tomato-based dishes that a few of the leaves are added to every jar of canned tomatoes. If they are added to the water in which shellfish is cooked, basil leaves impart a slightly spicy flavor that most seafood lovers find delicious.

Borage
(Borago officinalis)

This is the leading member of its group, the *Boraginaceae* family. Sometimes known as bee-plant, it is a luxuriant and hardy annual that grows to 2 or 3 feet in height. The leaves are oval, about 6 inches long and covered with gray hairs which look like fuzz and make them appear gray-green in color. Under long hours of bright light, the plant produces pale blue, star-shaped flowers that are not only lovely but may be used to impart a delicate flavor of cucumber to soups and salads.

Since the earliest days, when it was highly favored by the Greeks, borage has been thought to have the power to ward off melancholy. Pliny wrote that borage, crushed in wine, would drive away sorrow and bring courage. The saying, I, borage, bring always courage, a familiar phrase in England, was brought to that country by the Romans, who in turn acquired it from the Greeks. In 1756 English botanist Sir John Hill added, "Borage procureth gladsomness, it helpeth the giddiness and swimming of the head, the trembling and heating of the heart, it increaseth memorie and removeth melancholy." Various potions made from borage were also believed to beautify the skin.

Borage grows from large, rough, ridged seeds with cone-shaped bases. The seeds, which retain their fertility well, should be covered with only a thin layer of oil and kept moist until they germinate, which occurs very quickly. Even the poorest soil will grow borage, as long as the soil is not highly acid. The planter should be at least 8 inches in diameter and about that deep, for borage grows quickly and is a fairly large plant.

Borage does best when the planter soil is allowed to become almost completely dry between waterings. Growth is fastest at high temperature, but it does fairly well in the home environment and will even tolerate a touch of frost.

Light should be as bright as you can easily manage—certainly no less than 1000 foot-candles, and preferably more. As the plant grows larger, providing light to the lower leaves can be a problem that you may want to overcome by moving the plant outside. Or you can treat the plant as you would a small shrub, using artificial light overhead and letting the natural light that streams through a window provide for the lower leaves, or beaming an incandescent growth lamp upward to light the lower branches.

Both the leaves and flowers are used, and both are delicious, but don't try to get both from the same plant. If the flowers are allowed to open, the leaves are apt to become tough and slightly bitter. These are day-neutral plants, but with a decided preference toward long hours of lighting, so if you want indoor borage to flower, provide light that is twelve or even sixteen hours in duration.

Borage matures in six to eight weeks and provides several cuttings of leaves even during that brief period. The leaves are at their very best when snipped from the plant just before use, but they are among the easiest of all herbs to dry—just spread them on cheesecloth in a warm spot.

Tender leaves add a delicate cucumber flavor to salads, but they are also excellent when cooked like spinach, as people have been cooking them for centuries, or when mixed with spinach itself. They are delicious when chopped and added to bean, pea, or tomato soups, and they do much to improve the taste of cooked cabbage. Chopped, they also make a more than passable substitute for parsley.

The flowers may be used to add color and flavor to salads, but a more traditional use is to float them in iced beverages, especially those containing red wine (claret). The flowers also may be candied by dipping them in beaten egg white, then in sugar, and setting them on wax paper to dry. Such candied flowers are among the oldest sweets, and they have long been used to give a unique touch of flavor to wines and cordials.

Burnet
(Sanquisorba minor or Poterium sanquisorba)

Also known as pimpernel, burnet is a member of the rose family. A native of the north temperate climates, people have known it since ancient times but did not widely cultivate it until after the Middle Ages.

Burnet is a hardy, perennial herb; the plants are easily started from seed. Plants send up twelve to eighteen graceful stems with compound leaves, which are topped by oblong white or rose-colored flower heads.

The planter for burnet should be fairly wide—9 inches or so in diameter—to allow for the spreading crowns, but it is not necessary that it be deeper than 5 or 6 inches. Soil should be slightly alkaline, but potting soil is acceptable. Several seeds should be started, planting them half an inch deep, and the seedlings thinned to leave only the strongest single plant in the pot.

Burnet will tolerate nearly any conditions you choose to give it. If it is left outside throughout the winter, it will continue to send out tender young leaves even after most other plants have long since been killed by the cold. Indoors, under artificial light, its spreading mat of leaves will grow well under just a few hundred foot-candles of light, so it is a good plant for growing on the fringes of your indoor garden, where light is weaker than directly under the center of the tubes. Since flowering is unimportant, it can be given as many hours of light as you choose to provide.

Cut the young and tender leaves as they are produced. Fresh leaves will add a cucumber taste to salads, though the flavor is more pungent than that of borage, and they also make an excellent garnish for cold drinks. Dried leaves make an excellent herb vinegar and are also used for brewing herb tea.

Chervil

(Anthriscus
cerefolium)

This member of the carrot family is native to all of Eurasia and has been used for hundreds of years in much the same way as parsley, one of its close relatives. In appearance, too, it is somewhat like parsley, but lighter green in color, with finely cut, fernlike leaves. Some varieties produce a tuberous root that can be cooked and eaten as a vegetable.

Chervil requires a fairly loose soil through which the water drains with ease, so the soil should contain at least some sand. Like many other members of its family, chervil has weak seeds which germinate poorly, so the seeds should be sown rather thickly across the top of the planter soil. Germination takes about fourteen days, and the soil should be kept moistened until the first sprouts appear. As soon as the seedlings are 2 to 3 inches high, they should be thinned to stand about 4 inches apart.

This annual plant is by nature a shade-loving plant, so providing light is never a problem. You should be able to grow it in any but a north-facing window, and perhaps even there; and you can certainly grow it with even the most basic artificial light arrangement. Giving it long hours of light at intensities of up to 1000 foot-candles will promote incredibly fast growth, as will maintaining a high level of moisture in the soil.

The flavor of chervil is delicate and licoricelike, often compared to the taste of anise. That flavor is better preserved by freezing than by drying. The first of the tender young leaves will be ready to cut for freezing about eight weeks after planting. Each plant should provide several cuttings.

This delicate flavor is pleasant in many dishes—all kinds of fish and most chicken recipes, for example. As the flavor is extremely mild, chervil can be used more generously than most herbs. Try adding it to cream of spinach soup, tossed salads, or potato salad; or sprinkle it generously, just before serving, on lamb, roast beef, veal steaks, or broiled chicken. Chervil also has the remarkable characteristic of enhancing the flavor of other herbs, which explains why it is such an important component in the *fines herbes* of the French culinary art.

Chives
(Allium schoenoprasum)

Chives are by far the most delicately flavored member of the onion family, *Liliaceae*. As with most other members of the clan, this plant has magic and superstition in its background. Legend has it that when Satan fled the Garden of Eden, garlic shot up where he

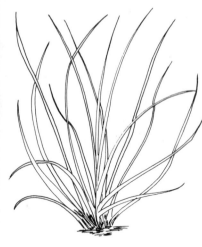

touched his left foot, chives from beneath his right. Be that as it may, chives were grown by the Chinese at least as early as 3000 B.C., and later were introduced to all of Europe by the conquering Romans. They were a favored herb in Charlemagne's garden.

Chives are hardy perennials which may be grown from seed or from division of the clumps. Starting the plants from seed can be chancey, because chive seed does not remain viable for any length of time and germination is erratic in any case, so buying starter plants is the best way to assure a supply.

Soil for growing chives should contain a high percentage of sharp sand or even fine gravel, mixed about 50-50 with rich loam or potting soil. Use about a 5- or 6-inch pot and plant the seed thickly, or start a single bulb in each pot. In either case, the chives, once they have started, will multiply rapidly; you will need to thin them now and then by taking up some of the bulbs and setting them in new pots.

Even the lowest light will support chives, as evidenced by the fact that people grew them indoors long before the invention of any type of artificial lighting. Growth is faster, however, when the light is more intense and of longer duration. You will probably not want to use the precious space beneath your artificial lights for growing chives but will prefer, instead, to keep a pot or two of them growing on a windowsill, in the time-honored fashion.

Chives send up tubular leaves that grow 8 to 12 inches tall, with rounded heads of lavender flowers rising a little bit higher. The flowers are as attractive as many ornamentals, but if you are growing chives for use in the kitchen, the leaves must be snipped before the flowers have a chance to develop. Flowering causes the stems to lose their mildly piquant flavor, as does drying or freezing.

Chopped chives are excellent in soups and salads, stews and casseroles, omelets and scrambled eggs. They are commonly added to sour cream for a sauce for baked potatoes, sprinkled on vichysoisse or other soups, and used as a garnish for cooked vegetables. In short, chives are used whenever a mild taste of onion is desirable.

Dill
(Anethum graveolens)

This member of the carrot family often grows wild in many parts of the world. The early Greeks used it to flavor dishes as well as for a decoration, which was woven into garlands and wreaths. The name derives from an old Norse word, *Dilla*, meaning "to lull," for dill was thought to have a soothing effect on crying babies. It also has a history of being used as a weapon against witchcraft and as an ingredient in love potions.

Dill is an annual which reaches a height of 2 or 3 feet. It can be grown in nearly any type of soil, but the planter should be at least 8 inches deep to allow for the taproot (the long root that grows downward from the plant). Seed germination is poor, so the seed should be sown rather thickly—about fifteen or twenty seeds to the inch—and later thinned so that plants stand about 3 inches apart. Cover the germinating seeds with about one-fourth inch of very fine soil or vermiculite at the time of planting.

Dill is an easy plant to grow, but it needs brighter light than most other herbs. When grown under light with an intensity of only 1000 foot-candles, the main stems develop quickly, but the plants do not produce the normal number of leaves, nor are they of normal size. Even at 1500 foot-candles growth is not as it would be in direct sunlight. And unlike most other herbs and foliage plants, dill does not seem to accept longer hours of light as a substitute for intensity. If you have a light setup capable of producing 2000 or more foot-candles of light, you can probably grow dill in an indoor garden. If not, you can grow it on the patio or balcony, setting it where it will receive as much direct sunlight as possible, perhaps after getting a jump on the season by starting the plant indoors.

The leaves of dill, which are blue-green and feathery, like those of fennel, are most widely used. But dill is also a flowering plant that produces, under the right photoperiod, tiny yellow flowers that are borne in umbels, and which also have their uses.

According to the scientists who compiled *Growth,* a biological textbook, dill will blossom only when provided with eleven hours or more of light. Growers can prevent blossoms by depriving it of light of this duration, or encourage them by extending the hours of brightness.

The fresh leaves are best when chopped and used sparingly. They go well with cottage cheese, cream cheese, potatoes, or potato salad. A bit of dill taste also goes well with broiled or fried fish, and the leaves are sometimes added to the water in which shrimp is to be cooked.

If the flower umbels are picked just before the tiny blossoms open, they may be used fresh to make dill pickles or dill vinegar, or dried and saved for later use.

Dill that grows outside will be pollinated and produce seeds, which are extremely useful either whole or ground. They are excellent with beets, cucumbers, beans, eggs, seafood, or in a large number of fish sauces. Their best-known use, of course, is in pickling, where they have few peers.

This is another of the *Umbelliferae* that is grown for its fresh foliage and seeds. It originated on the shores of the Mediterranean and has been used for at least three thousand years, starting with the Egyptians. To the Greeks it was a symbol of victory and was used to crown heroes. The Romans used it for the same purpose, but soon learned to eat the stalks raw or cooked, just as they are eaten in Italy today. The Romans took fennel to England, and there it found quick acceptance as both food and medicine—it is one of the principal healing herbs, widely believed to benefit the eyes. It was also used to cure obesity, as it was believed to dull the appetite that caused the condition.

Fennel is usually grown as an annual, but only because it cannot tolerate cold weather; actually the plant is a perennial. As a perennial, some fennel varieties can grow to a height of about 5 feet with heavy heads that need support; but sweet fennel, the variety *dulce* that is described here and which is the variety most readily available in this country, grows to only about half that high and has much thicker stems.

Fennel will grow in almost any soil that does not contain clay. Seeds should be sown about twelve to the foot, and the seedlings later thinned to stand about 4 inches apart in every direction. The thinnings can be added to any salad you happen to be making at the time.

Fennel needs more water than most other plants. The soil should be kept moist at all

Fennel

(Foeniculum vulgare dulce)

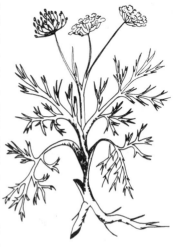

times, and this is one of the few plants for which daily watering is suggested. Never let the soil become completely dry.

The plant needs long hours of the brightest light you can provide. If you give it twelve or sixteen hours of light at 1000 or 1500 foot-candles, some foliage will grow, but the leaves will be widely separated and the edible stalks will be spindly and weak. It will do far better if you allow it to grow in direct sunlight, perhaps bringing it in for continued growth under lights before the first frost has a chance to damage it.

The handsome green feathery foliage of the fennel plants can be cut at any time after the plants have become established. The stalks can be left to develop and thicken, later cutting them for use like celery, though when they are grown under artificial lights, they will seldom achieve the thickness of that vegetable.

Fennel has a natural affinity for fish that great chefs have recognized for many centuries. Nearly any grilled or broiled fish is good when stuffed with fennel leaves. The leaves also make an excellent potherb, especially when cooked together with spinach. They may be used in many soups or chowders, especially those with fish or seafood ingredients. They may also be chopped and added to roast chicken or lamb, but only with discretion and immediately before serving.

Garlic
(Allium sativum)

This flat-leaved onion of the lily family is thought to be native to western Tatary (Siberia), where it spread to all temperate parts of the world. The Greeks and Romans grew it, and it is mentioned several times in the Bible. Like many of its relatives, it is linked with witchcraft and superstition, especially for its alleged ability to ward off vampires and other evils of the night.

Garlic is a perennial that grows from top sets or from divisions of the bulbs. Seed is seldom available, but garlic sets, the cloves into which garlic bulbs can be divided, are sometimes referred to as seed. Garlic bulbs from the grocery store will do quite well for planting. Usually these bulbs have about ten cloves each, which are planted separately. There are two common types, one pink and the other white, and the latter grows faster and easier than the former.

Garlic is one of the easiest of all plants to grow, indoors or out. While rich, sandy loam is the ideal soil for its cultivation, it seems to do well in almost any soil as long as the soil is several inches deep, to accommodate the roots. Its flat leaves are not altogether unattractive, so the garlic makes an excellent border plant. Rather than fill a planter with garlic alone, you will probably prefer to keep a few plants growing among your other vegetables and herbs, in those little corners that might otherwise go to waste.

Plant the clove 2 inches deep, spaced 3 inches apart or 3 inches away from the roots of other plants. Do not set garlic in with plants that require frequent watering, as garlic is very sensitive to this. Garlic does best when the soil is allowed to become thoroughly dry, then given a good soaking. When the stems become about 12 inches high, water should be withheld as long as possible, for this encourages bulb development while discouraging top growth. If the plants winter outside, bulb growth will continue throughout all but the coldest weather, providing extra-large bulbs for use the following spring.

Light for growing garlic is extremely easy to

provide, as the plant seems to accept nearly any intensity or duration of light. Growth is faster under bright light of long duration, of course, but the flavorful bulbs can also be grown in any window that receives as little as three or four hours of sunlight daily, or under just a pair of fluorescent tubes.

When top growth stops completely and the stems dry out and bend under their own weight, garlic is ready to pull. Dry it in any spot that does not receive direct sunlight, then remove the tops and roots with shears, leaving 1 inch of top and half that much root on the bulb; then store in a cool place.

Ginger
(Zingiber officinale)

A member of the *Zingiberaceae,* or ginger, family, this herb originated in southern Asia and spread from there to Africa, the West Indies, and Jamaica. One of the most beautiful of all tropical plants, it was grown and used in the Orient for centuries before Marco Polo brought it back to Europe at the end of his journeys. Spanish explorers brought it to America in the sixteenth century.

Ginger is grown much like the ornamental cannas. Very stout stems rise about 3 feet high from fleshy rhizomes, which are the source of the familar spice. Leaves surrounding the base are oblong and 8 to 12 inches long. Yellow-green flowers with purple lips are borne on tall spikes.

Ginger can be grown from pieces of fresh ginger root that you can buy in grocery stores. The entire piece of root should be set 3 inches deep in fertile soil that contains absolutely no sand or gravel. The pot should have a diameter of at least 8 inches, preferably more.

Ginger requires about ten months to mature, and growth will be greatly slowed if the plant is exposed to chilling temperatures during that time. As a matter of fact, temperature may be the single most important element in growing ginger. The plant can be, and often has been, grown to maturity at ordinary room temperature, but growth is greatly enhanced by warmer temperatures and higher humidity, as in a greenhouse. If greenhouse facilities are unavailable, choose the warmest spot in the home for growing this plant and provide all the humidity possible.

Soil for growing ginger should be kept moist but not soaked, as this plant is native to regions of frequent rain. Frequent watering will do it no harm.

Light for growing ginger need not be extremely high in intensity, but it should be of long duration. Providing 1000 foot-candles for twelve or more hours daily will do, and flowering will be enhanced if part of that is natural sunlight. But flowering is not necessary to the growth of the roots used for spice.

At the end of the tenth month following planting, dig up the entire plant and cut away all the top growth. Wash the roots in scalding water and dry them in direct sunlight until they will break with a snap. Set aside a piece or two for the next planting.

The rest of the dried roots may then be finely ground for use in cooking and baking, though you might prefer to candy a few pieces by boiling them in a thin syrup made of sugar and water and setting them on wax paper to dry.

Lavender
(Lavandula spica, L. officinalis, or L. vera)

Several lavenders, all belonging to the same genus of the *Labiatae* family, have been grown through the centuries and treasured for their fine, clean fragrance as well as for the delicate flavor they impart to herb tea, wine, jelly, or vinegar. Early Phoenicians, Greeks, and Romans used lavender in their rituals, and French kings later paid high prices for a bit of lavender with which to perfume themselves.

By the nineteenth century the culture of lavender had become so common that every housewife tucked a sachet made from it among her linens, and most people knew that the tips of the flowers added a brisk flavor to desserts and drinks.

The lavenders are perennials, but none is hardy where winters are severe. Young potted plants are sometimes available at garden centers, but lavender may also be started from seed. Seed germinates best in early spring or late fall, even when started indoors, demonstrating a phenomenon that is seen in many plants and which is far from understood by science.

Lavender grows about 2 feet tall, becoming a semishrub with a tendency to sprawl and cover an area of a foot or two in diameter; thus a large tub planter is needed for growing it. The soil should contain plenty of sand or even gravel, but must be entirely free of clay.

Seed can be started indoors in the late fall, and the plants will grow fairly well under 1000 foot-candles of artificial light or in a sunny window, producing gray-green, fragrant leaves an inch or two in length and providing a strong plant for blossoming the following spring. Even if it is maintained indoors and provided with fourteen to sixteen hours of light daily, the lavender may produce a few of the tiny flowers that are borne on long thin spikes, but at least part of that light should be natural. The plant will produce far more abundantly if, during the summer, the plant is set where it will receive six or more hours of sunshine each day.

Winter or summer, indoors or out, water

should be given only sparingly to lavender, for this is a plant which thrives under arid conditions. The plant should be kept indoors throughout the winter and its food and water reduced to only that which is needed for survival. Thus maintained, the life span of lavender plants is four to seven years, after which they die out and must be replaced.

Blossom production will be increased if flowers are not picked the first year. After that the flowers should be cut before they fully open for best color. To dry lavender for sachets or flavoring, cut when the first flowers are fully open and others on the spike are spreading; then lay them out in a warm place until they are dry.

Lemon Balm
(Melissa officinalis)

This member of the *Labiatae* family is one of the oldest herbs and is frequently mentioned in the Old Testament. It originated in the Middle East, like so many other herbs, and found its way around the shores of the Mediterranean. Its name is the Greek word for honeybee, and for more than two thousand years, it has served to attract those pollinators. Aside from its attraction for honeybees, as recently as the eighteenth century, people thought it had powers to restore youth, prevent baldness, and bestow longevity. There is an old Arab saying that balm tea makes the heart merry and joyful, and one early English author added, "Balm, cordial and exhilarating, sovereign for the Brain, strengthening the Memory, and powerfully chasing away Melancholy."

The plant is one of the very easiest to grow. It is a perennial capable of growing as tall as 24 inches, but it is easily started from seed and may be kept cut back to keep the plant small for indoor gardening. The plant, with leaves that are 2 to 3 inches long, about 1 inch wide, and strongly scented with lemon, has a tendency to sprawl and spread, so start only a few seeds in a planter that is wide—such as a window box—but not necessarily deep. Seed germinates in about fourteen days.

Any soil will do for growing lemon balm, but it should be kept moist. The plant thrives at room temperature but prefers a little extra humidity, so placing it near other plants will help.

Light for lemon balm is no problem. In nature it prefers shaded areas where the light is filtered by the leaves of other plants, and people grew it indoors long before the invention of artificial lighting. It will grow very well in any window area you have, or in the fringe areas under your artificial lights where it will receive a few hundred foot-candles of light for several hours each day.

The leaves of lemon balm are used in perfumes and toilet waters and to flavor many commercial liqueurs, including benedictine and chartreuse. For home cooking, the fresh leaves, finely chopped, make a delicious addition to salads of all types, and they are excellent when sprinkled over vegetable soup or fish chowder. The dried leaves are at their best steeped in boiling water to make a tea that is brisk with the flavor of mint and lemon.

Marjoram
(Origanum marjorana)

Known also as sweet marjoram, this is one of three species of its genus which are grown as flavoring herbs, the other two being oregano and pot marigold. Of the three, this one has the finest flavor.

Sweet marjoram is native to the Mediterranean region and has been cultivated as a flavoring herb since the earliest recorded days of history. Early writers such as Pliny and Albertus Magnus praised its fragrance. The Romans and Greeks used it as a symbol of fertility, and in India it is associated with magic and superstition.

Marjoram is an attractive, bushy plant capable of growing 12 inches tall but more likely to be low and sprawling. The leaves are small, gray-green, and rounded at the ends. Under long hours of adequate light, the plant produces tiny white flowers, but these are unimportant for cooking. The plant is a perennial, but most growers start it from seed and treat it as an annual.

Soil for growing marjoram does not need to be rich, but it should, ideally, be well limed. A generous handful of crushed limestone added to enough potting soil to fill a 6- or 8-inch pot makes a good medium for growing marjoram. Plant several seeds, then later thin out all but the strongest plant.

Seed germination is slow, requiring at least fourteen days. During this period the seeds require constant moisture, which is best provided by covering the pot with a layer of damp peat moss.

The plants are very slow to grow, yet they require more nutrition than most other herbs. The plant food you use should have a high amount of nitrogen in its formula.

Marjoram can be grown on a bright windowsill, but it does much better when given long hours of bright light, for it is a sun-loving plant. With twelve hours of light at 1000 foot-candles daily, the plant does far better than in most windows, and when it receives more intense light for the same duration, the increased rate of growth is almost startling.

After a first plant is well started and has become slightly woody, new plants may be started by pulling off branches and setting them in pots of moist sand until roots form. You may then repot and care for the rooted young plants exactly like those started from seed.

Marjoram does best if it is allowed to go into dormancy during the winter months. During this dormant period keep the plants in a cool place out of direct light; allow the soil in the pot to become almost, but not quite, dry.

Fresh leaves may be cut for kitchen use when the plants are 4 or 5 inches tall. Cut the flowering tops before the flowers have a chance to open; the tips may be dried. Fresh or dried, marjoram is used principally in meat dishes. Stews, meat loafs, gravies, poultry stuffing, and sausages of all kinds are improved by just a small touch of this herb. Rubbing fresh leaves on meats before roasting gives them the slight touch of flavor sought by knowing chefs, and many game and fish dishes also profit from a dash of sweet marjoram.

Nasturtium
(Tropaeolum minus and T. Majus)

These are the only important members of the Tropaeolaceae family, the nasturtiums. *T. minus* is a dwarf variety, *majus* a climbing vine. Both have been grown in flower beds since they were introduced to Europe from Peru in the sixteenth century. The dwarf species, *T. minus,* is best for indoor gardening or for growing where outdoor space is limited, as in pots or window boxes.

The word *nasturtium* derives from Latin words meaning "to twist the nose," which hints at the pungency of the herbs of this family. Its original European name was Indian cress, since it originated in South America, but in 1574 a Spanish physician, Niccolo Monardes, gave it the present name. It was then taken to Europe and planted in the special garden of Louis XIV, and in France today it continues to see use as a sophisticated salad green.

The plant is a tender annual with kidney-shaped leaves. Easily started from seed, it does best in a rich but sandy soil. Several seeds can be started in a 6- or 8-inch pot, then thinned out to the strongest plant, and even the thinnings may be used to add a spicy, peppery taste to a salad.

Nasturtium will grow very well at room temperature, but it is killed by the slightest touch of frost. Containerized plants should never be put outside too early or too late in the season.

Potted plants receiving several hours of bright sunshine each day will produce bell-shaped flowers in various shades of yellow, orange, and red, and it is entirely possible that some of your inside plants may flower. However, for culinary purposes, flowering is not necessary; nasturtium is grown for its pungent leaves, which develop easily under long hours of light—artificial, natural, or any combination of the two. Just a pair of 40-watt fluorescent tubes should be adequate if they are on for at least twelve hours daily, but brighter light will do no harm.

The fresh leaves are very rich in vitamin C. Though they are sometimes used as a garnish, they are at their very best when chopped and used to flavor bland cheeses—cream cheese and cottage cheese, for example—or when used as a substitute for watercress, to which they are related.

Oregano
(Origanum vulgare)

Origanum derives from two Greek words—*oros,* meaning "mountain," and *ganos,* meaning "brightness, beauty." They refer not to the plant itself but to its native home, the mountains surrounding the Mediterranean. Actually the plant appears to have started in the Middle East; the Greeks and Romans, who valued it as a food flavoring and also as a tonic, spread it across Europe. In Greece and Rome newly married couples were crowned with a wreath of oregano as a symbol of hoped-for happiness, and the Greeks placed similar wreaths on the graves of departed loved ones to help them rest in peace.

Oregano, like the marjorams to which it is very closely related, is a tender perennial which is usually treated as an annual. It is also known as wild marjoram, but its leaves have a distinctive flavor all their own, stronger and far more peppery than marjoram.

Oregano may be started by dividing the crown of existing plants, or from seed. The seed is very tiny, so the seedlings are slow to develop and must be nurtured carefully while young. They should be planted to a depth of less than one-quarter inch in fairly rich soil, then thinned out when the seedlings are 2 or 3 inches high. The soil should be kept moist but not wet. A 6-inch pot will hold one or two first-year plants, but a larger planter should be provided if you hope to grow the plants to full size. The plants are capable of living for years and can develop into small shrubs 2 or 3 feet high.

Oregano will grow fairly well under light of only 1000 foot-candles, but growth is much faster when the plants receive brighter light or when the plants are grown where they can receive natural sunlight. But if they are grown outside, they should not be exposed to severe frost. They should be allowed to go into dormancy for two months each winter, with reduced light, water, and nutrition.

Under the proper conditions of lighting, oregano will produce tiny pink-lavender flowers, but these should not be allowed to open. Cut the leaves and flowering tips from the plant just before flowering occurs, then dry them quickly in a warm, well-ventilated place. Strip the leaves from the stems before storing them.

Oregano may be the most useful of all the herbs. Most Italian dishes that have become popular in the United States contain it; no pizza tastes right without it; and it provides exactly the seasoning needed for gourmet-quality spaghetti sauces—but these only hint at the variety of ways in which it may be used. Try sprinkling the chopped leaves on roast beef, lamb, or pork. Add them to salads. Use oregano on peas, beans, or lentils. Add it to scrambled eggs, omelets, and cheese spreads. Use it to give a new flavor to potato salad. With oregano always growing close at hand, you will constantly discover even more ways in which this peppery herb can add to your dining pleasure.

Parsley
(Petroselinum crispum)

Parsley is a member of the *Umbelliferae*, which probably originated on the island of Sardinia in the Mediterranean. It was one of the first plants used for making wreaths to crown Greek athletes and give to loved ones as a token of affection. The Romans wore such wreaths at banquets in the belief that the parsley absorbed the fumes given off by wine and prevented drunkenness. They also used parsley to flavor their food and ate it after meals to take the odor of garlic from their breath.

Use of parsley seems to have continued unabated through the ages. The monks of the

Middle Ages grew it in their monastery gardens for its medicinal qualities as well as for its food value, and nearly every early herbal suggests it as a tonic for one ailment or another. That parsley is good for the health was not really confirmed until the twentieth century, when nutritionists discovered that the deep green leaves are excellent sources of vitamins A, B complex, C, and E, in addition to calcium and iron.

Parsley is a hardy biennial but is almost always grown as an annual because the leaves are crisper and tastier the first year. It is often considered a difficult plant to grow because of its remarkably long germination period, which is three to six weeks. Germination can be hastened by soaking the seeds for twenty-four hours before they are planted.

Soil for growing parsley should contain no sand. A rich potting soil will do quite well, as will a rich loam that contains some well-rotted organic matter. Seeds should be thickly sown ¼-inch deep in a 5- or 6-inch pot, and the soil should be kept well moistened until germination occurs. Do not place the pot under artificial light at this stage.

When the seedlings are 1 inch high, thin them to stand at least 3 inches apart, and give the plants more light. The light need not be intense, as parsley is a plant that does very well in the shade. Placing the pot on a windowsill, where it will receive three or four hours of indirect light daily, will do, or you can set the pot in the fringe areas under your artificial lights, where the light will meter at only a few hundred foot-candles.

No longer is parsley considered simply a garnish to be left on the plate along with the paper panties of the lamb chop. No herb bouquet is complete without a generous sprig of parsley, and, therefore, no herb garden is really complete without a few pots overflowing with its greenery. If the plants are healthy, you will be able to cut them repeatedly, but even so, you will find so many uses for parsley that you will probably need several plants.

Since its flavor is so mild, parsley can be combined with many foods, even several in the same meal. It works well in meat dishes, seafood, soups, salads, omelets, vegetables, and poultry. It provides the greatest flavor and nutrition when it is freshly chopped into the dish as it is just about to be removed from the stove and placed on the table. One tablespoon of minced parsley, taken with each of the three daily meals, will provide the minimum daily requirements of vitamins A and C—which is a good reason for adding it to your home garden.

Rosemary
(Rosmarinus officinalis)

A member of the *Labiatae* family native to the shores of the western Mediterranean, the Greeks and Arabs grew rosemary for its fresh fragrance; it was used in England and France as early as the eleventh century.

The Latin name of the plant means "dew of the sea," which comes from its habit of growing so close to the seashore that it was often touched by salt spray. The Greeks soon attributed to it the ability to strengthen the brain and the memory, and it is probable that Shakespeare thought he was stating scientific fact when he wrote, "Rosemary, that's for remembrance," for the alchemists of his time were devout believers in this myth.

Medieval herbals attributed many more mystic properties to rosemary. The head of the boar, served at Christmastime, was garlanded with a wreath of rosemary, and the herbals advised that the wreath had powers to "make thee light and merry," to "deliver thee of all evil dreams," and to "preserve thy youth."

Rosemary is a tender perennial which, when mature, resembles a miniature pine tree. It commonly grows to a height of about 3 feet, but has been known to reach 5 feet when grown outside in warmer climates. Its leaves are needlelike and gray-green to dark green, and its flowers are pale blue or lavender. It makes a good specimen plant to grow in a pot or tub, but because of its size, lighting it entirely and adequately artificially can be a problem.

Soil is one of the keys to growing rosemary. The soil must be light, dry, and very alkaline. Commercial potting soil will do only if it is mixed with enough pulverized limestone to raise the pH to 8.5 or higher. Rosemary can be very easily started by sowing several seeds in such soil, then thinning the plants out as they grow, leaving only the strongest specimen in the tub.

Providing light for a young rosemary plant is no problem, and the leaves will develop quite well under 1000 foot-candles of light given for twelve or more hours daily. But as the plant grows older and turns into a young shrub, getting light to all its leaves becomes more difficult. At this stage you may prefer to grow it on your porch or patio, bringing it in during the winter if you live north of Virginia; the plant, which is nearly evergreen, will live with even less light during the winter months, and it can be returned to the porch or patio after winter is over; or you may choose to keep it indoors at all times, providing light for the lower foliage by spotlighting the plant with a pair of incandescent growth lamps beamed upward.

Rosemary needs long hours of light for flowering, which occurs only after the second year.

But the plant is grown primarily for its aromatic leaves, which may be cut and dried at any time after the plant has gotten a healthy start.

Rosemary has a resinous and very pungent taste and must be used sparingly. It is good when sprinkled lightly over lamb or rare roast beef, or in beef stew and ragout of veal. Cauliflower, green beans, peas, and potatoes are among the vegetables that are improved by a touch of rosemary, and it adds an interesting flavor to jellies, especially those which have an apple base. Rosemary tea is made by steeping 1 teaspoon of leaves per cup of boiling water.

Sage
(Salvia officinalis)

The Latin name of sage comes from the Latin *Salveo*, "I am well." The Romans learned its cultivation from the Greeks and put sage in many cooked dishes—and probably these dishes included the first sage stuffings for rich meats such as pork and duck. The Romans took it to England, the English brought it to America, and in both countries it remains a favorite herb.

Eat sage in May, and you'll live for aye, is an old English jingle that expresses one long-held belief about the mystic properties of this herb. People in medieval England took that claim so seriously that sage was included in nearly every meal, and before the introduction of tea from China, the English drank sage tea entirely. The Chinese later became so fond of the herb that they would gladly trade two pounds of tea for one pound of sage.

There are dozens and dozens of species of sage, all with more or less the same flavor in varying strengths and with a variety of subtle overtones. *Officinalis*, the one described here and the one most commonly used for food, is a hardy and rather woody perennial with pebbly, grayish-green leaves about 3 inches in length. Its flowers are bluish-purple, but the plant is usually cut back for use before these have had a chance to open. The shrub can grow to about 2 feet, but it accepts pruning well and can be kept to a smaller size for easy handling and for growing under artificial lights.

Sage grows readily from seed, and germination takes about fifteen days. The soil need not be rich, but it must contain absolutely no clay, and adding some sand for drainage is a good idea. The pot should be at least 8 inches in diameter, and several seeds should be planted at a shallow depth. The seedlings can later be thinned to the strongest plant.

Young seedlings will do quite well in a sunny window. As the plants develop, however, they should be given long hours of the brightest light you can provide. They can be grown under 1000 foot-candles of light, but for really fast growth and lush foliage, light of higher intensity is preferable. Really robust plants are produced by full sunlight or light intensities of 2000 or more foot-candles.

Harvest these distinctively smelling leaves at any time by stripping them from the branches. Keep the plants cut back to a height of about 8 inches, which encourages the plant to spread outward and develop bushier foliage. A plant should yield two cuttings each year, but no cuttings should be made during winter, when light, food, and water must be reduced so that the plant can become semidormant. A sage plant may live for four or five years, but the older plants tend to produce less foliage, so you may want to start new plants well in advance of that time.

This you can easily do by cutting a few sprigs from the older plant and setting them in moist sand until roots have developed, then planting them firmly in proper soil. Do not make these cuttings during winter.

The flavor of sage is so strong that the herb must be used very gently. A few chopped parsley leaves added to sage will help tone down the flavor and prevent its overwhelming the dish to which it is added. Although sage is most commonly used in pork and poultry stuffing, it is also good when added to sharp cheese spreads or butter that is to be used in basting fish. You can make aromatic sage tea, which is said to be good for a sore throat, by pouring a cup of boiling water over a teaspoonful of the chopped leaves, allowing them to steep for five minutes, and adding sugar to taste.

Savory
(Satureja hortensis)

There are more than one hundred species of savory, including the well-known winter savory *(S. Montana)*, which is a perennial. But the most satisfactory is the one described here, the species often known as summer savory, an annual that is extremely easy to grow.

Savory is native to southern Europe and has been used since about the third or fourth century. It was highly prized by the Greeks and Romans, the latter of whom took it to England. Charlemagne included it in a list he wrote in A.D. 812 describing the plants he wanted in his kitchen garden, and it was one of the plants brought to America by the early colonists.

Summer savory grows to a height of about 12 inches, with small bronze leaves on bushy stems. It is a very fast growing plant, reaching its full size about sixty days after planting, so a single planter can be used for several crops during the course of a year.

Seed should be planted ½-inch deep and about 6 inches apart, in any good garden loam or potting soil. If the plants seem crowded as they develop, thin them to provide more room. Use the washed thinnings as if they were leaves from mature plants. As a matter of fact, savory is at its best when it is very young, so this is an excellent way to get the most out of a planter.

Savory does not need a great deal of light. It can be grown in any window box—inside or out—that receives a few hours of sunlight daily, and it will develop quite well under a pair of 40-watt fluorescent lamps.

Savory is, however, extremely sensitive to overfeeding. For that reason, and since the plant matures so quickly, do not fertilize it at all; simply allow it to feed on the nutrients in the soil.

Pull plants that you plan to dry before the tiny purple flowers have a chance to open. Strip the leaves from the stems and dry them; then crumble them and carefully store them in airtight bottles.

Savory is delicious with any vegetable. A sprig added to the water in which cabbage is cooked will help hold down the strong cabbage odor; and the herb goes so well with string beans that in Germany and Switzerland it is known as *Bohnenkraut,* or "the string bean herb."

Aside from its uses with vegetables, summer savory will enhance nearly all stews, gravies, sausage dishes, veal and pork dressings, and poultry stuffings. It is, all in all, a very useful herb—and subtly delicious.

Tarragon
(Artemisia dracunculus)

A member of the *Compositae* family, tarragon (sometimes called French tarragon) is a bushy perennial which grows to about 18 inches and bears very narrow leaves about an inch long, with a mild anise or licorice flavor. It is one of the plants currently being grown in the hydroponic kitchen garden at the Waldorf-Astoria.

Tarragon is native to eastern Europe, the Orient, and especially the Himalayas. The Greeks and Egyptians cultivated and used it as early as the fifth century B.C., and it is mentioned in the writings of Hippocrates.

Tarragon did not appear in Europe until at least the twelfth century, but then it won quick acceptance and is now greatly esteemed in France and Italy—where some chefs call it the king of herbs.

Sad to say, tarragon rarely produces viable seed. It can only be propagated by root division, which means you must start with plants. Tarragon is so popular, however, that young plants are commonly available at garden stores and nurseries. Such plants are usually potted in suitable soil and containers, so you need only nurture them along to maintain a steady supply of tarragon for the kitchen.

Tarragon will grow in sun or in partial shade, and indoors it will do quite well under artificial light. If you grow it as a patio plant, you will only need to move it indoors during extremely cold weather, but it should be sheltered from strong winds at all times.

Propagation of tarragon is made by root division, which should be done when the plant is two to three years old. Take up the entire plant and divide the roots so that the divisions have a minimum of two shoots each. Set the divisions in very sandy soil and keep the soil well moistened until the new plants have had a chance to become firmly rooted.

Tarragon leaves may be picked at any time. If they are to be preserved for later use, freezing is preferable to drying. Perhaps the best way to preserve the tarragon flavor is in vinegar, for these leaves make the most famous herb vinegar of all.

You can impart the delicate flavor of leaves of tarragon to steaks, roasts, and fowl by rubbing the meat with the leaves just before putting the dish in the oven. Tartar sauce, lemon-butter sauces, and salad dressings all benefit from tarragon, and it has few peers when used with seafood. As a matter of fact, it has few peers among the herbs!

Thyme

(Thymus vulgaris)

There are at least sixty species of thyme, but this broad-leaved variety is by far the best for the home gardener, especially for growing indoors under artificial lights.

Thyme is another herb which originated in the Middle East and spread to the shores of the Mediterranean, where it still flourishes. In Italy, Sicily, Greece, and Spain, wild thyme plants are among the most common of "weeds."

Thyme was one of the herbs ancient Greeks burned in tribute to their gods, and in that same era it symbolized strength and bravery. In medieval times an infusion of thyme was added to the bath water of warriors, to bestow strength and courage, and thyme tea was considered a cure for headaches, hangovers, and nightmares. In the last century in America, dried leaves were used in closets to keep away moths, and now, of course, it is among the most popular of the herbs for cooking.

Thyme, yet another member of the *Labiatae* family, is a perennial that grows to a height of not more than 12 inches, usually less. It is a gracefully trailing plant that is easily started from seed and just as easily raised in pots.

Sandy soil is the best for growing thyme. Plant the seeds, which are very tiny, to a shallow depth, and keep the soil thoroughly moistened until germination occurs—about ten days. Do not allow the soil to dry out until the seedlings are large enough to be easily visible. When the seedlings stand 2 to 3 inches high, they may be transplanted into individual 6-inch pots or thinned to leave the strongest specimen in a pot of that size.

Propagation may also be done from cuttings taken from a strong plant and rooted in moist, sandy soil; by layering the trailing stems by pulling soil over them until they root; or by division of the crown. The best thyme for the kitchen comes from young plants, so new plantings should be made every two or three years.

Water the thyme plants only when the soil becomes very obviously dry. Thyme, even more than other plants, is easily killed by too much moisture around its roots.

Thyme will grow in nearly any level of light that is provided, but when the intensity of light is less than 1000 foot-candles, the plants become nearly dormant and growth is incredibly slow. To maintain a steady supply for the kitchen, therefore, you should provide long hours of bright light—at least 1000 foot-candles, and preferably more.

To dry thyme for later use, cut off the tips of the stems as far back as the stem is tender. This should be done before the tiny blossoms have had a chance to open. Tie the stems in loose bunches, then hang them in a warm, well-ventilated place to dry. Strip the dried leaves from the stems and store them in an airtight container.

Thyme has a very strong, pungent flavor, and too much of it can easily overpower the other ingredients in a dish. But if it is used with restraint, it adds a subtle flavor to almost any dish, particularly when a racy tang is desired.

Thyme has a natural affinity for seafood and is indispensable in clam chowder. Added sparingly while the soup is cooking it is excellent, and it has a wide range of uses in making gourmet sauces and gravies. A pinch adds real zest to ordinary tea.

Watercress
(Nasturtium officinale)

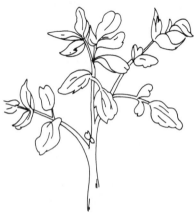

Sometimes listed as a vegetable because of its use in salads and on sandwiches, this favorite is listed here as an herb because of its growth habits and because it is more frequently used as flavoring in soups, stuffings, and sauces.

Watercress, with its pungent and peppery flavor, is a hardy European perennial native to the north temperate regions, where it grows in streams and along their boggy banks; it has spread to similar areas in North America. Not only tasty, it is also an extremely good source of vitamins A, B, and C, as well as phosphorus and iron.

To start watercress from seed, sow it in a pot of rich, loose soil and place the pot in a pan of water under artificial lights or on a sunny windowsill. Change the water in the pan daily. When the seedlings are large enough to be handled with ease, transplant them to individual pots.

Temperature is of the utmost importance in growing watercress. The pots should be kept standing in pans of water, and the water must be changed daily and kept cool at all times. Some growers even add a few ice cubes to the water in the pan when the temperature climbs.

As the young plants develop, they should be thinned to stand a few inches apart where their roots enter the soil. Use the washed thinnings exactly like the mature cress, so no waste is involved.

Watercress, as the name implies, needs far more water than most other plants. The plants should be watered every other day, the soil being thoroughly soaked each time. Under no circumstances should the soil be allowed to dry out.

Watercress will grow well under almost any light conditions. By nature it is a shade-loving plant, so the light does not really need to be intense. This is a good plant, then, for setting on the edges of artificially lighted areas where the intensity of light is apt to be low, or for growing in window areas where the hours of light are likely to be short.

If seed for watercress is unavailable, which is too frequently the case, cress may be grown from bunches you purchase in the store. Be sure the bunch is as fresh as possible, with no trace of yellow on the leaves. Plant the stems with their roots directly in pots standing in water, or allow the roots to develop by placing the bunch of cress in a glass of water, which must be changed at least once a day. Do not submerge all the leaves, for some must be above the surface to supply the plant with carbon dioxide. When the plants are well started, set them in soil and treat them exactly like those started from seed.

Once it is well started and healthy, watercress can be snipped repeatedly; a few plants will probably supply as much as you need. It mixes well with romaine, escarole, parsley, spinach, or chicory and can be used as a substitute for most of these. It is sometimes cooked as a potherb but is far better when mixed with other greens.

the vegetables

Unlike herbs, which are so similar to one another in their needs, cultivation, and manner of growth, the plants that we use as vegetables come from a large number of plant families and hence have differing requirements that cannot be set forth in general ways. Even two members of the same plant family may have altogether different needs for light, soil, water, and nutrition. For that reason it is futile to attempt a general description of their cultivation; the specific growth requirements of each plant appear in the text dealing with that plant.

Botanically speaking, many of the plants we use as vegetables are fruits, which means they may require pollination, as with the cucumbers. This does not necessarily mean they are more difficult to grow—it simply means the grower has another step in the growth process to which attention must be given.

Also by botanical definition many of the plants that we use as vegetables would be more correctly defined as herbs. They are grouped here according to their use, however, and not according to their exact botanical nature.

You can start most of the vegetables from seed. Selection of the proper variety often plays an important role in home gardening. Many of the standard varieties produce sprawling plants with heavy root structures that require far more soil and space than the indoor gardener can readily provide. But now new plant varieties have been developed that help solve the problem. Cucumber, squash, and many other favorite vegetables are now available in bush or dwarf varieties that can be grown in very small amounts of soil, and often these varieties produce vegetables equal in size to those harvested from larger plants of the same species. For gardening fun, or where space is extremely limited, you can grow many vegetables in miniature form—plants that produce tiny replicas of their larger brethren.

With many of the vegetables, proper duration of light is extremely important, not only to achieve blossoming as a prelude to fruit production, but also to avoid the problem that has plagued gardeners, indoors and out, for numberless years—"bolting to seed."

Bolting is a part of the photoperiod effect. The number of hours of light a plant gets may determine whether a plant develops as you wish or whether it will suddenly shoot upward and prepare to produce seed before it has reached a state of edibility. In the outdoor garden this usually occurs when seed starts too early or too late in the season. This frequently happens with radishes and some varieties of lettuce.

The outdoor gardener can combat the problem of bolting only by carefully selecting growing sites—sunny spots for some plants, shady spots for others—and by carefully following the seasons. But gardeners using artificial lights create their own seasons and so can overcome the problem of bolting easily.

A few of the vegetable plants are not suitable for indoor gardening. Corn, potatoes, and the various grains, for example, require too much space to be grown in this fashion; and others, such as broccoli, will not develop properly when grown indoors. These plants you will not find mentioned in the section which follows. But you will find many plants that are very easy to grow, others that can be grown with moderate ease, and some plants that are a real challenge to grow. No matter what your skills and equipment, you will find some plants that will increase your gardening enjoyment and your dining pleasure.

Beans
(Phaseolus nanus)

The great family *Leguminosae* includes all common garden, snap, string, and stringless beans whose immature pods are cooked and served or whose seed is dried and cooked. There are more than 200 types and 1,500 varieties, but *P. nanus,* the bush bean, is the one best suited for the indoor garden, not only because it requires less space and is more easily lighted than the climbing varieties, but also because it is far more attractive. A single plant, or even two, will not provide enough beans for a family for a year, but the plants are fun to grow and reasonably attractive, and can provide a fairly small but highly delicious supply of beans for adding to soups, salads, and cooked dishes.

Pole beans or climbing beans sometimes achieve a height of 8 or 10 feet, making the entire length of the plant very difficult to light. The bush beans described here, on the other hand, usually grow only about 15 inches high and have a very shallow root system, making them far more desirable for growing in limited space. Like most of their relatives, they are native to North America, where they were cultivated by the Indians. Beans were known in the Old World, but they belonged to another genus, *Dolichos.*

If you live in any area of the country with three or more frost-free months, you may want to grow a few containers of bush beans on your porch, patio, or balcony. They will grow well there with little care, but as they are very tender and killed by the slightest touch of frost, they should not be set outside until all danger of frost is past. If you live in a very warm region, do not place the plants in direct sun or set them where they will be exposed to heat reflecting off concrete; temperatures above 95 degrees will injure both the flowers and the pollen. Outside plants should be given some protection from rain, which causes the blossoms to drop. With these precautions outdoor plants can be grown by the same techniques used for growing indoor or greenhouse plants, which are as follows:

Seeds and Soil By far the most popular of the bush-bean varieties are Top Crop, Contender, Wade, Tendergreen, and Bountiful, but if you prefer wax beans, choose Brittle or Pencil Pod. The seed germinates in four to seven days, and the beans mature in six to eight weeks, depending on variety and conditions. Beans can be picked from each bush in successively smaller amounts for at least four weeks after maturity, and subsequent plantings can be made so that one plant will be ready to bear as another is ready to die. A packet of seeds contains far more seed than you will probably want to plant, but any excess can be used for growing bean sprouts, if you wish, as described under Sprouts (pp. 197–198).

Beans grow best in a slightly acid soil with the pH 5.8 to 6.5. Some sand in the soil also helps, but under no circumstances should the soil have a high content of clay. Nor should the soil have a high nitrogen content, which promotes foliage growth while reducing the number of edible pods produced by the plant.

Soil for growing bush beans need not be deep, but the planter should be large enough, if it contains a number of plants, to allow the plants to stand 4 to 6 inches apart. Growing them closer together will promote fungus diseases. If the soil is reasonably rich at the time of planting, no additional fertilizer should be needed to bring the plants to maturity, and high-nitrogen fertilizers should not be used under any circumstances.

Beans

Planting   Beans should be planted in drills 1 inch deep, the seed spaced about 2 inches apart. After germination they can be thinned to provide the required 4 to 6 inches between plants. If beans are planted in cold wet soil, they will not germinate but will rot. Room-temperature soil is ideal for planting.

Water   Beans tolerate a wide range of moisture in their natural environment, but they are easily killed by water standing around their roots. They are capable of withstanding relatively long periods of dryness, so it is better to be on the safe side and water them infrequently and only when the soil shows an obvious need for water.

Temperature Beans grow best at temperatures ranging from 65 to 85 degrees, with optimum growth at the higher end of the range. The higher temperatures are easier to achieve in a greenhouse, of course, but there one must be wary of allowing temperatures to climb too high, which will result in no growth at all. A warm room or the space beneath a skylight will do nicely, and cooler night temperatures will not harm the plants.

Light Beans need the brightest light you can provide. Some authors suggest that the plants can be made to bear under 1,500 foot-candles of light, but there is good reason to doubt this. The suggested minimum is 2,000 foot-candles, preferably more. This is really a plant for growing in a light room, a greenhouse, or under the most elaborate light arrangements.

Duration of light is also important. Although bush beans are a day-neutral plant capable of blossoming in a wide range of day lengths, scientific experiments show that they have a decided preference for shorter days—not more than 13½ hours of the brightest light you can give them. Keeping the days relatively short will cause maximum production.

Harvest Snap beans can be picked when the pods are almost at their full size but are not yet showing the outlines of the enclosed seeds. At this time they should snap easily and be stringless. Shell beans should be picked when the beans are clearly discernible within the pods. They are at their most flavorful when cooked and served within minutes of picking.

Beets

(Beta vulgaris)

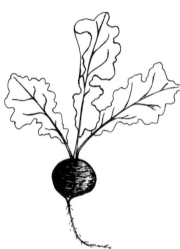

Actually a biennial herb, this native of Europe and North Africa is an excellent root vegetable for indoor gardeners, even when space and resources are somewhat limited. Don't plan on giant beets the size of turnips, however—think instead of growing them only until they are bite-size, tender, and sweet, and plan on using the leaves, which are excellent either cooked or raw in salads. Both the edible roots and the leaves have been used as foods since about the third century A.D., but it was not until the sixteenth century that improved varieties made the beet a garden favorite.

Seeds and Soil   Beet seeds consist of two to six seeds in a dry fruit husk, which must be softened before the young shoots can emerge. Soaking the seeds in water for about twelve hours before planting, therefore, hastens germination. If you do this, germination should occur about ten days after planting. Dozens of varieties are available, but Early Wonder, which matures in about sixty days under the right conditions, is probably the all-time favorite.

Beets absolutely refuse to grow in any soil that is too acid. The best soil for them has a neutral pH, which means they can be grown in most commercial potting soils. Adding some sand or perlite will provide the better drainage that is needed for optimum growth. The soil in the planter should be at least 6 inches deep, and the planter should be large enough to allow the developing beets plenty of room—a minimum of 3 inches between plants, preferably a little more.

Planting   After soaking the seeds, plant them ½-inch deep in moist soil, set 1 to 2 inches apart. Keep the soil very moist until the young seedlings emerge. When the seedlings are a few inches tall, thin them to stand at least 3 inches apart. Failure to thin them at this time will greatly retard root development. There is no waste when beets are thinned, as the young thinnings may be used in salads or cooked as an addition to other vegetable dishes.

Water Beets need more water than most other root vegetables. How often you water depends greatly on the temperature and the ability of your soil to retain moisture, but the soil must never become completely dry. Covering the pot with a layer of damp sphagnum after each watering will help slow down evaporation and keep the soil constantly moist, thus assuring faster growth and a quality crop.

Nutrition If the soil is rich in nutrients at the time of planting, additional plant food may not be needed. If you are using your own soil mix, however, and fertilizer is needed, feed the plants when they have just been thinned. Plant food for beets should have a high nitrogen content.

Temperature Beets will do very well at room temperature, but the roots are extremely sensitive to heat and dryness. When they are grown at higher temperatures, they develop smaller roots that are tough and stringy, while developing abundant top growth. For this reason greenhouse beets are better grown in winter than in summer, and beets grown indoors under artificial light may do just as well as those you grow in an outside planter under natural sunlight, where you have no way to control the temperature.

Light Because beets produce no seed until the second year and chances are good that you will pull them well before that, photoperiodism is not an important consideration in growing them, nor do they show a strong tendency to bolt to seed. This means that the duration of light can be extended, if need be, to compensate for its lack of intensity.

Many growers report that beets will develop if they receive 1000 foot-candles of light. However, as with many root crops, development will be faster and more natural with 1,500 foot-candles or more of light. Provide light for at least twelve hours daily, but if growth seems slow, raise that to sixteen or even eighteen hours out of each twenty-four-hour period.

Harvest   Pull beets when they are just a little over 1 inch in diameter. Cut the tops about an inch above the edible root, leaving the stub of their stems to prevent bleeding during cooking. The tops, which are rich in vitamins A, B, and C, calcium, and phosphorus, are best when cooked very briefly in boiling water and seasoned to taste.

Brussels Sprouts
(Brassica oleracea)

This member of the family *Cruciferae*, a close relative of cabbage, is not an easy one for the home gardener. Even in an outdoor garden it is so slow to develop, requiring five or six months when started from seed, that it must be grown from young plants started in a greenhouse. Its sprouts or buds may also fail to develop properly under artificial light alone; therefore, this is really a plant for the home greenhouse; or it can be started under artificial light, then moved to an outdoor area and grown to maturity there.

The plant is native to the coast of Denmark and both sides of the English Channel. A development from wild cabbage, it seems to have appeared as a cultivated plant before the sixteenth century in the area around Brussels, Belgium, but it was not widely grown until the nineteenth century. A slow-growing biennial that reaches from 2 to 4 feet in height, depending on variety, it produces tufts of cabbagelike leaves at the top of a leggy stalk, with lower leaves that are spaced further apart. The edible portions—the familiar sprouts or buds—form in the axils of the lower leaves, and those nearest the bottom of the stalk develop first. Because of its rather odd appearance, the plant is frequently grown as a curiosity. These sprouts are best when matured in cool weather and can even use a mild touch of frost.

Seeds and Soil Select a dwarf variety such as Catskill or Long Island Improved. Standard varieties send down a deeper taproot, requiring more soil and more space than you will want to provide. The dwarf plants will grow no more than 2 feet high and will require soil about half that deep, yet each plant will yield about a quart of sprouts.

Seeds will germinate at a temperature of 45 degrees or more. If the seeds are started indoors in late winter or early spring, the seedlings will be 7 or 8 inches high by mid-summer, when they will be ready to be shifted into an outdoor area and grown to maturity, then harvested following the first frost. If the plants are to be grown in a greenhouse, seed should be started in the summer and the plants matured during the winter, because this is a plant that is easily killed by high temperatures such as those which occur in the summer greenhouse.

The soil should be a rich mixture of sand and loam. Its pH should be 6.0 to 7.0, with a high nitrogen content. Adding a nitrogen-rich plant food to the soil in which brussels sprouts are started is advisable. The planter should be at least 10 inches in diameter.

Planting Start the seeds ½-inch deep in the container in which they are to grow, or in a layer of vermiculite over soil if they are to be transplanted. Keep the soil moist at all times. Providing the plants with 1000 foot-candles of light will take them through the seedling stage, until they are ready to be set where they are to grow to maturity. Pinching off a few lower leaves at this time—when they are 7 to 8 inches high—will make the plants produce more heavily.

Water Like cabbage and all its relatives, brussels sprouts need a great deal of water. The soil must be kept moist at all times, and the plant must be watered more frequently as the plant grows and begins to form its buds. A layer of mulch will help hold down evaporation while also helping to keep the roots cool.

Brussels Sprouts

Nutrition Brussels sprouts feed heavily on nitrogen. About two or three weeks after they pass the seedling stage, they should be fed a nitrogenous fertilizer, and they should have another feeding when the first buds begin to form. When this feeding is given, tear off the lower leaves to make room for the sprouts and to concentrate all the food into the forming of the edible parts of the plant.

Temperature Cool temperatures are essential for the cultivation of brussels sprouts, which makes them not a good plant for the summer greenhouse, where cooling can be a problem. When they are set outside, the plants also need some protection from the blazing noonday sun, especially when they are grown in southern regions. Select your coolest spot for growing this crop, and, if possible, leave the plant outside until it has been nipped by frost.

Light It might be possible to grow this plant to maturity using only artificial light of great intensity, but any attempt to do so must be regarded as an experiment. This is one of the plants where natural sunlight is an absolute requirement, at least given our present knowledge.

Intensity of light is not the real problem, for the plant grows quite well in the shade and would grow to maturity under light of relatively low intensity; the problem is in *how* it will grow under artificial light. Because foliage tends to grow toward, as well as parallel to, the source of artificial light, the sprouts simply refuse to take proper shape under such illumination. Probably there are other unknown causes for this phenomenon, but it is a problem that prevents the proper development of several heading plants—notably cabbage and lettuce—under artificial light. However, after the sprouts have started to form and their shape is defined, they will bear normally under even the lowest level of artificial light—1000 foot-candles or even less.

Harvest The first sprouts picked should be those lowest on the plant, although they will not be as firm as those which appear later near the top. They should be picked before they show any signs of yellow. Tear away the leaf below the sprout, then twist the sprout off its stalk.

All sprouts which are budding and in which the shape is defined at this time will mature, as long as the plant is protected from freezing. In some instances plants may continue to produce sprouts for five or six months. Just move the plant to your coolest room, keep its roots provided with moisture, give it a little light, and harvest the sprouts as they swell.

Cabbage
(Brassica oleracea capitata)

Native to Greece, Britain, and France, cabbage has been cultivated since before recorded history. A member of the mustard family, *Cruciferae,* it is known to have been grown by the Egyptians, the early Greeks, and the ancient Celts. Although it is generally regarded as an easy plant to grow, in most of its forms cabbage is not really suited to indoor cultivation or growing under artificial light. It is a plant that needs a lot of space and that has an odor that can be imparted to carpet and furnishings, and its heads fail to form properly for the reasons mentioned in the entry for brussels sprouts. However, there are new dwarf varieties available that require less space and are suitable for growing in window boxes or as patio plants, and some of the larger varieties may also be desired as greenhouse plants.

Seeds and Soil Literally hundreds of varieties are available, and most seed companies now offer at least one miniature variety, such as Dwarf Morden, which develops a head about the size of a softball. Standard cabbage varieties are divided according to the seasons—early, mid-season, and late. In most of the United States, the late cabbage varieties are easiest to grow. Cultivated as described here, they need at least 5 gallons of soil for each plant.

Rich, moist loam with a pH of 5.5 to 7.5, is the ideal soil for growing any member of the cabbage family. Garden loam that contains a good deal of humus or well-rotted organic matter is perfect. Enriching the soil with phosphorus well in advance of planting helps provide faster and better growth.

Dwarf varieties can be grown in a pot with a diameter of 8 inches or more, or several can be grown in an oblong window box. The soil should be at least 6 inches deep, for even dwarf varieties of cabbage are biennials that send down taproots.

Planting Seeds should be started in a warm room, preferably one where the temperature ranges from 70 to 75 degrees. Seed will germinate in ten to fourteen days. After the seedlings emerge, the temperature should be reduced to 60 degrees or less. Seedlings can be started where they are to grow, starting several and thinning them, or they can be transplanted when they are about 3 inches tall. Start dwarf seedlings in May or June, placing them in a sunny window or under 1000 footcandles of artificial light; then move them outside after about five weeks for a crop that will be ready to harvest in the fall or early winter.

Water Soil in which cabbage is grown must be kept constantly moist to assure development of the heads. If the plants are allowed to dry out and then are watered, the heads are likely to split open. You can prevent cracking of the cabbage head by using a trowel to break some of the lateral roots near the surface. Covering the planter with a thick layer of mulch helps maintain the moisture.

Nutrition Several weeks after the cabbage plant has passed the seedling stage, it should be fed with a nitrogenous fertilizer. Or you can also apply cottonseed meal or blood meal, both of which are readily available at garden centers, around the plants, which will then be carried to the roots by subsequent waterings.

Temperature   Cabbage does best at cool temperatures. At night, especially, high temperatures will slow growth. During the day the plant should not be set where it is exposed to heat reflected off concrete or stone. Plants can withstand temperatures as low as 20 degrees over short periods. However, if they are exposed to freezing temperatures for a month or more and then touched by warmer air, the plants bolt to seed in a way that is almost impossible to stop.

Light   Cabbages need full sun, but it must be cool sunlight. Avoid western exposures and reflected heat. After the heads have developed some further growth will result if you display them under artificial light of enough intensity—1500 foot-candles or more should do. But since this is one of the relatively few plants that can be left outside after the start of the frost season, and since it gives off an unpleasant odor, it is probably best not to bring cabbage inside.

Harvest   The flavor of cabbage improves if the heads are exposed to a touch of frost, another reason for leaving plants outside. However, cabbage heads may be cut and used as soon as they are firm. The firm heads are simply pulled up and the roots cut away. They must be kept in a cool place. All except the most coarse outer leaves are eaten, either cooked or raw. By the way, the strong flavor of cabbage results from the breakdown of sulfur compounds in the leaves, and this breakdown does not occur unless cabbage is cooked too long, cooked at too high a temperature, or cooked in too much water. If you prevent too much contact with water at high temperature (by steaming it, for example), it is one of the mildest vegetables you'll ever taste.

Carrots
(Daucus carota)

One of the easiest of all vegetable plants to grow under almost any light, this is the leading member of the carrot, or *Umbelliferae,* family. Actually a biennial herb that produces in the first year an edible yellow or orange root topped by feathery foliage arising in a circle from its crown, during the second year of life it bears flowers and seeds at the top of a tall stem. But carrots are grown as annuals, of course, since only the edible roots of the first year are wanted.

Carrots are native to Europe and Asia. They were cultivated by the early Romans and Greeks, who described many varieties, including some that were red, in their literature. Today carrots are cultivated throughout the world and hundreds of varieties are available. The edible roots can be long and tapered, short and stubby, or miniatures the size of your little finger, depending on the variety you choose.

Seeds and Soil The long and tapered varieties require deeper soil and take longer to mature. For this reason the short and stubby varieties are best for growing in limited space. Some popular varieties of the short type are Nantes and Danvers Half-Long. These mature from seed in about sixty-five days. Nearly every seed company now offers at least one midget variety of little carrots that are a delight to serve whole, either raw or cooked.

One midget variety that I personally tested is Short 'N' Sweet, which produces tiny carrots in about sixty-five days.

The best soil for carrots is a rich loam with plenty of sand, or a potting soil to which sand has been added. Ideally, the soil should be slightly acid with a pH between 5.5 and 6.5, but you can also grow carrots in a neutral potting soil.

Soil should be at least 6 inches deep in the planter, even for miniature varieties. Carrots send down feeder roots that go several inches beyond the tip of the carrot, so providing a deeper planter is a good idea. The other dimensions of the planter are determined by how many carrots, of which variety, you intend to grow. You can grow eight or ten carrots of most standard varieties with careful spacing in a pot with an 8-inch diameter. About a dozen of the miniatures can be grown in a pot of the same size.

Planting   Carrot seed germinates slowly, and germination can be erratic under even the best conditions. The first sprouts are very weak, so soil resistance must be held to a minimum by soaking the soil before planting, then covering the seeds with a half-inch of soil that has been loosened by sifting. Or seed may be germinated before planting. To do this, spread the seed in a thin layer between two sheets of wet blotting paper and store them in a refrigerator until white root tips begin to break through the seeds. You can then sprinkle the germinated seed over the soil in the planter and cover it with another layer of moist soil. Seed should be sown thickly—about a half-dozen seeds to the inch—and thinned later.

When seedlings are 2 to 3 inches high, thin them to stand ½-inch apart in all directions. Thin just after watering, so the soil around the

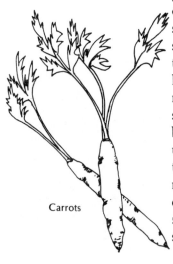

Carrots

remaining plants will not be disturbed. When the carrots are ½-inch in diameter at the crown, thin them again to stand 1½ inches in every direction. These thinnings will be large enough to use in salads or to cook with other vegetables.

At the same time as the second thinning, the shoulders of the carrots (the upper part that joins the green top) should be covered with soil. If this is not done, exposure to light will cause chlorophyll to develop and turn the exposed parts green.

It is very important to thin carrots. Crowding them will not give you more carrots—it will result in no carrots at all. If new plantings are started at intervals of about two or three weeks, in other pots, you can maintain a fairly good supply. Carrots that are even slightly crowded will have a tendency toward toughness and irregular shape.

Water Except during the very early stages of growth, when the soil should be kept moist to aid germination, carrots are able to withstand long periods without water and actually seem to thrive under the driest conditions. It is best, therefore, to water infrequently—certainly no more often than every seven or ten days. When water is given, however, the plants must be flooded. Remember that the feeder roots are below the carrot itself, and water must get down to these roots.

Nutrition If the soil is fairly rich to start with, carrots should need little fertilization. However, if growth appears slow, a feeding of high-phosphorus plant food may be in order. Never apply a nitrogenous fertilizer to carrots, as it stimulates branching of the roots and causes the carrots to develop skins that are thick, rough, and scaly.

Temperature The best temperatures for growing carrots are 60 to 70 degrees, which means the average home is just right. If carrots are grown in an atmosphere above 70 degrees, they will not lengthen properly, and below 60 degrees they fail to develop the right color and flavor.

Light Since no seed is produced until the second year, photoperiodism plays no important role, bolting is not a problem, and long hours of light can be provided to induce better growth. It is possible to grow carrots under only 1000 foot-candles of artificial light given for twelve or more hours each day, but growth will be very slow and the carrots will not develop normally. However, if you increase the intensity of the light to 1500 foot-candles for the same period, the rate of growth will be almost normal. Carrots grown in outdoor planters should be set where they will receive several hours of full sun each day.

Harvest Standard carrot varieties should be pulled and used when they are just over a half-inch in diameter at the shoulders, the midgets when they are about half that size. They are best flavored and most tender if they are not allowed to grow to their full size. To store them, cut off the tops and leave just about an inch of stem, which locks in the flavor. Remember, though, that carrots are most crisp and flavorful when taken directly from soil to table, with perhaps a brief detour to the cooking pot.

Celery
(Apium graveolens)

Another member of the important carrot or *Umbelliferae* family, celery is a biennial native to the marshy areas of Europe, Africa, and India. Known in ancient times, it was not cultivated until the seventeenth century. It has

been grown hydroponically, in greenhouses, and under artificial lights in experimental light laboratories, but it is a very difficult plant to grow, even outdoors. Try it only if you are ready for a challenge.

The problems have more to do with moisture and nutrition than with light. Celery, which grows 12 to 18 inches tall, has a very shallow root system, yet it needs far more nutrients than most other plants. It is also a marsh plant that requires constant moisture. Providing for those needs is difficult, but it can be done.

Seeds and Soil The very richest soil is needed for growing celery. It is nearly impossible to make the soil too rich. Celery will grow in any soil with a pH between 5.2 and 7.5, with 6.0 regarded as ideal. Enriching the soil with plant food before planting will help, and mixing in some humus, if it is available, will aid in keeping the moisture content high. Soil in the planter need not be deep, but the other dimensions of the planter should be large enough to provide 4 inches in all directions between mature plants. Seed should be blight resistant, preferably one of the Pascal strains.

Planting Seed is germinated in darkness. During the germination period temperatures should be in the 60s during the day and in the 50s at night. Seed may be started where the plants are to grow by scattering the seed thinly over the soil, then covering the seed with a thin layer of sand or vermiculite. The soil must be kept very moist until germination occurs, but water should not be poured directly over the seeds. Water given from the bottom is preferable; or you can start the seeds hydroponically.

When the young seedlings emerge and begin to take root, they need light of gradually increasing intensity. Move them from the dark area to one where they receive some indirect light, then to a slightly brighter spot, and finally to a spot where they will receive some direct light, either artificial or natural. They should not receive direct light until they stand about 3 to 4 inches high. By this time they will be ready to thin to stand 4 inches apart. After the thinning, add another layer of loose rich soil to the planter, banking it up around the seedlings so they are rooted about 3 inches below the surface. Throughout these early stages of growth, sudden fluctuations in temperature must be avoided, for no stalks will form if the plants are exposed to these conditions.

Water Celery needs a constant supply of water, and plenty of it. In the outdoor environment it grows best in regions that receive as much as 2 inches of rain weekly. This means that the soil is almost constantly soaked. Hydroponics is one way to solve the moisture problem. Other growers report success as a result of keeping the planter set in a larger container of water and submerging the pot to within 3 inches or so of its top. Frequent watering from the top is the least desirable method and should be used only as a last resort. But the soil must be kept constantly moist by whatever means.

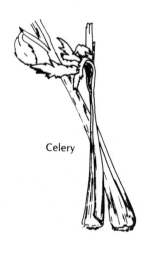

Celery

Nutrition Because the plant has such a shallow root system yet is a heavy feeder, providing proper nutrition is the greatest problem in growing celery. Hydroponics, which constantly washes the roots with nutrient-enriched water, is the obvious answer. In soil the plants should be fed at ten-day intervals, using an all-purpose formula such as a 10-8-22, which can be dissolved in water and given as the plants are watered. Feeding can be reduced as the plants reach maturity.

Temperature Celery absolutely requires cool temperatures that do not fluctuate. Temperatures above 75 degrees will almost certainly stop growth or kill the plants. For this reason greenhouse plants are best grown in winter, and patio plants must not be set where they are exposed to reflected heat. Temperatures beneath a skylight are also likely to be too high.

Light Providing light for celery is no real problem, unless you attempt to give the plants light that is too intense. This is one of the plants that truly needs shade. If you grow it in outdoor containers, set it where it receives protection from the burning rays of the noonday sun. Greenhouse plants should also have some protection; set them in the shade of other plants or use muslin to filter out the brightest light.

Actually celery appears to adapt itself to most levels of light as long as it is not too intense, according to the brightness provided as the young plants are developing and are first exposed to illumination. Reports indicate that it has been grown under intensities as low as 1000 foot-candles, as well as at levels more than twice that high. Adapt it slowly to your own lighting situation and give it twelve hours of light daily.

Harvest Growing celery from seed requires about six months. At the end of the fifth month, the celery should be blanched. This is done by covering the lower part of each plant with a paper collar. Gather the leaves and stems close around the plant, then wrap and tie thickly folded newspaper around the stems, allowing about 4 inches of the leaves to protrude at the top. Bank a little soil around the bottom of the paper to help hold it in place. The paper excludes light and thus whitens the base of the celery.

At about the end of the sixth month, cut the plants' roots immediately below the soil surface, then use the stalks and leaves at once, either raw or as flavoring in soups, stews, and stuffings.

Chinese Cabbage
(Brassica chinensis)

This leafy vegetable of the mustard family, known to the Chinese as *bok-choy* or *pak-choi*, is an extremely prolific plant that is easy to grow. The heading Chinese cabbage, *B. pekinensis*, known in the Orient as *pe-tsai*, requires much more space and is not recommended.

Chinese cabbage has been cultivated in the Orient for nearly two thousand years and is believed to have been developed from wild mustard, a close relative. It was introduced to Europe before the middle of the last century, but did not become popular in America until recent times.

The plant grows to a height of about 16 inches. Its leaves are green and slender, each divided by a crisp white midrib. All leaves are edible, either cooked or raw in salads, and several cuttings may be made before the plants grow to maturity, when the leaves become slightly tougher and are suitable only for cooking.

Seeds and Soil   Select any loose-leaved variety, such as Crispy Choy, which will germinate in about seven days. A packet of seed contains far more seed than you will use in a single year, but the seed keeps well and can be used in later plantings; or you can use it as a substitute for mustard seed in recipes calling for that seasoning.

Any soil except that which is very acid—6.0 or less—can be used for growing Chinese cabbage. The most important requirement is that the soil hold water well, as most commercial potting soils will do. The soil in the planter should be at least 6 inches deep. The plants will tolerate more crowding than most vegetables, but you should allow for 2 or 3 inches between roots. A window box will easily hold a dozen plants, perhaps even more.

Planting Always start Chinese cabbage where the plants are to grow, as the seedlings are nearly impossible to transplant without destroying them. Seeds should be planted ½-inch deep and about 2 inches apart. Firm down the soil above them and thoroughly water it. When the plants are about 3 inches high, thin them to stand about 4 inches apart; use the thinnings in salads. When they stand about 6 inches high, thin them again and use the thinnings as cooked greens; or snip them near the base of the leaves, which will leave the plants in place to produce a later cutting.

Water Like many of its relatives, Chinese cabbage needs a constant supply of water. Especially when the plants are young and more actively growing, they may need water daily, depending on the quality of the soil and many other factors. The top inch or two of soil should be very moist at all times.

Nutrition If it is grown in a rich loam or commercial potting soil, a crop of Chinese cabbage should reach maturity without further fertilization. If growth slows noticeably during the latter stages, however, a feeding of high-nitrogen plant food may help.

Temperature Chinese cabbage demands cool temperatures for best growth. If it is grown outside, it must be protected from hot sun. It will stand very light frost but is killed by freezing temperatures. If temperatures approach 80 degrees the plant will almost certainly bolt and produce few edible leaves. Temperatures in the 50s are best for growing this plant.

Light Chinese cabbage should be given at least 1000 foot-candles of light while young; growth will be faster with brighter light. Keep the young plants under lights about eight hours daily. After the plants are well started, growth will continue at lower light levels, a phenomenon that can be seen in many plants. Healthy plants that are approaching maturity will continue to develop quite well if they are set in a window that receives a few hours of cool sunlight each day.

Harvest Chinese cabbage requires about eighty days to reach full size. However, in about half that time the young plants are far more tender and flavorful, and leaves are ready for cutting. Use the youngest leaves for salads, mature ones for cooking. The thick white midrib of the mature leaf is sometimes used as a substitute for celery.

Collards
(Brassica oleracea acephala)

Doubtless one of the earliest cultivated forms of cabbage, collards were known to the Greeks and Romans. The plant is a biennial herb capable of growing 2 or even 3 feet high, but most cultivated varieties are far smaller and easier to handle.

The plant produces coarse, cabbagelike leaves at the top of a stout stem. Young leaves are used in salads, older ones for cooking. Young or old, they are rich in Vitamins A and C, as well as in minerals.

Seeds and Soil   Vates, which does not grow nearly as tall as other varieties, is the recommended choice. The seed germinates quickly and easily, and plants reach maturity in about eighty days. Each plant will yield at least two crops, so only a few plants, started at carefully selected intervals, will provide all the collards you can use during the course of a year.

Any soil with a pH between 5.5 and 6.5 will grow the best collards. Potting soil may be used, but adding a little peat moss will improve it, and some sand should also be mixed in to improve the drainage. The planter should have a diameter of at least 10 inches and should be at least 6 inches deep. A planter of this size will provide for a single plant grown to maturity.

Planting   Sow the seed thinly to a depth of ½ inch. As the seedlings develop, thin them to stand first 2 inches, then 4 inches, apart, finally reducing them until only a single plant stands in the pot or until plants in a larger planter stand at least 18 inches apart. Use thinnings in salads or cooked as greens.

Water   Although they will tolerate a certain extent of dryness, collards will grow faster and taste better if the soil around their roots is moist at all times. The plants consume more water as the upper leaves begin to develop.

Nutrition   If the soil is rich at the time of planting, collards should need no fertilization until about the time the tuft of upper leaves begins to spread. At that time they should be fed with a nitrogenous plant food. The maturing plant will exhaust the nutrients needed for growing more collards or any other member of the cabbage family, so new soil should be put in the pot if any of these are to be grown.

Temperature   Collards tolerate a wide range of temperatures. If you live south of Virginia, they can be grown outdoors during the winter. They will stand summer heat, but some cooling should be provided if plants are grown in a greenhouse during the summer.

Light   Collards will also grow under a wide range of light intensity and duration. However, growth is faster under bright light of long duration. Where only artificial light is provided, light intensity should be at least 1500 foot-candles for twelve or sixteen hours daily. A sunny area is best when growing them on the patio.

Harvest   Pick leaves from collard plants when they are almost full size but before they have had a chance to become tough and woody. For salad, the youngest leaves from youngest plants are by far the best. When you are picking leaves, allow the main stem to stand to produce a further crop. Any collard plant that is not exposed to freezing temperatures should provide at least two crops, and an indoor plant may continue to produce new leaves for several months.

Cucumber
(Cucumis sativus)

This popular member of the gourd family probably originated in Asia or Egypt, but because it has been cultivated for thousands of years, its origins are uncertain. It is, however, known to have been cultivated in greenhouses by the early Romans and is relatively easily grown under artificial light. Because of its commercial importance, scientists have studied the cucumber intensely, and so its requirements for growth are better established than those of many plants.

Seeds and Soil Standard cucumber varieties produce trailing vines that may spread several feet in all directions. These also send down very deep taproots that require large amounts of soil and space. On the market now, however, are several bush varieties that are very compact and require far less soil. All seed companies offer at least one of these varieties. Burpee's Bush Champion is one. This variety bears cucumbers as large as 11 inches in length. A single plant may be grown in a 6- or 7-inch pot, and three plants may be grown in a 12- or 13-inch planter. Other cucumbers may be grown in limited space by using hydroponics.

Light loam or potting soil will grow cucumbers. The pH should be 5.5 to 6.8. Either soil should be well enriched with nitrogen before planting the seeds. The formula should be about 15-30-15, or a few ounces of cottonseed meal can be stirred in as a source of nitrogen. Sifting the soil to loosen it will provide for a better start. Seed germinates in eight to ten days, and cucumbers mature in about sixty days.

Planting Loosen the soil to the bottom of the planter. Sprinkle a few seeds over the top, then cover them with about an inch of soil. Moisten lightly and give them full light. Throughout the early stages of life, until blossoms begin to appear, cucumber growth can be stimulated by long, even continuous lighting. When seedlings are about 6 inches tall, select the strongest plants and pinch out the weakest ones. Do not attempt to pull them up, as their roots will almost certainly be tangled with those of the seedlings that are to remain. For reasons having to do with pollination, you should grow at least two plants to maturity.

During the early stages of life, cucumbers will grow far faster if higher temperatures—up to about 80 degrees—can be provided. This is not absolutely essential, but temperatures should be kept at least in the high 60s.

Water As they are composed of such a large percentage of water, cucumbers are among the thirstiest garden vegetables. Not only do they require soil that will hold moisture for their roots, but they can do with a constant source of water that they may draw upon as needed. Watering potted plants thoroughly once a week may serve, but adding individual water tanks is preferable, especially where cucumbers are rooted in large planters. The water tanks should be put in before planting.

To install a water tank, dig a hole beside where the seeds are to go, large enough to accommodate a small clay flower pot sunk to its rim. Plug the drainage hole. Plant the seeds a couple of inches away from the pot. This pot can be filled with water daily, which will seep slowly through the pores of the unglazed clay and supply the cucumber roots with constant moisture. However the moisture is supplied, the plant will use far more water as it begins to blossom and produce fruit.

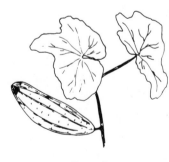

Cucumber

Nutrition Cucumbers are fairly heavy feeders, especially with regard to nitrogen. The soil should be enriched with nitrogen prior to planting, but later feedings of a 15-30-15 plant food dissolved in water may be helpful. Two feedings should carry the plant through to maturity. Keeping the soil surface covered with cottonseed meal and watering through the layer is another way of providing needed nutrients to the roots.

Temperature Cucumbers grow best when daytime temperatures are 70 to 75 degrees and night temperatures are not lower than 60 degrees. A spot beneath a skylight or in front of a sunny window will probably provide the extra warmth needed for optimum growth indoors, or it can be provided by using incandescent growth lamps. But these slightly higher temperatures are not an absolute requirement—cucumbers can be, and have been, grown at room temperature. Outside plants should not be exposed to frost.

Light Cucumbers are day-neutral plants, meaning they will blossom under a wide range of day lengths. However, several scientific studies have determined that the greatest number of blossoms will be produced if the plant—as it approaches the flowering stage—receives exactly 8 hours of light of high intensity—up to 4000 foot-candles—where, it has been found, growth and fruit production level off. Light of this high intensity can only be provided in a special light room, a greenhouse, beneath a skylight, or with direct sunlight, but there are several approaches you can take that will help you provide adequate light for growing cucumbers.

Remember that 4000 foot-candles is the requirement for optimum growth. There are accounts of cucumbers growing under far weaker light. The problem is that few of these accounts say *how many* cucumbers were grown. Probably you should not attempt to grow cucumbers unless you are able to provide at least 1500 foot-candles of artificial light,

supplementing that with some natural sunlight. It is worth noting that natural sunlight
of relatively low intensity will produce more
blossoms than even the brightest artificial
light.

Where cucumbers have been grown under
less than optimum light, reports indicate that
longer hours of illumination are preferable.
Providing sixteen hours of light at 1500 foot-
candles may not produce optimum results, but
it is adequate for some blossoming and fruit
production.

All cucumbers—including the so-called bush
varieties—have a tendency to climb. This can
be of advantage in providing light to all parts
of the plant. By providing a string or trellis for
the clinging tendrils, the vines can easily be
trained to grow in ways that will take fullest
advantage of available light.

Pollination Cucumbers produce male and
female flowers on the same plant. The male
flowers, which appear first, greatly outnumber
the female. Female flowers are easily recognized by the miniature cucumbers that develop behind them. Pollen must be transferred
from male to female, as described in Chapter
4. However, more fruit will set if pollen from
the male flowers of one plant is transferred to
female flowers of another. Therefore, I suggested growing at least two plants.

Harvest Picking may begin as soon as the first
cucumbers are of desirable size. Cut the stems
with shears about an inch from the cucumbers.
If any cucumbers show signs of yellowing on
the vine, remove them at once, for they will
slow or stop production.

A relative of the potato that is native to the tropics, the eggplant is usually grown as an annual, but only because it is so easily damaged by frost. Actually the plant is a perennial or semishrub capable of living four to six years, depending on the variety and conditions. Capable of producing fruit without outside pollination, it is an extremely beautiful plant that is fairly easy to grow. Plants have attractive gray-green foliage, large lavender blossoms, and produce fruit that can be black, purple, green, yellow, or white. The fruit can be as small as an egg or as large as a dwarf melon, depending on the variety.

In southern Asia the eggplant has been cultivated for many centuries, but did not appear in Europe until the Middle Ages and even then it was grown only as an ornamental. As food, it has never been highly popular in the United States, but that is at least partially due to the fact that it needs a longer growing season than is found in many parts of this country.

Seeds and Soil All seed companies offer dwarf plants, many of which yield full-size fruits. New Hampshire is one variety that matures fruit about seventy-five days after planting and requires far less room than standard varieties. Garden centers and discount stores around the country sometimes sell yellow and white varieties as seed for growing "egg trees," but these are simply more colorful types of eggplant. Each plant from a standard variety will yield about eight fruits; smaller-fruited varieties will yield two or three times that number. Flavor is generally better in the small varieties.

Eggplant is a heavy feeder, with a root structure that penetrates deep into the soil, so depth must be considered when you are choos-

Eggplant
(Solanum melongena)

ing a planter. A 5-gallon barrel or tub-type container is suitable.

Soil should be rich and porous, but with enough sand or perlite to provide good drainage. The pH should be no lower than 6.0, no higher than 8.0. Before planting time it should be enriched with a plant food having a 15-30-15 content. Adding about 2 pounds of compost to the soil for each plant is an even better idea, if this is available.

Planting Plant seeds ¼- to ½-inch deep and keep them at a temperature of around 70 degrees until germination occurs. Start several seeds, as the emerging plants are very fragile and some seedlings are likely to be lost. They can later be thinned to the desired number of plants, or transplanted to individual pots after they are 3 inches high and strong enough to stand the shock of being moved.

If you transplant them, the plants should first be "blocked out" by running a sharp knife through the soil midway between the plants, cutting their roots. Shield plants from direct light following this operation, and keep them well watered. A week after the cutting of the roots, the plants may be lifted, transplanted, and once again placed beneath lights.

Water Eggplant is among the thirstiest of vegetables, especially when it is setting fruit. Soil should be thoroughly drenched at least once a week and should not be allowed to dry out while the plant is actively growing, for this will reduce production. If a plant is maintained as a perennial, however, water should be drastically reduced for two to four months following the harvest, to allow the plant a period of rest.

Eggplant

Nutrition When the plants are about 3 inches high, give them a feeding of plant food, preferably one using a 15-30-15 formula. Four weeks later they should be fed again, and from that time on feeding should be biweekly. Never pour fertilizer directly over the stems, and reduce the nutrients to zero after the harvest if the plant is to be held over.

Temperature Very young plants do best when the temperature is 65 to 70 degrees during the day and about 55 degrees at night. After they have passed the seedling stage, however, optimum growth and fruit production results at much higher temperatures at night. Such temperatures are easier to maintain in a greenhouse, beneath a skylight, or in front of a sunny window. Your outdoor spaces may also provide these temperatures, but you must move the plants indoors before the first cold weather. Plants that are to be held over should be kept in a cool room during the period of dormancy.

Light   A day-neutral plant that will blossom under a wide range of day lengths, eggplant also seems capable of accepting nearly any intensity of light. One grower I contacted has brought a plant to production in an east-facing window that receives not more than four hours of light daily, and there are reports of eggplant being grown under only 1000 foot-candles of artificial light. If you can provide 1500 foot-candles of light for twelve hours daily, you can almost certainly grow eggplant. Because fruit production increases when the rate of growth is faster, providing even brighter light should increase the yield. Fruit production will also increase if some of the light is natural.

Harvest   Eggplant fruit may be picked when it is one third to fully grown. Wait only until a high gloss appears on the skin of the fruit before picking it. Stems of the fruit should be cut with a sharp knife to avoid breaking the branches. Not only are the young fruits more tender, with a better flavor and fewer seeds, but picking them will sometimes stimulate the plant to further production. Unbruised eggplant may be stored for several months in a cool place.

Kale
(Brassica oleracea acephala)

A nonheading relative of cabbage, kale is thought to be the first member of its family cultivated by the early Greeks and Romans. Its leaves contain ten times as much vitamin A as an equivalent amount of green lettuce and when cooked, about three times as much vitamin C as an equivalent weight of orange juice. Not only nutritious, it is an extremely easy plant to grow, indoors or out. South of Virginia it can be grown outside during the winter, and just about any home in the country will have a window with enough light for growing indoor plants.

Seeds and soil   Seed for three different types are available through most seed houses—Scotch, Siberian, and flowering kale. Each can be had in dwarf form. Dwarf Blue Curled Scotch is best from a horticultural viewpoint, but flowering varieties offer beauty as well as utility.

Soil should be fertile but sandy, with a pH of 6.0 to 8.0, such as two parts potting soil and one part sand. Kale also needs plenty of calcium, so adding some ground limestone or crushed eggshell to the planter soil will also help. Soil in the planter should be at least 6 inches deep; the other dimensions will be determined by how many plants you intend to grow; plants need to stand 3 or 4 inches apart in all directions.

Planting   Broadcast the seed thickly over the soil in the planter, cover them with ½-inch of soil that has been loosened by sifting, and water thoroughly. Young plants will stand a lot of crowding, so they need not be thinned until they have grown large enough to provide a meal from the thinnings. Thin, as mentioned, to 3 or 4 inches all around.

Water   Kale will survive and grow with very little water, especially after the plants are well started. Give water only when the soil becomes obviously dry and growth appears to slow down. Depending on the characteristics of the soil and the size and number of the plants, watering will probably be needed only at intervals of seven to fourteen days.

Nutrition   Plants will need no further nutrition until they approach maturity, at which time the rate of growth may become slower. At this time they should be fed with a 5-10-5 liquid plant food; feeding may be repeated each time the plants are watered.

Temperature   Kale is a plant that does best at cooler temperatures. It should never be exposed to the heat beneath a skylight or in a summer greenhouse. Growth will slow noticeably whenever the temperature climbs into the high 60s.

Light   Kale was being grown on ledges in sunny windows long before the introduction of artificial light, revealing how little light it needs. Grow it in any but a north-facing window, or place it under low-intensity artificial light for long hours each day, which will provide good growth and prevent its bolting to seed.

Flowering kale produces clumps of blue,

purple, or red flowers, depending on the variety. These flowering varieties are relatively new and commercially unimportant, so little is known about their photoperiod. The seasonal nature of the plant, which flowers in autumn, however, strongly suggests that flowering can be induced by treating it as a short-day species—providing it with not more than nine hours of light daily as it approaches the flowering stage.

Harvest   Kale is seldom eaten raw because its leaves are a little too coarse for salad. The very young leaves are not so coarse, however, and may be used for this purpose. Leaves mature about sixty-five days after seed is planted.

As the first leaves approach maturity, strip the largest outer leaves from the plant and leave the smaller inner leaves on the plant to grow. New leaves should be ready for picking in a month or so, and healthy indoor plants can be made to produce for several months.

Kohlrabi

(Brassica oleracea
caulorapa)

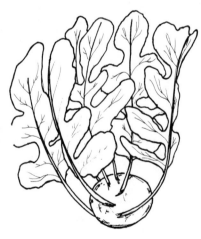

This cousin of the cabbage is a biennial herb with a swollen, bulklike stem from which its leaves arise. The bulbous stem, which is rich in calcium and vitamin C, may be eaten raw or cooked, but the plant is more often grown as a curiosity than for its food value. Kohlrabi has been cultivated since the sixteenth century but has only recently begun to gain any popularity in this country.

Seeds and Soil   White and purple varieties are available. For best flavor select one of the white varieties, such as Early White Vienna; for a touch of color select Purple Vienna. Seed germinates in about ten days, and bulbs are ready for picking about seventy days after seed is planted.

A rich loam or potting soil that holds water well is essential for growing kohlrabi. Soil should be at least 6 inches deep, and you should provide at least 4 inches of surface area for each plant you hope to grow. Growth of kohlrabi is not greatly affected by crowding, but crowded plants must be handled carefully at harvesting.

Planting Broadcast seed over the soil in the planter, cover them with half an inch of sifted soil, and water well. Keep in a cool but well-lighted place, and thin the seedlings when they stand about 3 inches high. A window box 36 inches long should hold not more than eight or nine plants.

Water Water is a key element in growing kohlrabi. The soil should be constantly moist to the touch. Under no circumstances should the plants be allowed to go longer than a week without being watered.

Nutrition Overfeeding easily harms kohlrabi. By starting with a rich soil, you should be able to grow plants to maturity without further feeding. If growth slows noticeably, however, you might want to give the plants one feeding of 5-10-5 plant food added to their water.

Temperature Like cabbage and many of its relatives, kohlrabi needs cool temperatures. South of Virginia it can be grown outside during the winter months. Temperatures above 65 degrees will cause slower growth and will result in woody bulbs with a strong flavor. Provide temperatures in the 50s, if possible, at all stages of growth.

Light Provide long hours of light of 1500 foot-candles or more. Some accounts state that kohlrabi has been grown with as little as 1000 foot-candles of illumination, but the growth would surely be slower under those conditions, and fast growth produces better flavor in this vegetable. Bulb growth may also be stimulated by thinning the leaves and allowing the bulbous stems to receive more light.

Harvest Bulbs should be picked before they exceed 2 inches in diameter. Bulbs larger than that become woody and lose their delicate flavor. Since potted plants are likely to stand close together, remove the bulbs by cutting the stems just below the bulbs, leaving the roots in the soil. Roots of crowded plants will be entangled and, if one plant is pulled, its neighbors may suffer fatal injuries.

Leeks
(Allium porrum)

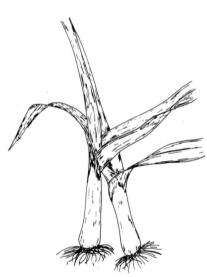

The leek is a biennial herb of the onion genus of the lily family. By far the sweetest and most flavorful of the onions, it grows wild in Switzerland, Africa, and scattered parts of the United States. The Greeks and Romans cultivated it, and it was said to be so highly prized by Nero that he insisted on having it served at his table at least several times each week. Few plants are easier to grow.

The leek, in case you are not familiar with it, is a bulbless onion with hollow leaves that are flat rather than round. The thick stem, which is akin to an elongated bulb, is used wherever a delicate touch of onion flavor is needed.

Seeds and Soil American Flag is the most readily available seed variety. The seed germinates in about 7 days. Mature leeks appear in about 120 days, but leeks of scallion size are ready in about 85 days, and even before that the thinnings may be used in salads.

Soil should be porous and especially rich in nitrogen. Woodland soil, which naturally contains a lot of humus, is ideal for growing leeks. Two parts potting soil and one part sand will serve, as long as the pH of the soil is between 6.0 and 8.5. A pot with an 8-inch diameter is large enough for growing about a dozen leeks to maturity, but several times that many can be started in the pot and the thinnings used as they grow.

Planting Sprinkle the seed thickly, then cover with ½-inch of loose soil and water thoroughly. Provide full light (2000 foot-candles). When the seedlings appear and attain a height of about 3 inches, thin them to stand about 1 inch apart. When they are about 5 inches high, thin them to stand about 2 inches apart in all directions. Keep the soil very moist through these early stages of growth. Use the thinnings as a substitute for chives or scallions, depending on size.

Water If the soil is light and porous and holds water well, watering thoroughly at weekly intervals will suffice.

Nutrition Nitrogen is the essential nutrient, and leeks can hardly be given too much. A 10-5-5 formula plant food, dissolved according to the manufacturer's instructions and given with the weekly water, will fill this need.

Temperature Leeks do well under a wide range of temperatures, but growth slows if the air becomes extremely hot—in the 90s or above. On the other end of the scale, they will tolerate all but severely cold weather, so window-box or patio plants may be left outside until well after the first frost.

Light   Leeks can be grown using 1000 foot-candles of light for at least twelve hours daily, but growth will be slow and the leeks will not thicken as they should. Under 1500 foot-candles for the same daily time period, growth is far better, and when the brighter light is provided for sixteen hours daily, the leeks grow almost normally. Growth appears to level off at about 2000 foot-candles.

When the leeks are about as thick as your little finger, bank soil up around the lower 2 or 3 inches of each plant. Excluding light will blanch the lower part of the leek, improving both its appearance and its delicate flavor.

Harvest   The principal use of leeks is to provide flavor rather than sustenance, so they are simply pulled as needed.

Lettuce
(Lactuca sativa)

The cultivated form of lettuce was developed from the wild prickly lettuce native to Europe and the Orient. Grown and used at least as early as 500 B.C., lettuce is a shallow-rooted, hardy annual. Five basic types are now grown, with the loose-leaf, or nonheading, type best suited for growing under lights, while the other types may be grown in outdoor containers or under the conditions found in a greenhouse.

Seeds and Soil   For leaf lettuce select Salad Bowl, Simpson, or any of the Grand Rapids strains. For the greenhouse or patio select Great Lakes, an iceberg variety; and for growing in a large window box or to produce a few deliciously edible novelties, select Dwarf Morden, which yields heads about the size of tennis balls. Seed germinates in six to eight days.

Lettuce does best in a sandy loam with a pH between 6.0 and 8.5. Adding ½-pound of rock phosphate to each square foot of soil will enhance growth. Soil for growing lettuce need not be deep, but the planter should be large enough to assure that leaves of adjacent plants do not touch throughout the entire growing period.

Planting   Seed is planted ¼-inch deep and kept cool and moist until it comes up. Seedlings need low light, which should be gradually intensified by moving the plants closer to the light source as the plants grow larger. Thin seedlings as soon as they are large enough to handle. Thin standard varieties to about 8 inches between plants, but dwarf varieties need only about 4 or 5 inches around each plant.

Heading-lettuce varieties may be started indoors, then moved outside after the last hard freeze but while at least sixty days of cool spring weather remain. Outside and greenhouse plants should be set in shaded areas, or they may be damaged by the glaring rays of the sun.

Water   Keep lettuce constantly moist for best growth. Water plants whenever the soil becomes dry just below the surface. Each watering should leave the soil wet enough to form a ball when squeezed. The leaves of plants, however, should be kept out of contact with the moist soil, for this can lead to lettuce rot, which will spread through the entire plant. Spreading a layer of sand over the soil will prevent this affliction. Its need for constant water makes lettuce a good plant for growing hydroponically.

Nutrition   Lettuce is a fast-growing plant that should derive all its needed nutrition from an adequate amount of rich soil. However, after the first crop of leaf lettuce has been cut, later production may be stimulated by a generous feeding of fertilizer that is high in phosphorus and potassium and low in nitrogen.

Temperature Cool temperatures are essential at all stages of growth, which stops completely at 80 degrees or higher. If they are exposed to just a few days of such temperatures, heading varieties will never form heads, and even leaf lettuce will bolt to seed. If heads on outside or greenhouse plants have not formed before summer temperatures begin to rise, it may be necessary to protect them by moving them to a shadier, cooler spot or by placing a canopy of netting above them. Room temperature—55 to 65 degrees—is nearly ideal for all varieties.

Light Under no circumstances should any type of lettuce be exposed to far-red light, which causes it to bolt to seed without fail. This means you should avoid using plant-growth lamps, and lettuce should not be exposed to incandescent lighting. Warm White and Cool White fluorescents provide the only artificial light that should be used with this plant.

Too much light may be a problem with plants grown outside or in a greenhouse. Canadian studies conducted in 1965 revealed that lettuce tipburn is caused by light intensities of more than 7200 foot-candles. This can be prevented by shading the plants with cheesecloth, which should be placed high enough to allow good air circulation around the plants.

Lettuce production appears to level off at about 3200 foot-candles of light, according to accounts in the scientific literature. It can be grown, however, under light that is far less intense, provided very long hours of light are given. If 1500 to 2000 foot-candles of light are provided for sixteen to eighteen hours daily, growth will be fast enough to put a bit of lettuce on the table at fairly regular intervals. But if even low-intensity light is given continuously, the lettuce will be burned exactly as if the light were too bright.

Harvest For optimum flavor and crispness, use all lettuce as soon as it is picked. Cut the plants at soil level. Leave the roots of the leaf lettuce in the soil, keep them regularly fed and watered, and they will produce another crop in about sixty days, depending on variety. Some varieties will produce several crops during the course of a year.

Lima Beans
(Phaseolus lunatus)

An annual herb or vine of the pea family, lima beans originated in South America, as is evidenced by the fact that the dried seeds have been found in ancient tombs in Peru and Chile. From there they made their way to Florida, the rest of America, and, finally, to all temperate parts of the world.

Lima beans, like most other legumes, need no help in pollination. They do, however, require very, very intense light and high temperatures, so you probably should not attempt to grow them unless you have a special light room or a home greenhouse, or unless you have a sunny patio where a few potted plants can be grown during the summer months and then brought inside for a little continued production.

Seeds and Soil Select one of the bush varieties such as Henderson Bush Lima, as these are far more productive and require far less space than the vining types. Bush varieties also produce the first beans in as little as sixty-five days, whereas the vining varieties require at least an additional month to produce.

Each bush lima should have an 8- or 9-inch pot. Four or five plants are needed to produce a bushel of beans. The best soil is a sandy loam, but any soil except one containing clay may be used for lima beans. The pH should be slightly acid, about 5.5, so adding a little peat moss to neutral potting soil will result in better growth.

Planting   Soil should be at room temperature or slightly higher when seeds are started, as they will rot in cooler soil. Plant the seeds 3 inches apart and about 1½ inches deep. Provide full light until the seedlings are about 3 inches high, then thin out all but the strongest seedling in each pot.

Water   Lima beans will tolerate slight dryness of the soil more easily than water standing around their roots, which causes rotting and death of the plant. It is best, therefore, to water infrequently, letting the soil become dry to the touch and then flooding it thoroughly.

Nutrition   Phosphorus and potassium are the essential nutrients, but additional feedings of these should not be needed if the soil is rich when seed is planted. Avoid using nitrogenous fertilizer, as it will produce lush foliage but few beans.

Temperature   Lima beans require warm to very warm temperatures at night as well as during the day. Outside plants are killed by the slightest touch of frost. Maximum growth occurs when temperatures are in the high 70s or low 80s, making this one of the better greenhouse plants.

Lima Beans

Light Lima beans need the very brightest light possible—at least 3000 foot-candles and preferably more. When they are grown in phytotrons, they are frequently given light more than twice that bright—in at least a few instances as high as 7500 foot-candles, under which they continue to grow. So the light needed for growing these can only be had in a special light room, a greenhouse, or an outside area that is exposed to direct sunlight for several hours each day.

Duration of light is equally important. It has been established that the best photoperiod for this plant is nine hours of light during each twenty-four-hour cycle, making it a short-day plant. Unlike the many day-neutral plants, such plants will not accept longer hours of light as compensation for lack of intensity and will produce blossoms if the hours of light are shorter but not if the photoperiod is exceeded. During the summer when days are long, this may even cause problems for greenhouse growers, so it may be best to grow lima beans in the greenhouse during the shorter days of winter.

After the plants have blossomed and the legumes are formed, light of such extremely high intensity is not absolutely necessary. Beans will continue to develop, but slowly, if they are provided with about 2000 foot-candles of light. This means that outdoor plants may be moved inside, for display or for protection from frost and for prolonged production, if you have only that limited lighting capability.

Harvest Pick lima beans when the beans are clearly discernible under the swollen places under the pods. Do not allow the beans to become very thick or they will toughen. The first beans should be ready to pick about sixty-five days after planting, and each plant will yield several crops at intervals of about ten days following that before the plant is exhausted.

Mustard
(Brassica nigra)

While mustard is botanically an herb, it is placed here because growing enough seed to make the familiar condiment is not a viable project in limited space and because the leaves of this fast-growing annual are so often used as a vegetable.

Black mustard has been eaten since ancient times. It grows wild throughout Europe and the United States, is nutritionally superior to most other vegetables that are cooked as greens, and is one of the easiest of all plants to grow.

Seeds and Soil   Mustard can grow in nearly any soil but prefers a sandy loam, with a pH of 5.5 to 7.5. Soil can be as shallow as 4 inches. Plants need only 3 or 4 inches between bases, so a large number can be grown in the average window box. Tendergreen produces a crop faster than any other variety—as soon as thirty days after planting.

Planting   Sow the seed thickly to a depth of ½ inch. Water lightly. Place under artificial light or in any sunny window. As the young plants develop, thin them to stand 3 or 4 inches apart, using the thinnings in salads to give flavor to milder greens.

Water   Mustard needs very little water, and the plants can withstand very long dry spells. Water about biweekly, letting the soil become very dry before flooding it to the bottom.

Nutrition   Mustard is not a heavy feeder. The nutrients in any fairly rich soil should carry it through until at least the first crop is harvested. After that it can be fed with any plant food once monthly or each time a crop of leaves is cut.

Temperature   Room temperature is nearly ideal for mustard. It can stand cold weather or hot, but at high temperatures the leaves toughen and develop a strong flavor.

Light   Mustard will grow under nearly any light conditions. The light coming through any but a north-facing window will be fine for it, or it will thrive under just a few hundred foot-candles of artificial light. Give it light of long duration for faster growth.

Harvest   Leaves less than 4 inches high are best for salads. If leaves are to be cooked, let them grow 6 inches high. The leaves should be cut with shears. If the stems are not cut too close to the soil, each planting will yield at least a half-dozen cuttings at about thirty-day intervals.

Okra
(Hibiscus esculentus)

Known sometimes as gumbo, okra is a tropical member of the mallow family. Its origins are in Africa and Asia, and it grows wild along the banks of the Nile. Long grown as an ornamental, it produces yellow flowers with red centers, which are followed by edible pods that are red or green, depending on the variety.

Seeds and Soil   Okra can be grown in any soil with a pH close to neutral—6.0 to 8.0—as long as the soil holds water well. Since the pods are 90 percent water, this is another plant that should benefit from hydroponic gardening.

The best seed variety is Dwarf Green. Soil for growing this variety should be 9 inches deep, in a pot with about the same diameter. A hydroponic planter should accommodate three or four plants.

Planting If several plants are to stand in a large planter, seeds should be planted 9 inches apart. Soil must be warm at the time of planting, otherwise the seeds will rot. Seed will germinate in three or four days under full light. Okra is very difficult to transplant, so it is best started in the pot where it is to grow.

Water Okra needs constant moisture and will consume even more water as the pods begin to develop. A good way to supply this water is by providing individual water tanks, as described for cucumbers (see pp. 156–160).

Nutrition Avoid using nitrogenous fertilizer, as this will result in lush foliage but few pods of okra. If the plant is fed at all, it should be with food high in phosphorus.

Temperature Optimum growth occurs when the air temperature is in the low 70s, but growth is only a bit slower at high room temperature. Heavy frost will kill the plant.

Light Okra is a day-neutral plant that will flower in a wide range of day lengths; however, the results of at least one experiment suggest that the greatest number of blossoms are produced when the daily light is nine to twelve hours in duration. Flowering occurs over a long period of time, with each hermaphroditic blossom producing one edible pod of okra.

As for intensity of light, okra appears to have needs similar to those of cucumber, with which it is often compared. That it needs high light—certainly no less than 1500 foot-candles, but preferably a minumum of 2000—seems clear, so it is best to grow okra as a greenhouse plant or as an ornamental in the sunniest spot on your porch or patio. Lighting may be greatly reduced after the blossoms have fallen from the pods.

Pollination Like tomatoes, legumes, and many other fruits and vegetables that are produced from perfect flowers, okra will produce its pods without hand pollination. However, there will be more pods if you carefully insert a cotton swab into the center of each flower, thus assuring the transfer of more pollen; and fruit production may be further stimulated by spraying each blossom with a hormone compound such as Blossom-set (see pp. 77–79).

Harvest Pick okra pods a few days after the blossoms drop. They should be soft, with very small seeds. If they stay on the plant more than a few days, they become woody. The first pods should be ready for picking about fifty-five days after planting, with more pods ready to be picked every second or third day thereafter. Plants that are protected from killing frost, as in a light room or greenhouse, will continue to produce for several weeks after the first crop.

Onions
(Allium cepa)

Onions probably originated in Asia Minor, but they have been cultivated for so long that it is nearly impossible to establish their origins. The Old Testament mentions them, and they were used in the earliest days of Greece and

Egypt. Dozens and dozens of varieties are available today.

Onions are among the easiest vegetables to grow. However, it is best not to attempt to grow them to maturity, because growing the large bulbs that are suitable for slicing is very space-consuming. Settle instead for sweet young green onions, pencil-thin scallions, and even young thinnings that are used like chives.

Seeds and Soil   Onion seed does not remain viable long and should be planted within a year of purchase. Most seed will produce green onions in about fifty-five days. White and red varieties have the mildest flavor.

The best soil for onions is a sandy loam. Onions absolutely refuse to grow in soil containing too much clay. The best soil is mildly acid, with a pH 5.5 to 6.0. Soil should be about 5 inches deep. A pot with an 8-inch diameter is large enough to grow about a dozen green onions, more if they are to be picked at scallion size. Onions may also be grown in the borders around other plants, as their roots do not spread and will not interfere with growth.

Planting   Seed will germinate at any temperature between 45 and 85 degrees, but it germinates best at 65 degrees. Germination occurs in seven to ten days. Plant seed an inch deep, under soil that has been loosened by sifting. Seed should be sown rather thinly, the soil moistened thoroughly, and the pot set under lights. When the seedlings are about 3 inches tall, they should be thinned to stand about 2 inches apart in every direction. The first thinnings make a good substitute for chives.

Water   Onions need constant moisture. If the top layer of soil becomes completely dry at any time, the root will split and attempt to form two bulbs, with neither bulb developing as it should.

Nutrition A feeding of 10-5-5 plant food, given a month after planting, is suggested. Avoid pouring the nutrients directly over the developing bulbs.

Temperature Onions prefer temperatures slightly below 65 degrees for foliage growth, and slightly higher than that for bulb development. Outside plants will not be killed by a touch of frost.

Light Onions that are to be used as scallions may be grown with 1000 foot-candles of light. If you want bulb development, supply at least 1500 foot-candles. In either instance, provide long—twelve to sixteen—hours of lighting daily.

Harvest The entire length of onions is usable at any stage of growth. While they are thin as grass, they are chopped and used like chives. Scallions are usually pulled when they are about as thick as a pencil. Green onions are at their tastiest if they are pulled before a true bulb is fully formed—not more than fifty or fifty-five days after planting.

Peanuts
(Arachis hypogaea)

Peanuts are legumes that originated in South America, as evidenced by seed found in ancient Peruvian tombs. The vines, which grow 12 to 18 inches tall, make an attractive plant in a tub or half-barrel, but peanuts do require high temperatures and the intense light that can only be had in a special light room or by using the natural sunlight that is available.

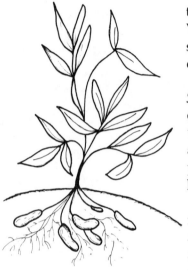

They require four to five months growing time—a longer season than is found north of Virginia—but you can beat the seasons by starting the plants indoors, then moving them outside after the last frost.

Seeds and Soil   Seed companies commonly offer two varieties—Spanish red peanuts and the Mexican brown variety. The Spanish nuts are larger and more flavorful, but the Mexican plants are more prolific. Seed may be in the hull or it may be shelled.

Soil for growing peanuts does not need to be rich in nutrients, but it absolutely must be acid, with a pH of 5.0 or lower. The soil must also be loose enough to allow the fruiting stalks to penetrate the ground, as the peanut is one of the few plants that bears its seed under the soil. The plant produces two sets of flowers, and after the lower set has been fertilized in the fashion of other legumes, they send out long peduncles, which bury their tips in the soil. The nuts form in the soil, on the tips of these peduncles. A mixture of two parts potting soil, one part sand, and one part peat moss will provide both the acidity and the looseness of soil needed for growing peanuts. A container that will hold at least 5, but preferably 10, gallons of soil is needed to grow peanuts. If you grow more than one plant in a container, the plants must stand at least 6 inches apart in all directions, so the planter should be wide as well as deep.

Planting   Plants to be grown in the greenhouse or light chamber may be started at any time. Plants for the patio or balcony should be started about March or April, so they can be moved outside in warm weather as soon as possible. At warm room temperature and under bright light, the seed will germinate in about seven days.

Start with a planter that is filled with soil to about 6 inches from the top, as more soil will be added later. Plant the seeds—hulled or in the shell, as they come from the supplier—an inch deep and about 6 inches apart. Water the young plants weekly and provide the brightest light possible; then, when the plants are several inches tall, fill the planter with very loose soil to its rim, banking the soil around the plants. This loose soil will make it easier for the peduncles to bury themselves, and the crop will be increased. Plants can be grown to this stage using 1500 foot-candles of light for twelve or sixteen hours daily, but from this point on they need light that is far more intense—at least 3000 foot-candles.

Water Water generously about once a week, after the soil becomes dry to a depth of about an inch. Avoid letting water build up until the soil feels very wet to the touch, for this will cause rotting of the roots.

Nutrition Avoid the use of any nitrogenous fertilizer, which will result in lush foliage while retarding the development of the nuts. Peanuts need very little in the way of nutrition, so the nutrients in the soil should provide for their needs.

Temperature Young plants will grow at room temperature, but optimum growth occurs when the air temperature is in the 80s and slows only when the temperature soars into the mid-90s or above. Thus even outside plants should have a southern or western exposure, if possible. Outside plants will die at the first touch of frost, but the peanuts will continue to develop beneath the soil as long as the weather does not become extremely cold.

Light Peanuts are long-day plants, which flower only when they receive twelve or more hours of light daily, and then only when this light is of very high intensity. In experimental phytotrons they are typically grown under at least 4000 foot-candles. Some flowering may occur at lower intensities, but not much. After the plants are a few inches high and have approached the flowering stage, they absolutely demand the most brilliant light that can be provided.

Harvest After the foliage turns yellow, dig up a few of the peanuts and examine the inner shells. They should show a rich gold marked by veins, and the nuts should be fully developed. If they have not reached this stage, leave the plants in the soil for a month or two longer; the peanuts will develop by feeding on food that is stored in the upper stems. Then pull out the entire root system and dry the peanuts by spreading them out for sixty days in a warm, well-ventilated place. Each healthy plant will yield about 150 peanuts, depending on variety.

Roast peanuts for twenty minutes in a 300-degree oven, then allow them to cool in the shell, which will continue the roasting process.

Peppers, Hot Ornamental
(Capsicum annuum)

A member of the potato family and native to the tropics, this annual grows to a height of about 12 inches, then produces tiny, white, self-pollinating flowers that are followed by tiny, cone-shaped fruit that can be yellow, orange, red, or white, but which is always extremely hot and spicy. Beautiful and easy to grow, this is a highly decorative plant that can provide all the tang needed for chili and similar dishes.

Seeds and Soil   Nearly every seed company offers the same variety, though usually they are offered as "Christmas" or "ornamental" peppers, with no mention of the fact that they are edible.

The best soil is slightly acid, with a pH around 5.0, and with enough sand to provide good drainage. Mixing two parts loam or potting soil with two parts peat moss and one part sand will meet the requirements, if the soil used is close to neutral. A 6-inch pot holds enough soil for a single plant.

Planting   Start seed away from direct light, though it does not require total darkness. Sow only 2 or 3 seeds in the pot, to avoid crowding, and cover them very thinly with soil. Water from the bottom in a pan or sink until moisture reaches the top layer of soil. Remove the pot from water and let it drain. Cover the pot with glass or plastic to help retain all possible moisture, and set the pot in a warm, dim place. After the seed germinates, remove the cover and set the plants under light. When the seedlings are 2 inches tall, thin all but the strongest one from the pot, transplanting the others if you wish.

Water   Spray the leaves of the plant frequently, at least once a week. The soil must be evenly moist, but not constantly wet. Water standing around the roots will kill the plants.

Nutrition   Feed the plants every four to six weeks, but avoid using plant foods that are high in nitrogen. If the soil is fairly rich in phosphorus to start with, the plant may need no fertilizer until about the time its blossoms begin to open.

Temperature The best temperature for growing ornamental peppers is 75 degrees, but they produce fairly well at room temperature. Fruit may drop from the plant before it matures if the temperature fluctuates too frequently.

Light Provide 1000 foot-candles for less than twelve hours daily. This is a day-neutral plant, but it shows a decided preference for shorter hours of daylight. Using natural sunlight, alone or in combination with artificial light, promotes maximum flowering.

Harvest The first peppers should mature about fourteen weeks after planting, and the plant may continue to bear for several months. New fruit will be white and turn yellow, red, or orange as it matures; peppers grow constantly hotter in taste as their color deepens. A healthy plant should produce all the hot peppers you can use. Be careful not to rub your eyes with the fingers that have been used in picking them.

Peppers, Sweet
(Capiscum frutescens)

Sweet peppers, also a member of the potato family, are natives of the tropics. They are grown as annuals in the outdoor gardens of North America because they are so easily killed by frost, but they are actually perennial plants, fully capable of developing into woody shrubs 7 or 8 feet high. The hot varieties, which produce fruit that change in color from green to red, yellow, or orange and become spicier with the change, are members of the same genus and are grown in much the same fashion.

Sweet peppers are a real challenge to grow. They require the kind of light that may be provided only in a greenhouse, a special light room, a solarium made bright by the largest skylight, or by using full sun. When set with fruit, however, they are an incredibly beautiful plant, and you may want to grow one on the patio or in the greenhouse and then move it in for a brief but spectacular period of display beneath your lights. As they prefer short hours of lighting, they are also good plants for growing in the greenhouse during the winter months.

Seeds and Soil   Most seed companies offer varieties that produce full-size fruit on compact bushes. These grow only about 18 inches high, do not sprawl over a large area, and require less soil for growing. They produce a large number of peppers in as little as sixty days, depending on variety. Recommended varieties are Merrimack Wonder, New Ace Hybrid, or Golden Calwonder, which, unlike the others, produces yellow fruit.

Peppers grow best in soil that is very sandy or that contains a great deal of humus. The pH should be 6.0 to 7.0. If wood ashes from the fireplace are available, stirring a few cupfuls into the soil will add potash and cause better growth and production. Each pepper plant will need a large container, at least 15 inches in diameter and 12 inches deep.

Planting   Pepper plants produce best if their growth is never interrupted, so it is best to start seeds where they are to grow. Plants for the greenhouse or light room may be started at any time. If peppers are to grow on the patio, you can get a jump on the summer season by starting them about eight weeks before the last expected frost, then moving the pots outside after the danger is past.

Germination is poor, so start about six or eight seeds in each pot and cover them with a thin layer of soil. These should later be thinned to the strongest seedling. Keep the soil very moist at all times, and provide the brightest light possible for long hours daily, to get the plants well on their way.

During the early stages of life, good ventilation is very important to peppers, so this must be provided for plants that are to be grown in the greenhouse. After the seedlings are a few inches tall, banking soil up as high as their lowest leaves will help support them until they attain some woody growth.

Water   In their early stages especially, peppers need a lot of water. Later in life, after their roots have developed, the soil can become somewhat dry between waterings. But the soil should be constantly moist until the plants are at least 6 inches tall and becoming bushy.

Nutrition   When the plants are a few inches high and have developed their first true leaves, they should be given their first feeding. Give each plant a cup of manure water, which is available at most large garden centers. If manure water is not available, dissolve a 15-30-15 plant food in the plant's regular water. Repeat the feeding at monthly intervals.

Sweet Pepper

Temperature   Peppers can withstand moderately cold weather without being killed, but they produce fruit only at higher temperatures. At blossom time the temperature must be between 65 and 80 degrees if fruit is to be produced. If the temperature exceeds 80 degrees, the blossoms and small fruit may drop without setting.

Light   Foliage growth will occur under 1000 or 1500 foot-candles of light, but far more intense light is needed for blossoming and fruit production. One account states that peppers were brought to maturity with only 2000 foot-candles, but even brighter light is strongly suggested. Peppers are, after all, sun-loving plants, and to grow a worthwhile crop you should plan on supplying light of at least 3000 foot-candles in intensity. Outside plants should get all the sunlight possible.

Peppers are day-neutral plants, capable of blooming under a wide range of day lengths. Some evidence indicates that the greatest number of blossoms are produced on shorter days—less than twelve hours of light—but this may not be true of all varieties.

Pollination   As with tomatoes and eggplants, to which they are related, pepper-plant flowers are hermaphroditic, and pollination will take place with no help from you. Fruit production will be increased, however, if you spray the blossoms with a hormone compound such as Blossom-set (see pp. 77–79).

Harvest   After blossoms have dropped and all fruit has set, fruit growth will continue under lower light, so maturing plants can be set under low-level lights for display, if you like. If plants are to be grown as perennials, light, temperature, water, and nutrition should all be greatly reduced during the winter, though temperature should not be reduced below 40 degrees or so.

Green peppers are ready to pick when they feel firm to the touch and have become heavy.

If they remain on the plants too long, they will begin to change color, becoming red or yellow, depending on variety. Red peppers should be rich in color before they are picked.

Branches of the pepper plant are brittle and break easily, so the peppers should be harvested by carefully cutting the stems ½ inch from the cap. Peppers keep best at 32 degrees.

Radishes
(Raphanus sativus)

The radish is a member of the mustard family and a cousin of cabbage. Its true origin is uncertain, though it probably descends from the wild species found growing throughout Europe, Japan, and much of North America. That it has been cultivated for many centuries is beyond doubt.

Radishes were a favorite vegetable in early Rome, Greece, and Egypt, and at the same time were being grown in China and Japan. All parts of the plant are edible—not just the familiar root—and in many countries, radishes are cultivated for the tops alone. Three basic types are grown for their roots—spring radishes, for the small red globes; summer radishes, which are long and white; and fall radishes, which may be black or white, round or long. All are relatively easy to grow.

Seeds and Soil   Most popular of the round red varieties are Scarlet Globe and Cherry Belle. White Icicle is the finest of the summer types. Of the round, autumn varieties White Chinese, Celestial, or Black Spanish are recommended.

Rich sandy loam is best for growing radishes. Soil from a woodland floor, which contains a great deal of well-rotted leaves or other humus, is ideal. The pH may be 6.0 to 8.0, but should be neither more acid nor more alkaline. The top 2 or 3 inches of soil must be very loose to allow bulb development. Roots are shallow, so the soil need not be deep. A pot with an 8-inch diameter will accommodate about a dozen radishes, and more if they are to be picked while they are very small.

Planting   Sow the seeds about ½ inch deep, fifteen or more to the inch. Soak the soil with water and keep it moist at all times. When germination occurs and the plants must be thinned, the thinnings, which are pungent with the flavor of radish, make a delicious addition to any salad. When the tops are about 2 inches high, the radishes should be thinned to stand about 2½ inches apart in all directions.

Water   A constant supply of water is the first key to proper root development. Give the plants light but frequent watering as soon as they stand a couple of inches high. A layer of moss over the pot will help preserve moisture while also keeping the soil and roots cool.

Nutrition   Plant food, if you use it at all, should not be nitrogenous, as this stimulates foliage growth at the cost of root development. It is far better to start with a rich soil and let the radishes feed on the nutrients it contains.

Temperature   All radishes, even the summer varieties, do best under cool conditions. It is especially critical that the soil be kept cool, so a layer of mulch should be kept over the pot. Fall varieties, if they grow on a patio, will stand light frost, but not the others.

Light   Spring and fall varieties need short hours of light; otherwise they will bolt to seed and produce no edible roots. Give these less than twelve hours of light each day. Summer varieties will attempt to bolt to seed under short hours of light, so give them more than twelve hours of light each day.

Light intensity should be 1500 foot-candles or more. It may be possible, as some authors state, to grow radishes under light that is less intense, but growth will certainly be slower, and for radishes that are firm, crisp, and mild in flavor, fast growth is essential; slow-growing roots, if they develop at all, will be tough and woody.

Harvest Spring and summer radishes should be pulled promptly when they achieve the desired size; this should be twenty to forty days following planting, depending on variety. Winter varieties require about sixty days to mature. If they remain in the soil too long, spring and summer radishes become woody. Winter varieties may be left in the pot and pulled as needed.

Shallots
(Allium ascalonicum)

It is difficult to think of a member of the onion family as being beautiful, yet the shallot certainly is, and it is also one of the easiest of all plants to grow, sending up its graceful, bright, green-blue stems under almost any conditions.

The shallot is a kind of multiplying onion that does not occur in the wild. Though it resembles garlic in some ways, it has a mild flavor that most gourmet chefs consider essential to the practice of their art. The plants develop gray, angular, pointed bulbs that are joined at the base but which lack the sheath that encloses the garlic bulb. Young plants are eaten whole, like scallions or green onions, and mature bulbs are used more like garlic, but with a milder, superior flavor.

Sets and Soil Shallots are best started from sets, which are divisions of the loosely joined bulb clusters that are sold over the produce counter at most grocery stores. If you buy sets from seed suppliers, look for the Louisiana variety, which is the only true shallot sold in this country.

Shallots will grow in any soil except that which is very, very acid—the pH no lower than 5.0. They send feeder roots down to a depth of about 8 inches, so the soil should be about that deep. They have no lateral roots, however, so they may be planted to stand very close together and will not interfere with other plant varieties in the same planter.

Planting Divide the bulb into cloves. Plant each clove about 1 inch deep, setting the cloves 3 inches apart or at least 3 inches from the main stem of any other plant already in the pot. Soak with water and set under lights. Sprouts will appear in seven to fourteen days. Several shallots make an attractive border around the edges of large planters, and new plants can be started each time the older ones are pulled.

Water Shallots grow best if the soil is slightly moist at all time; however, they are not harmed by long periods of dryness, so they can be watered as is convenient or in a manner that is compatible with the needs of any other plant the container might hold.

Nutrition Shallots are very light feeders and will thrive on the nutrition found in all but the poorest soil. However, bulb development may be enhanced by an occasional feeding of high-phosphorus plant food.

Temperature   Shallots are completely hardy and tolerant of almost any temperature they are given, though growth will stop under freezing conditions. Room temperature is nearly ideal for growing them.

Light   Shallots readily accept whatever light is available. They will grow almost normally under a few hundred foot-candles of light, as in a sunny window or under a pair of low-intensity fluorescents, yet they are not harmed by light that is very intense. Growth is greatly stimulated by increasing the duration of light.

Harvest   The young shallots may be pulled at any time after they appear and used like green onions; people eat both the tops and the bulb. If tops are cut near the soil, new ones quickly appear to replace them, and the minced tops may be used as chives. Cutting the top stimulates bulb development. Mature bulbs are ready to pull about five months after planting. With the tops cut off, the bulbs may be dried, then stored in a cool place after dividing a few to start a new planting.

Spinach
(Spinacia oleracea)

A member of the *Chenopodiaceae* family and closely related to beets and Swiss chard, spinach is cultivated in nearly all temperate parts of the world, having originated in China during the eighth century and reaching Europe about four hundred years later. It is an extremely easy plant to grow as long as you give some attention to its basic requirements.

Seeds and Soil   Spinach seed should be no more than a year old, for older seed is unlikely to germinate. Select any popular variety such as Viking, America, or Virginia Savoy, but not the so-called New Zealand Spinach, which is an altogether different plant.

Soil of the right pH is essential. Spinach will grow only if the pH is between 6.0 and 6.7. If the soil is more acid than pH 6.0, adding a little lime will bring it up to that point, but be careful about adding too much. The soil should also be very rich in nitrogen, or it should be enriched with a nitrogenous fertilizer before the seeds are planted. Never attempt to grow spinach in any soil mixture that includes peat moss, for this will sooner or later cause the soil to become too acid, which will kill the plants. The soil needs to be only a few inches deep, but the plants need to stand about 3 or 4 inches apart, so a large planter such as a window box is needed for a worthwhile crop.

Planting   Spinach seed should be germinated in the refrigerator. To do this sprinkle the seed over a damp blotter or paper towel, cover with another layer of the same, and store in the coolest part of the refrigerator for about five days. When small breaks appear in the seeds, indicating where the first roots will appear, the seed is ready to sow.

Do not start spinach at room temperature. This is critical. If temperatures rise into the 60s while spinach is less than six weeks old, it will be nearly impossible to keep the plants from bolting. Select the coolest spot in your home for young plants.

Sow the seeds ¾ inch deep, about 1 inch apart. Flood the soil with water and set the planter in light. The plants can be thinned as they become crowded; add the thinnings to other greens in salads or in cooking.

Water   Spinach needs far more water than most foliage plants. Healthy plants need water every third or fourth day. Mulch can help the soil retain moisture, but never use peat moss or sawdust as mulch, for these will cause the soil to become acid. Grass clippings, straw, or shredded aluminum foil may be used as mulch without causing this problem.

Nutrition Spinach is a fairly heavy feeder that requires more nitrogen than the other basic nutrients. Use a nitrogenous fertilizer on a weekly or biweekly basis, and increase the feeding at the first sign of yellowing of the leaves. Mix together a few ounces of blood meal and rock phosphate, both of which are available at garden centers, and sprinkle them over the planter soil to help provide further nutrition each time you water the plants.

Temperature Cool temperatures are best for growing spinach. After the plants are six weeks old, they may be grown at temperatures in the 60s, but even then cooler temperatures are preferred. This is one plant that will do far better in a cool room than on a warm patio or porch, and it would be very difficult to grow in a summer greenhouse, but it is an excellent plant to grow there during the winter.

Light Spinach does not need light of high intensity. It does, however, need light of short duration—nine hours or less out of each twenty-four-hour cycle. It will do very well in a window that faces east or south, or with 750 to 1000 foot-candles of artificial light, but it is likely to be burned if it is set in a window that faces west. Leaf burn, as well as bolting, may occur if the hours of light are too long.

Harvest Spinach reaches maturity in about forty days, depending on variety. Plants are considered mature when about six of the leaves have grown to a length of about 6 inches. However, long before any plant reaches maturity, you can begin to harvest tender young spinach. Just carefully cut away the outer leaves, allowing the central leaves to remain on the plants. The central leaves will then spring into growth, and this cycle can be repeated several times before growth slows and the plants must be allowed to mature. Cut mature plants just above the soil; be sure to dig the roots out before starting a new crop of any kind. Spinach, by the way, is tastier and more nutritious if it is cooked very briefly in a small amount of water, then allowed to stand for about five minutes, the pot covered, in its own juices.

Sprouts

Sprouts are the very easiest vegetable crop to grow and certainly one of the most nutritious. The most common sprouts are germinated from legume seed, principally the soybean, *Glycine soja;* green or golden gram, *Phaseolus aureus;* or the mung bean, *P. mungo.* However, any edible seed that produces a nonpoisonous plant can be sprouted for use as food. Usable seeds include grains, nuts, legumes, and a large number of vegetables. Any vegetable closely related to the potato or tomato should be avoided, as the leaves and stalks of these plants are toxic, and the same may be true of the sprouts.

A sprout is simply a young plant that might grow to maturity if it were not eaten. The sprouting process releases nutrients that are stored in the seed as food for the plant embryo. Thus sprouts contain a high concentration of vital minerals, vitamins, and protein needed for sustaining life. They are therefore excellent as food.

The basic process for sprouting is simple. Soak the seeds for twelve hours, drain, then place in a well-ventilated container such as a wide-mouthed jar with a cloth tied over the top. Invert the jar over a rack in a dark corner where the temperature remains constantly in the high 60s. At least four times daily rinse the seeds thoroughly in water of about 70 degrees, to wash away putrefactive bacteria and molds and as a means of refreshing the air in the jar. Full development of the sprouts should take place in two to seven days, depending on the type of seed. (Sprouts can, of course, be grown hydroponically, but since they are grown in darkness, its a waste of a lighted hydroponic planter to grow sprouts in it.)

No matter what kind of seed you are sprouting, they should be kept moist but not wet, and in a dark place. When the sprouts have developed, they should be drained thoroughly and refrigerated. Leafy sprouts may be left out in the light for a few hours, to increase their vitamin content before they are refrigerated.

Sprouts are at their most nutritious when they are used raw in salads. If they are lightly sautéed in butter or oil, however, they will transform an ordinary bowl of tomato, chicken, or vegetable soup into an exciting main course. Lightly toasted, they may be used as a substitute for nuts in cookies and fudge. Spicy sprouts, such as radish, will pep up any sandwich or give new life to a party dip. Mixtures such as lettuce, lentil, cabbage, bean, and sunflower need only a simple dressing to convert them into an unusual, tasty, and extremely nutritious vegetable dish.

Squash
(Cucurbita genus)

Squash probably originated in North America, but the evidence to support this belief is far from conclusive. The common name derives from a corruption of the Indian name for gourds, *ascutasquash*, certain types of which

they used, though they may not have cultivated them. Further compounding the confu-
sion about the origins of squash is the fact that
the genus includes not only all squash, but also
all pumpkins, gourds, and cushaws, and the
original species have become so mixed and in-
terwoven that not even botanists can sort
them out.

Two basic types of squash are cultivated,
both of which are grown for the fruit borne on
very tender annual vines. Winter squash are
large, slow-growing, hard-shelled varieties
that grow on long, straggling vines that may
spread as much as 20 feet and with root systems that require a great deal of soil. These
are obviously not suitable for growing in con-
fined areas. Summer squash, on the other hand,
grow very quickly, require far less soil, and are
available in compact bush form that makes the
plant easier to handle and to light. They can
be grown hydroponically or in soil, using artificial or natural light or a combination of the
two.

Seeds and Soil Summer varieties include the
yellow crookneck or straightneck types, the
green zucchini and coccozelle, and the white
scallop, or patty-pan squash. Early Prolific is
the recommended straightneck; Fordhook is
suggested for zucchini; and Early White Bush
is suggested for patty-pan squash. All produce
fruit on very compact bushes.

One squash plant can produce as much as 50
pounds of squash, depending on variety. The
seeds keep for years, however, so the excess
can be put aside for later planting or they can
be toasted and salted to make a delicious
snack.

Soil for growing squash should be rich but
sandy. The plants will tolerate soil that is a bit
acid or alkaline, but more fruit will be pro-

duced in soil with a pH between 6.0 and 6.5. Working some rotted leaves (any kind will do) into the soil will help it retain moisture and increase fruit production.

Even summer squash needs a fairly large amount of soil—at least a 5-gallon container and preferably one that is larger. Crowding of the root structure can seriously damage this plant. B & C West, manufacturer of hydroponic units, says their home unit will accommodate three squash plants. Some support should be available for the vines, as the fruit can become heavy. The vines are easily trained, so setting the planter on a large table or flat surface should be adequate.

Planting   Never attempt to transplant squash; start the seeds in the container in which they are to grow. In a large pot, plant 6 seeds in a circle about 1 foot in diameter, covering them with 1 inch of soil. Water them well and provide long hours of light. About fourteen days later thin out all but the two strongest plants; later reduce this to one. Do not thin by pulling, as the roots may be tangled and the remaining plants may be damaged; use shears to cut the stems just above the soil.

Summer squash needs only about sixty days of hot weather in which to produce a crop. This means that in nearly all parts of the country you can grow squash in an outside container during warm months, even if you have no light system with which to extend the seasons. By using lights to start plants indoors, however, you can lengthen the growing season and nearly double the crop.

Squash

Water   Squash plants need a soil that is uniformly, slightly moist at all times. Like cucumber, the edible fruit is composed mostly of water, so the plant will become far thirstier as fruit sets and begins to swell. At this stage plants may need even daily watering, depending on factors such as temperature. Water tanks may also be provided as for cucumbers (see pp. 156–160).

Nutrition Squash are heavy feeders. Once a week, along with their water, they should be given a cup of water-soluble plant food, the formula about 15-30-15. Liquid manure, available at some garden centers, is excellent food for squash.

Temperature Squash can be grown at room temperature but it does better when days are very warm, and nights cool. If you grow it in any artificial environment, provide the warmest conditions possible. Outside plants will be killed by the first heavy frost.

Light Squash are day-neutral plants, but with some preference for longer hours of light. According to the growers at B & C West, the maximum number of blossoms will be produced when the plants are provided with ten hours of natural or fourteen hours of artificial light. This may vary with the type of squash, but since the plants are day neutral, some flowering should occur on any reasonably long day length.

According to the same growers, squash has been grown under intensities of about 2000 foot-candles. Some suggest that even lower levels will serve, but any attempt to grow squash under weaker light should be regarded as experimental.

Pollination Male and female flowers are borne separately on the same plant. They are large and vaselike, yellow or orange, and very showy. The pollen inside the male is so profuse that it is clearly visible, and the squash can be seen developing behind the female, taking on shape and even some color, well before the flower opens. If male flowers open in advance of the females, the pollen may be collected on a cotton swab and kept for a day or two until a female flower is open and ready to receive it.

Harvest Summer squash should not be allowed to grow to maturity, when its seeds will become large and tough, its skin leathery, and its flavor strong. Long varieties may be picked when they are no larger than your finger and should never be grown to much more than 6 inches in length. The round patty-pan squash is ready for use when it is only 1 inch in diameter, and its diameter should never be more than 3 or 4 inches. In all cases the squash should be picked while the skin remains tender enough to break easily when pressed with the thumbnail. If the fruit is picked at this stage, the plant can be made to bear for quite some time. If, however, a few squash are permitted to become large and mature, they will sap the energy of the plant and production will stop altogether. Use a sharp knife to cut the squash from the stems, thus reducing the chance of damage to the rest of the plant.

Sweet Peas
(Pisum sativa humile)

Peas have been known since ancient times, and almost certainly originated in Europe and Asia. Many garden varieties are borne on annual vines that climb by means of tendrils to a height as great as 6 feet. The dwarf variety I describe here, however, grows to only about 12 inches, produces peas in a shorter time, and is far easier to grow. A single plant will not produce enough peas to be worthwhile, of course, but the plants are very attractive, especially when they are in blossom or laden with fruit, and several plants can be grown in a large planter of oblong design.

Seeds and Soil   The best dwarf pea varieties include Little Marvel, Laxton's Progress, and Alaska. A light sandy loam with a pH of about 6.5, is regarded as best for growing peas. The soil does not need to be rich in nitrogen but should be high in phosphorus and potassium. The soil should also hold water well. The soil should be fairly deep to allow for the root system, and the other dimensions of the planter should be large enough to allow about 4 inches between plants.

Planting   Peas can grow outside as long as cool weather prevails. They are not a good crop for the summer greenhouse, where temperatures are likely to be too high. If peas are to be grown on the patio, they should be started indoors under lights about eight weeks before the last hard frost of spring. Those to be grown to maturity under lights may, of course, be started at any time.

Soak the seed in water overnight. Sow the seed thickly—twelve seeds to the foot—in holes about 2 inches deep. Provide long hours of the brightest light possible, but keep the plants in a cool place. When the seedlings are about 2 inches high, thin them so they stand at least 3, but preferably 4, inches apart in all directions. When the size doubles again, provide some support, such as stakes, to keep them out of contact with the moist soil.

Water   Young roots are easily destroyed by too much water in the soil. Until the plants are well started, keep the soil lightly moist but never wet. Water should be slightly increased as the plants fill out, then increased again when the blossoms fall and the pods begin to develop. During this final stage of growth, it is very important that the soil be moist at all times.

Nutrition   Never feed peas with high-nitrogen plant food. Instead, three or four times during the life of the plants, feed them with a water-soluble plant food rich in phosphorus and potassium.

Temperature   Keep the peas cool at all times. Ideally the temperature should be in the 50s. Growth is slower in the 60s and may stop altogether in the high 70s; the blossoms will fall under these warmer conditions. At the other extreme, the plants will tolerate temperatures in the 30s, but will refuse to blossom and set fruit when temperatures fall that low.

Light   There are accounts of peas reaching maturity with only 1500 foot-candles of light. However, they are not harmed by extremely brilliant light, and so 2000 or more foot-candles is suggested, with some natural light included if possible.

The peas are day-neutral plants, but they demonstrate a decided preference for long hours of lighting. Outside, plants will blossom and produce some peas if they receive a few hours of direct sunlight each day. Inside, where you control the hours of lighting, peas should receive no less than twelve hours of light each day, preferably sixteen hours or more, followed by uninterrupted darkness.

Pollination   Like all legumes, peas are truly self-pollinating. However, production on inside plants may be increased by gently shaking each plant while it is in the blossom stage, and there are indications that production may also be stimulated by spraying the blossoms with a hormone compound (see pp. 77–79).

Harvest Peas are ready to pick about eighty days after planting. They should be picked as soon as the pods are filled out but before they show any sign of losing color. They are at their very finest while immature, tiny, and soft, but picking them then greatly reduces the size of the crop. They should be cooked as soon as they are taken from the plant, for within two hours their natural sugar converts into starch, greatly altering the flavor.

Tomatoes
(Lycopersicon esculentum)

Tomatoes are native to tropical America, where the Indians cultivated and ate them long before the arrival of the first European explorers. The name derives from the Mexican Indian name for the fruit, *tomatl,* and contrary to popular belief, the tomato was among the first plants exported to Europe from the New World, having been planted in European gardens as early as the sixteenth century. Thomas Jefferson planted them at Monticello in 1781, and in that same century they were introduced to the Orient. Tomatoes of those early years were ribbed and as likely to be yellow as red; the smooth tomato we know today did not come into being until the nineteenth century, about the same time that plum tomatoes were developed.

Though outdoor gardeners grow the tomato as an annual because it is so readily killed by cold weather, it is actually a perennial that is capable of living for several years. Its closest relatives are potatoes and tobacco, and slightly more distant relatives include eggplant, peppers of all types, and flowering petunias. The tomato itself is a beautiful plant when laden with fruit and it is relatively easy to grow, either under lights or as a movable potted plant, but careful consideration must be given to selecting the right variety.

Tomato

Seeds and Soil Most tomatoes develop on vines that will continue to grow taller as long as the growing season lasts. These are known as indeterminate vines. Not only can providing light to all parts of the plant become a problem, if not an impossibility, as the plant becomes extremely tall, but it is also difficult to provide space for the root system of such a plant. Most varieties of tomatoes have large root systems, which spread approximately to the same extent as their tops; thus if you intend to grow a tomato vine that stands 6 feet high, soil of the same depth would have to be provided, which is clearly an unworkable idea in an apartment garden.

This problem can be avoided by planting tomatoes that grow on "determinate" vines, which produce a certain amount of foliage growth and then stop growing while the fruit sets and ripens; many of these have been developed in recent years. There are also dwarf varieties, which produce smaller fruit, and cherry tomatoes, which, though they produce extensive vines, do not have such heavily developed root systems.

Among the tomatoes that grow on determinate vines are Fireball, Urbana, and Sioux, the last of which produces globe-shaped fruit that is slightly flattened. Tiny Tim and Pixie Hybrid are the best of the true midgets, producing tomatoes on vines no higher than 15 inches. Small Fry Hybrid is the suggested cherry tomato.

Even determinate vines require fairly large amounts of soil—a 5- to 10-gallon container that should be wide as well as deep, to accommodate the lateral roots. Midget and cherry tomato plants each need a pot at least 9 inches in diameter. All can be grown hydroponically, to save on space.

Tomatoes grow best in sandy loam that is just below neutral in acidity, with a pH between 6.0 and 7.0. Two parts neutral potting soil and one part sand is about right. Enriching the soil with phosphorus by adding a cupful of bone meal to each pot of soil prior to planting will give the plants a boost and cause earlier production.

Planting   Tomato seed germinates in eight to ten days. Even if they are provided with long hours of bright light, they require about nine weeks in which to reach the large seedling stage. Since they are so slow-growing, if tomatoes are to be matured outdoors, they should be started about nine weeks before the last spring frost, thus allowing them plenty of time to bear before they are killed by the first frost of autumn.

Since germination is poor, start at least three seeds for each plant you hope to grow. Seeds should be planted 1 inch apart and ¼ inch deep. The best temperature for germination is 70 degrees. The young seedlings will tolerate continuous lighting, so provide the longest possible hours of light. Growth levels off at about 1500 foot-candles, so brighter light is not needed at this stage. The minimum level of light for reasonably good growth is 1000 foot-candles.

Two weeks after planting, when the plants have developed their second set of leaves, thin all but the strongest plants from each pot. Keep the soil slightly dry through this stage. When the plants stand about 8 inches tall and their leaves are beginning to spread, they should be given the brightest light you can provide—not less than 1500 foot-candles, but ideally 2000 or more. Outside plants must receive at least six hours of sunlight daily. Plants should also be staked at this time.

Water   Tomatoes are able to withstand long periods of dryness far better than they can tolerate water standing around their roots. For this reason it is best to water them infrequently, certainly not more than once a week. Let the upper soil become perceptibly dry, then give the soil a good soaking. More water will be needed as the fruit sets and begins to swell.

Nutrition   Phosphorus is the key nutrient in growing tomatoes. Give plants a water-soluble food that is high in phosphorus but low in nitrogen on a weekly or biweekly basis, though this may be reduced when the tomatoes are nearing maturity. Too much nitrogen in the food will result in lush foliage and few tomatoes. If a plant is maintained for a long period of time, however, it may begin to show signs of nitrogen deficiency: purple stems and yellow upper leaves. If this occurs a single dose of nitrogenous fertilizer is recommended.

Temperature   Tomatoes need warm temperatures, but not too warm. All growth stops at about 95 degrees, so greenhouse temperatures must be carefully watched during the summer. Less fruit is set if night temperatures stay above 80 degrees for any length of time. A high room temperature of 68 degrees is adequate for good production. Plants are killed by temperature that drops to 32 degrees or lower.

Light   Since the tomato is a favorite research plant, we know a great deal about its responses to environmental factors. Experiments made as early as 1957 established that, even though the tomato is a day-neutral plant and capable of blossoming in a wide variety of day lengths, it produces more flowers and produces them sooner when it receives exactly nine hours of light during each twenty-four-hour cycle. Plants getting light of this duration, flowered ten to fourteen days sooner than those provided with sixteen hours of light each day.

Tomatoes have been brought to maturity using just 1000 foot-candles of light, but only under carefully controlled laboratory conditions, which usually include stripping many of the leaves from the plant to allow for better distribution of light. Even under these conditions fruit production is much greater under more intense light, so the home grower should plan on providing not less than 1500 foot-candles for tomatoes.

Darkness is also important, so tomato plants should not be set where they may be exposed to spillage from street lamps and other light sources. Unless the plants are given at least seven hours of uninterrupted darkness during each twenty-four-hour cycle, they will refuse to bloom, no matter how adequate the lighting.

Pollination The blossoms will set fruit without artificial pollination, but more fruit will be set if the stems are very, very gently shaken while in flower or if each flower is sprayed with Blossom-set, the hormone compound developed for use on tomatoes (see pp. 77–79). The hormone spray should be used not more than three times.

It takes forty-five to fifty days to produce ripe fruit from a blossom. If you carefully prune suckers and side branches after the first fruit has set, the plant will be stimulated to

Tomato

increased production, making it possible to have fifty or more tomatoes on a standard or midget plant and twice that many on a cherry-tomato vine.

Harvest   Allow the fruit to ripen fully on the vine. Vine-ripened tomatoes are far richer in vitamin C than those that are picked before they are fully ripe. Full ripeness usually comes about seven days after the fruit shows the first traces of red.

Never pick a tomato by attempting to pull it directly away from the plant, for this may damage the branch. Instead, twist the fruit gently on its stem, tipping it slightly sideways as you twist. This bit of caution will help keep the plant healthy and productive for many, many months to come.

selected fruits
and berries

Bananas, strawberries, kumquats, oranges and lemons, pineapples and peaches, even an occasional cup of coffee made from beans picked from your own indoor tree—these are just a few of the fruits and berries you can add to your apartment garden.

One of the major horticultural developments of this century has been the introduction of a large number of self-pollinating dwarf fruit trees. Where once even outside growers were unable to grow many fruits without the presence of a pollinating tree of another variety, the self-pollinating varieties make it possible to produce fruit with only a single tree. (This means only that the trees will accept pollen from their own blossoms, of course; in most instances, pollen must be transferred from the male parts of the flowers to the female, as described in Chapter 4.) Dwarfing of the trees assures that they will remain small enough to grow in a limited area, even though the fruit they produce is of normal size.

However, not all the fruit varieties described in the following pages are new. Many are small trees—natural dwarfs—that have been around for centuries. Many of these have long been favored as houseplants, though not every home gardener realizes that they can be made to bear fruit.

A few of the fruit-bearing plants can be started from seed. But most cannot, because of their manner of propagation or because of the method by which the plant is dwarfed, so it is usually necessary to start by buying young stock. Dwarf trees are usually created by grafting a young bud from the desired fruit variety onto a dwarfing rootstock; if, however, seed from the fruit is planted, the resulting plant will revert to type, sending up a full-size tree that, in most instances, will not bear. Dwarf stock is readily available from most large nurseries or from the suppliers listed in the Appendix.

Some of the fruit-producing plants are very easy to grow, requiring relatively low light and very little care. A number of them are moderately easy to grow, needing brighter light and a great deal more attention. Some present a real challenge, requiring not only the very brightest light but the most careful attention to all parts of the artificial environment.

But easy to grow or challenging, the plants included in this section have this in common: they are beautiful as well as productive, worthy additions to any indoor garden.

Banana

(Musa nana)

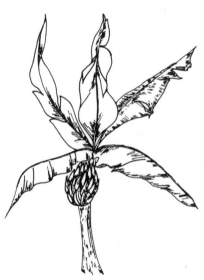

Bananas, which are among the oldest known fruits, were once called figs because old legends said that the leaves Adam and Eve wore were actually banana leaves.

A large number of banana varieties grow throughout the tropics, on plants that are up to 25 feet tall. Some produce fruit as thick as the human arm. The dwarf varieties, however, seldom grow taller than 5 or 6 feet, and they bear clusters of tiny but deliciously edible bananas. Dwarf bananas are also among the most interesting plants for the home garden.

The banana plant is actually a fast-growing herb. The stalks are composed of several layers of tightly compressed leaves. The flower clusters force their way up through this tightly packed stalk after it reaches its full growth, then emerge at the top to droop over all sides of the leafy crown. The flowers at the tip have only stamens, so they produce no fruit. The flowers around the base of the cluster are hermaphroditic, however, and these produce fruit with no pollination. The bananas grow in whorls around the base of the fruiting stalk, with fifteen or twenty bananas in each whorl.

After bearing a single time the leaf stalk dies back to the true stem of the plant, its underground rhizome. New suckers on which further fruit is produced constantly rise from this rhizome, so fruit is produced by a healthy tree about once every twelve months.

Stock and Soil Dwarf varieties are Lady-finger, Jamaica Dwarf and, simply, Dwarf Banana. Nurseries usually offer rhizomes, suckers, or young plants that are already potted. Because they produce no viable seeds, bananas can only be propagated by separating suckers or secondary shoots, from the parent plant or making cuttings of the rhizomes. Suckers are usually only available in March or April, so it may be necessary to order them well in advance.

Bananas may be grown in any soil, but they do best in one that contains a great deal of humus. Good drainage is essential. Mixing one part well-rotted manure (once manure rots it is odorless), if you can obtain it through a nursery, to three parts soil, will help provide the heavy nutrition needed by the banana plant. The planter should be at least 36 inches in diameter and 18 inches deep.

Planting Plant the rhizome or sucker about 12 inches deep. Cover it with potting soil or a mixture of potting soil and well-rotted manure. If you are starting with a young plant, remove all but one sucker, then allow this to grow and bear its fruit before you cut it back and allow another sucker to grow. After the plant has produced its first crop, it may be allowed to send up three or four fruit-bearing tops at a time, depending upon its vigor.

Water The soil for growing bananas must be kept wet at all times—not just moist but wet. In the natural environment bananas grow best in regions that receive as much as 100 inches of rainfall annually, so it is extremely difficult to give them too much water. Humidity should also be as high as possible.

Nutrition Bananas are extremely heavy feeders. Because of their fast and heavy growth, they need plenty of fertilizer in addition to that which is already in the soil. It is almost impossible to feed the plant too heavily or too frequently. Give water-soluble plant food each time you water the plant, increasing its strength if the growth shows any signs of slowing. Covering the soil with a mulch of rotted manure, compost, or even grass and leaves will help provide more food for this hungry plant.

Temperature Bananas will bear fruit at high room temperature—68 degrees or so. However, growth and fruit production are stimulated by higher temperatures. The greenhouse is the ideal location for this plant. Placing it beneath a skylight, where temperatures are warmer for at least part of each day, will help, as will setting it close to a high window that faces south or west. If you choose to set the plant outside during the summer months, be aware that the plant will produce no fruit if it is touched by the slightest frost. Heavy frost may cause it to die back to the soil; however, the rhizomes will not be killed unless they are exposed to freezing weather.

Light The banana plant does not need extremely bright light, but it does need light over its entire length, which is composed of leaves, and this creates some minor problems. If only overhead lighting is provided, the lower parts of a tall plant may suffer. The problem is best overcome by providing artificial light from overhead while letting the slanting sunlight that comes through a sunny window provide for the lower leaves, or by combining the overhead lighting with one or two spotlight-type growth lamps beamed on the lower part of the plant. About 1000 foot-candles of light, supplied to all parts of the plant, is adequate.

The plant will blossom, and thereby produce fruit, on any adequate day length. However, like many tropical plants, it does best when given less than twelve hours of light in each twenty-four-hour cycle; nine hours is the amount most frequently suggested.

Harvest   The entire whorl of bananas may be cut from the tree as soon as they are sizable, then set in a cool and shady place to develop their sugar, color, and flavor; or they may be allowed to ripen on the tree. After you have cut the bunches from the tree, the stalk that produced them must be cut back before another sucker is allowed to develop and take its place. The tree should continue to produce for about six years before the rhizome must be replaced.

Cantaloupe
(Cucumis melo)

Cantaloupes are the fruits of tender annual vines that are thought to have originated in India. Members of the melon genera of the family *Cucurbitaceae,* most cantaloupes are borne on sprawling vines above massive root systems, making them impractical as containerized plants for the indoor garden. But that refers only to the standard types. Dwarf cantaloupe varieties are now available with bush-like vines that spread not more than 36 inches and which almost beg to be added to your garden.

Seeds and Soil   Suggested dwarfs are Minnesota Midget, which, about seventy-five days after planting, produces eight or more 4-inch

Cantaloupe

melons—just right for individual servings; or Short 'N' Sweet, which produces its fruit in about the same number of days. At least one dwarf honeydew plant, Oliver's Pearl Cluster, is available, and there is no good reason why it could not be grown by the techniques described here, as its needs are nearly identical.

Cantaloupes need a sandy loam with a pH that is very close to neutral. Ground limestone should be added to any soil which tests below 7.0. Cantaloupes absolutely will not grow in soil that contains too much clay, nor will they tolerate any soil mixture which includes peat moss.

Melons also need a great deal of humus in the soil to help retain moisture. If well-rotted manure or compost is available, adding about 2 pounds of this to the potting soil will provide all the humus that is needed. The planter for growing melons should be at least 18 inches deep and 24 inches across. This is also an excellent plant for growing hydroponically, but I'd suggest you grow only one plant per unit, not three as suggested by the manufacturers.

Planting   Plant eight to ten seeds in a circle with a radius of about 6 inches in the center of the planter. Cover the seeds with ½ inch of soil that has been loosened by sifting. Water well, and provide full light. When the seeds germinate, thin out all but four or five plants from the planter. When the young plants have developed four to six leaves each, remove all but the two strongest plants from the tub.

One problem is that melons need a long, hot growing season—longer than is found in the northern parts of this country. If you intend to grow cantaloupes in an outside container, you can overcome this problem by starting the plants under lights, then moving them outside when the days become hot and the nights are no longer too cool.

Water Cantaloupes need an abundance of water from the time they are seedlings until they are almost full-grown. Only after the fruit has set and started to ripen should water be withheld. They will greatly benefit from individual water tanks, as described for cucumbers (see p. 158).

Nutrition The cantaloupe is a very heavy feeder. Even when compost or manure is added to the growing medium, the plant and its young fruit can stand additional nutrients, given biweekly. One water-soluble formula I have used with success is 15-30-15.

Temperature The plant will grow quite well at high room temperature and may set some fruit. However, fruit production is far greater when temperatures are in the 70s, and maximum production occurs when temperature reaches the 80s. Night temperatures should also be warm; fruit does not develop properly if night temperatures fall into the low 50s.

These high temperatures clearly suggest a greenhouse or special garden room with separate temperature control as the best place for growing cantaloupe. However, the area beneath a skylight or directly in front of a sunny west window, where daytime temperatures are increased by the sun, may serve; or the air around the plant can be made a few degrees warmer by the use of incandescent bulbs.

Light The plant itself will flourish and blossom if it is provided with only 1000 footcandles of light. Brighter light—1500 to 2000 foot-candles—is needed, however, if the fruit is to achieve normal size and ripen properly.

One problem arises because blossoms and fruit are borne in the lower leaf axils. If overhead lighting is used, much of the light may be blocked by the large upper leaves, and the light that does reach the lower area will be weakened by distance. The problem is best overcome by supplementing the overhead lights with an incandescent plant-growth lamp that can be beamed directly on the lower area; or the situation may be improved to a lesser extent by snipping away a few of the upper leaves. The plant flowers best when it receives nine to fourteen hours of light daily.

Pollination   Pollination is the same as for squash (see pp. 201–202). However, after the fruit has set you should carefully pinch off all but six or eight of the young melons. The nutrition that would have gone into these will be used by those which remain, and the plant will then produce larger, prettier, and tasty fruit.

Harvest   Cantaloupes are ripe when their stems begin to separate from the fruit. A crack may appear all around the stem when the melon is ready to pick. If you lift it and give it the slightest twist, it should come free of the vine easily.

Fruit on outside plants will not ripen if temperatures drop into the low 50s. These may be picked to ripen inside under lights or in a warm, sunny window. All cantaloupes develop a better flavor if, after they are picked, they are stored in a warm place for a couple of days. If you store them at 50 to 55 degrees, they may be kept for as long as three weeks.

The coffee tree probably originated in Ethiopia, gaining its familiar name from the province of Kaffa; it most likely spread from there to Arabia, then Sri Lanka, and finally South America. The Arabs cultivated it as early as the fifteenth century, and by the eighteenth century it was being raised for culinary purposes in the greenhouses of Louis XV of France. These royal trees were the ancestors of many South American trees of today.

The coffee tree makes a striking specimen plant. It is also very easy to grow. Fully capable of developing into a large tree but easily kept to manageable size by judicious pruning, the tree has large, evergreen glossy leaves and bears dense clusters of fragrant white flowers that give way to clusters of green cherrylike fruit, which change through various shades of green and golden brown until, when they are fully ripe, they turn bright red. An indoor tree may be decked out in blossoms, green fruit, and fruit in all stages of ripeness at any given time. It is for such beauty that the coffee tree is best grown, for most trees yield only about a pound of coffee a year—enough for a bracing cup now and then, but hardly enough to cause Folger's any worry.

Seeds and Soil Named varieties are not offered by the seed companies, which offer their seed simply as Arabian coffee. A package of seed contains about a dozen coffee "beans," and you will need them all since germination is poor.

Soil for raising coffee must be somewhat acid, with a pH of about 4.5 to 6.0. It should also be well drained. A good mixture for the potted tree is two parts loam, one part peat moss, and one part sand.

Young plants will need only a 5- or 7-inch pot. At the end of its first year, the plant

Coffee
(Coffea arabica)

should have about a 12-inch pot, and as it goes into its third year of life, move the plant into at least a 5-gallon container.

Planting Before planting seeds, carefully peel off their outer husks. Make a mixture that is 85 percent water and 15 percent Clorox or other liquid chlorine bleach, and soak the seeds for twenty minutes. Spread soil about 1½ inches deep in a shallow container. Sow the seeds well apart, covering them only to about the thickness of the seed. Place the container in a warm location but out of direct light. The best temperature for germination is 75 degrees. Keep the soil moist, never allowing it to dry out until germination occurs; then reduce the water slightly but not enough to cause the plants to wilt.

After transplanting them into individual pots, water the plants well.

Water As a native of shady tropical forests, the coffee tree likes plenty of moisture in soil and air. It should be watered plentifully during spring and early summer, but sparingly during winter, when it will need a rest. The aim should be to keep it moist at all times except when it is resting. The soil should always be well drained, and at no time should it get excessively wet and boggy. A layer of peat moss over the soil will help it hold moisture, thus reducing the frequent watering that may cause excess moisture to build up in spots.

Coffee

Nutrition The coffee tree is a relatively light feeder, deriving much of the food it needs from any healthy soil. However, a monthly or bimonthly feeding of water-soluble plant food, with a formula 5-10-5 or so is suggested. Give no nutrition during the winter months, when the plant should rest.

Temperature The ideal temperature for growing coffee lies between 65 and 70 degrees, making it an excellent plant for growing indoors. It will tolerate some variation in either direction, including very light frost. It is easily harmed by very high tempertures, however, and is not really a good plant for the summer greenhouse.

Light The coffee tree does not need extremely bright light. On plantations it is ordinarily grown in the shade of larger trees. Setting the tree in a bright window, where it can receive from 500 to 1000 foot-candles of light for several hours daily, or putting it beneath 1000 foot-candles of fluorescent light, will be adequate, though floodlights may have to be added if the tree grows extremely large. Light in the greenhouse must be filtered with netting. Older trees will tolerate brighter light.

This is a day-neutral plant, but it blooms best when the light is less than twelve hours in duration.

Pollination The flowers are hermaphroditic, and some fruit may be produced without hand pollination. However, touching the center of each blossom with a cotton swab, as described in Chapter 4, will cause the tree to bear more fruit. Never use a hormone compound on these blossoms, as it may destroy the viability of the pollen.

Special Culture Coffee trees are fully capable of growing too large for your apartment garden and so pruning may be necessary to keep the plant under control. Before you start clipping, however, it is essential that you know the peculiar growth characteristics of this plant.

A central stem is always dominant, and the primary lateral branches grow in pairs opposite each other and horizontally from this central stem. These may branch to give secondary laterals, and the secondary growth may branch again. All these branches will spread out on about the same plane and at right angles to the central stem. No upright branches grow from the horizontal laterals, but only from the central stem. If the central stem is cut back, more upright stems will grow, and from these will spring more lateral branches like those growing from the central stem.

All upright branches should be cut while they are very small, and the central stem should be clipped when it threatens to reach a height of about 4 feet. This causes branching of the primary lateral growth. The secondary lateral branches should be thinned out so that only one is left at each node. Find the first node with two laterals, then cut one away. Move to the next node and cut away the lateral on the opposite side. This helps stimulate branching instead of upward growth, and greatly increases fruit production.

Harvest   The coffee tree will not bear fruit until it is three years old, though it may blossom before that time. It will be bearing fully by its fourth year and may then go on providing coffee for fifty years or more. The coffee is ripe when the cranberrylike fruit is a very bright red in color. Each fruit contains two coffee beans.

These beans should be spread on a pan and roasted in a 350-degree oven until they take on the familiar rich brown color we associate with coffee; be sure to turn them frequently so the roasting is uniform.

They'll not provide a great deal of the beverage, but having a cup now and then can be a fulfilling experience, especially if it's accompanied at breakfast by juice squeezed from fruit you've grown yourself.

Figs have grown in Syria, Iran, and the Mediterranean countries since the dawn of time and played an important part in mythology and religion. They are relatively easily grown, but selection of the proper variety is absolutely critical for success.

It is nearly impossible to grow Smyrna figs, even in most outdoor gardens, in this country. This is because of the way they must be pollinated. To understand this, you must understand the way this strange fruit is constructed.

A fig is a collection of many fruits, which grow inside a fleshy receptacle. The outer wall of the fig is actually a stem with a specialized cavity. Inside this appear a number of flowers, some male and some female. In the Smyrna fig all the flowers are female, and it would appear that they are doomed to die unpollinated. And that is exactly what happens without the presence of a very specialized wasp, *Blastophaga psenes,* the fig wasp, and a nearby caprifig tree from which the wasp can carry pollen. This process, known as caprification, requires not only the presence of the fig wasp and the caprifig tree, but also a great deal of technical help from the grower. Since the fig wasp can survive in very few parts of the United States, the Smyrna fig is beyond the reach of most growers.

Figs of the common type, however, produce their fruit asexually, and any pollination or seed production which follows is not necessary to the production of fruit. Trees of the San Pedro type produce two crops, but only the

Figs
(Ficus carica)

first crop is produced asexually, and so the second crop will be lost to the indoor or greenhouse grower.

Stock and Soil   Texas Everbearing Fig, available from Burpee's, is the most readily available dwarf fig. It grows to a height of 4 or 5 feet but may be kept pruned to even smaller size. The tree is evergreen and an extremely attractive addition to any garden. Magnolia is a variety that is capable of becoming a very large tree, but which accepts pruning so well that you may be able to keep it under control. Young trees grow extremely fast when conditions are favorable, and may bear a crop the first year.

Figs grow best in a sandy loam that contains plenty of plant nutrients. They will tolerate soil that is very alkaline but not soil that is acid. The pH should be no lower than 5.0. A mixture of two parts neutral potting soil and one part fine sand is good.

Planting   Give the young tree as much soil as space allows; the container should hold at least 5 but preferably 10 gallons of soil. It will look out of place at first, but the plant grows so quickly that plant and container will soon be matched. Set the plant at least 2 inches lower than it grew in the nursery. If you want a more bushlike growth rather than a tree, set the short trunk portion entirely under soil so that leaders will develop and cause secondary upright growth. Water well, so soil will be washed between all the roots.

Water   The soil should be kept slightly moist at all times. This is best done by covering the soil with a mulch, preferably of manure, which helps provide the nutrients the plant needs. In addition, the leaves should be sprayed with

Fig

water at least every other day. Reduce the amount of water when fruit is on the tree, for too much moisture at this time ruins the taste of the fruit.

Nutrition Fig trees almost always refuse to bear fruit if they receive too much fertilizer. Allow the tree to go its own way as long as it appears to be doing well; then at the first sign of drooping, feed it a nitrogenous fertilizer or liquid manure. In the autumn of its second year and every autumn thereafter, it should be repotted, adding at that time 4½ ounces of superphosphate and 2½ ounces of sulphate of potash to the soil. Give no nutrition during the winter, when the plant must rest.

Temperature Fruit can be produced at any temperature between 65 and 80 degrees. Plants will tolerate some cold but not severe freezing. If they are left outside during cold weather, they may show no signs of damage, yet later crops may be greatly curtailed.

Light Figs need relatively low light, but the entire tree must receive it. This is less of a problem if the tree is regularly pruned and kept small. Adequate light is 1000 to 1500 foot-candles, which is best achieved by setting the tree near your brightest window and supplementing the sunlight with overhead fluorescents, or by beaming incandescent growth lamps on the unlighted parts of the tree. Greenhouse light should be filtered through netting. Outside plants should get long hours of sunlight, but should not be exposed to the glare from brick or concrete.

If you are using artificial light, long hours of lighting are suggested, though the fig is day neutral, at least in the everbearing varieties.

Harvest Everbearing figs may produce two or three crops a year. The fruit is mature when it is soft to the touch and can be easily removed from the stem with a gentle twist. If the fruit is less sweet than you feel it should be, it can be made sweeter by picking it before it ripens on the tree and placing it in a warm spot until it softens. As a dessert, fresh figs have few rivals when they are cut in half and soaked for an hour in orange liqueur, and they are extremely rich in vitamins A and C.

Grapefruit
(Citrus paradisi)

The origin of the grapefruit, more correctly called the pomelo, is lost to history. The first Florida planting was made in 1823, but no fruit was produced until 1885. Some of the original trees, which grew to more than 60 feet, were still growing and bearing fruit as late as 1940. Until recently it bordered on idiocy to suggest that this fruit could be grown in the home, the greenhouse, or even in any but the very warmest parts of the United States, if only because of its size. But all that has changed with the recent introduction of the Dwarf Marsh Grapefruit.

This true dwarf produces clusters of three to six seedless fruit that develop without pollination. The tree is remarkably beautiful, with shiny evergreen foliage, and can be kept to a height of 3 or 4 feet by regular pruning. At least one enthusiast, a young man named William Madonna, is now raising his own grapefruit tree indoors in Rhode Island. The tree is now in its fourth year of life. It is bearing well, he says. He moves the tree outside for about ninety days each summer, but at all other times it is kept beneath a pair of 40-watt fluorescent lights, placed at a distance of 18 inches above the tree—very low light indeed for a fruit tree.

Stock and Soil   The Dwarf Marsh variety, offered by Four Winds Growers (see Appendix),
is the only readily available dwarf variety.
Trees are shipped as bare rootstock, packed in
damp peat moss. Four Winds offers two sizes,
one suitable for planting in a 2-gallon container, and the other needing a 5-gallon
planter. The latter size is suggested, because
you will get an older tree that should already
be off to a healthy start.

Sandy loam is the best soil for grapefruit.
Soil should be slightly acid, with a pH of about
5.5 to 6.2, so adding peat moss to the loam or
potting soil is advisable. Before planting it is
also a good idea to incorporate a few ounces of
rock phosphate and granite dust into the soil.
As these break down, they will assure the tree
a healthy start.

Planting   Be absolutely sure the planter is
large enough to hold all the roots with no
crowding whatsoever. A very large planter
that will hold about 10 gallons of soil is ideal.
Fill the planter, then dig out a hole large
enough for the roots. If any of the roots are
damaged, cut them away until the cut shows
live, undamaged tissue. Set the tree in the hole
so that it stands just a little higher than it
stood in the nursery. The juncture of the main
roots and the trunk should be just about even
with the top of the hole.

Fill the space around the roots with soil. Be
sure to fill in carefully around the roots, leaving no air pockets. When the hole is filled to
within about 2 inches of the top, run water in
it to wash the soil down among the roots.
Shake the tree several times while you are filling and watering the hole, to help settle the
soil. Allow all excess water to drain away, then
fill the hole with dirt, leaving a shallow inden-
tation that slopes toward the trunk at the cen-

ter of the planter. Water the soil thoroughly, being sure that it is completely moist to the level of the lowest roots.

Water During the first two weeks after you set the tree in the planter, the roots of the young tree must receive constant moisture. It may be necessary to water it three times a week. During the rest of its first year, it should be watered once every week to ten days. During later years the trees are best watered less frequently, but will require more water each time. When you give water it is important to flood the container so that water runs out the bottom and leaches soluble salts from the soil. Check outside trees frequently and water them if the soil crumbles when you pinch it between your fingers. Spray or mist the foliage weekly to remove dust. Keep the humidity very high at all times, or the tree may refuse to blossom and set fruit.

Nutrition Bill Madonna, who raises those grapefruit in Rhode Island, says the trees do best when they are fed every tenth day—except during winter months, when they are resting—with a complete fertilizer that contains trace elements plus a chleating agent, such as Ortho-Gro. He also suggests using fish emulsion now and then. Any high-phosphorus plant food will help initiate flowering and setting of fruit. Switch to a nitrogenous fertilizer during the summer.

Temperature The Dwarf Marsh Grapefruit will blossom and produce fruit with temperatures ranging from 50 to 80 degrees. However, fruit may drop from the branches if temperatures exceed these limits by only a few degrees. The lower part of the range may also

cause the fruit to be bitter and slow to ripen.
Keep trees away from drafts when they are
indoors.

One way to meet these requirements is to
move the trees outside following the last frost,
then move them back inside as autumn approaches. While they are inside the trees
should be maintained at 68 degrees.

Grapefruit

Light The tree will probably not blossom if
given more than twelve hours of light daily. It
should also be protected from spillage from
other light sources, especially incandescent,
during the period of darkness.

If you move a tree outside, set it in a shady
area for about ten days, then place it in full
sun. This allows it to adjust to the change and
prevents leaf burn. Greenhouse grapefruit
should be placed in the shade of other trees, if
possible.

While it is possible to maintain a tree under
a low-level light and possibly have it produce
some fruit without setting the tree outside,
brighter light is suggested for a tree that is to
remain always indoors. Place the tree under
1500 foot-candles of light, add all the sunlight
that is available, and you will almost certainly
get better development of fruit.

Harvest The fruit is very slow to develop.
After the tree blossoms and the fruit appears, a
period of nine to ten months is required before
the fruit is ready to pick. During that period
the tree may blossom again and attempt to set
more fruit, but it should not be allowed to do
so until its fourth or fifth year; small secondary
fruit should be picked from young trees as
soon as it appears, thus letting the older fruit
have all the nutrients. The skin of a ripe
grapefruit will usually contain a mixture of
pigments, primarily green fading to yellow.

They are best picked by cutting them from the tree with half an inch of stem attached and then cutting away the stem. They will keep for several weeks with proper refrigeration.

Kumquat
(Genus Fortunella)

This is a genus that includes about six evergreen shrubs or small trees, and which is so closely related to the citrus trees that crosses between the two are very easy to make. Kumquats differ from citrus trees in that they have small fruits with acid pulp and sweet edible skins or rinds. A British plant hunter, Robert Fortune, brought the first kumquat trees to Europe from China and Japan in 1846. Extremely decorative, they were grown indoors long before the invention of fluorescent lighting.

Standard kumquat varieties may grow 6 or 8 feet high, but dwarf varieties seldom grow taller than 2 or 3 feet. All parts of the trees are sweetly scented, with dark green glossy leaves, fragrant white flowers, and miniature fruit that give them the appearance of a tiny orange, lime, or lemon tree, depending on the variety.

Not only are the kumquats available as dwarfs, but they can also be had in what can only be described as a variety of "flavors." There are limequats, citrangequats, and even lemonquats, though the last is a curiosity that growers rarely offer. These varieties are created by special grafting techniques, and the result is a tree that bears fruit with a combination of flavors; the limequat tastes, for example, like a cross between lime and kumquat, which is exactly what it is. Fruit of any type seldom exceeds 1½ inches in diameter, and all types have agreeably spicy, edible peels. You can grow any type by the methods which follow.

Stock and Soil   For kumquats with orange-flavored fruit, select any true dwarf variety such as Nagami, Neiwa, or Marumi. These produce fruit about the size and shape of an olive. One crop is produced each year, usually in spring or fall, but inside trees may bear a second crop.

If the taste of lime is to your liking, choose the Dwarf Eustis Limequat, a prolific little plant that bears year round. At any given time it may display blossoms and fruit in all stages of ripeness.

For fruit similar to tangerines, in taste if not in size, try growing the Dwarf Calamondin Citrangequat, which produces acid fruit that can be left on the tree until needed. (Most citrus suppliers listed in the Appendix offer these varieties.)

Sandy loam is the best soil for growing kumquats. Soil should be slightly acid, with a pH around 5.0, so adding some peat moss to the growing medium is a good idea. The tree is likely to die if the pH goes above 7.5.

Before planting, enrich the soil with a few ounces each of fish emulsion, coarse phosphate rock, and granite dust, all of which are available at plant centers. These should go under the roots of the young tree to give it a healthy start.

It is possible to grow a kumquat tree in only 2 gallons of soil; however, a much larger container is suggested. A tree set in 5 or 10 gallons of soil will not need to be repotted after a few years, as it will if you use a smaller container. This avoids the sometimes deadly shock caused by transplanting.

Planting The procedure is the same as for planting grapefruit (see pp. 229–230).

Water The soil must not dry out, nor should the roots stand in water. The planter should be flooded each time water is given. The leaves should be sprayed with water weekly to keep them free of dust. If you set a tree outside during the hot summer months, check the soil for moisture daily to assure that it does not dry out. Provide inside trees with the most humid atmosphere you can manage.

Nutrition Kumquat trees are heavy feeders. They need regular doses of a complete plant food that contains magnesium, manganese, copper, and other trace elements, as well as high concentrations of nitrogen, phosphorus, and potassium. Use the NPK formula 20-20-20, and fertilize the tree once monthly, unless the tree is in dormancy. In addition, you should give the plant about 1 pound of 6 percent nitrogen carrier over the course of a year, and at least double that amount as it gets older. If blood meal, cottonseed meal, or well-rotted manure (which, by the way, is odorless) is available, covering the soil with a thin layer will help provide more nutrients and trace elements.

Temperature Kumquat trees are more resistant to cold than are the citrus trees and can withstand quite lengthy cold periods. However, they will cease to grow altogether if the temperature falls to 50 degrees or lower, so plants grown in a greenhouse may need some heat during the winter. Fruit sets very well at room temperature, but may drop if temperatures rise into the 80s for any length of time, as they may in a greenhouse. Fluctuating temperatures may bring about the same result.

Light Kumquats can be grown with relatively low light, in a sunny window, for example, or with fluorescents suspended overhead, providing 1000 foot-candles to the upper extremities but even less to the lower leaves; however, they do benefit from brighter light and, if possible, you should provide illumination of higher intensity. If you move it outside during the summer months, allow the tree to adapt to the brighter situation by placing it first in the shade, then in full sun.

The tree does best with twelve hours of light followed by twelve hours of uninterrupted darkness.

Pollination Some fruit may be produced without pollination, but the crop will increase greatly when the flowers are hand pollinated. Never use a hormone compound on kumquat blossoms, as there is some evidence that the acid contained in these compounds destroys pollen. Most growers ship trees of a size and age that should blossom and bear fruit in the first year after planting, the crop increasing in subsequent years.

Harvest After fruit is set, kumquats require about two months to develop and ripen. The flavor is best when they ripen on the tree. Ripe fruit of orange varieties may yet show some yellow and green when mature. Limequats are light yellowish green when ready. All can be removed from the tree with a gentle twist. The peel as well as the pulp is edible in all varieties and may be eaten fresh or preserved either in syrup or by being candied.

Kumquat

Lemon
(Citrus limon or
C. limonia)

Lemons were introduced to Europe at about the same time as oranges, and were brought to America by the early Spanish explorers. Because of the high acid content of the fruit and the limited number of ways in which it may be used, lemons have not been commercially planted to the same extent as oranges. But the lemon tree, which will thrive in any reasonably bright, warm, and humid situation, has long been a favorite of indoor gardeners. It is an undeniably charming house plant that provides green beauty, heady fragrance, and an abundance of fruit throughout the year for many, many years. One grower in Oregon has an indoor lemon tree that has been bearing fruit for nearly twenty years—and she provides no artificial light at all, only the sunlight coming through a large west-facing window.

Stock and Soil   Two outstanding lemon varieties are commonly offered as dwarfs: the Meyer and the Ponderosa. Developed from stock that originated in the more rigorous part of China's temperate zone, these hardy little shrubs grow about 3 feet tall. Either type will produce far more lemons than the average family can use.

Both types are evergreen, having lush foliage throughout the year. Their blossoms are pinkish-white and delectably fragrant, and either plant is likely to have ripe and unripened fruit on it at any given time, even as more blossoms are forming and opening. The Meyer produces far more lemons, but those borne by the Ponderosa are often gigantic, frequently weighing more than 3 pounds apiece.

When you order a young lemon tree, you should specify that it be grafted onto trifoliate rootstock, which produces a smaller and hardier tree. Never accept a graft made on grapefruit rootstock, which produces a shrub subject to sudden decline when it is grown indoors.

The healthy young tree you select should have the budded joint at least 6 inches above soil level. The thickness of the tree above the joint should be almost equal to the thickness of the rootstock below. If the trunk is definitely thinner, it may mean that the rootstock or bud was diseased or that the root was budded more than once. The graft should appear as a smooth joining that is well healed. Bark on the rootstock should be smooth, clean, and yellowish, never rough and graying.

It is better to obtain a large one-year tree than a tree that took two years to reach the same size. Only a healthy tree can grow fast enough to be large in a single year. A one-year-old tree can be distinguished by the leaves that will still be growing out of the trunk just below the main branches. These drop off after the first year of life. You can also determine the age of the tree by measuring the diameter of the trunk an inch above the union of the bud and the rootstock: it should be ⅜ to ¾ of an inch wide.

The young tree should have a root ball of about 12 inches. Soil inside this root ball must not be broken away by jarring or by allowing the roots to become dry. If the nursery sells bare rootstock, as many do, the roots must be kept moist with damp peat moss until planting. Bare rootstock should never be kept in pails of water, which invites fungus diseases.

Sandy loam is the best soil for growing lemons. The soil should be slightly acid, with a pH between 5.0 and 7.0. The ideal pH is 5.5 to 6.2. A pH above 7.5 will almost certainly result in the death of the tree.

The planter should be at least 18 inches wider than the root ball and deep enough to contain the roots with absolutely no crowding. By setting the planter in the largest, deepest planter your room can comfortably accommodate, you will afford it the best chance to provide the enjoyment for which it was purchased. Before planting it is wise to enrich the soil with 2 or 3 pounds of well-rotted manure, if available, as well as with a few handfuls of coarse granite dust and phosphate rock.

Planting   If the roots are bare, the procedure is as described for planting grapefruit (see pp. 229–230). The procedure for planting balled rootstock differs only in that no roots are trimmed, and after the tree is set in the soil, the burlap is untied, folded back, covered with more soil, and left to disintegrate.

Water   During the first fourteen days after it is set in the planter, the young lemon tree must be kept constantly moist. It may be necessary, during this period, to water it three or four times a week. During the remainder of its first year in the planter, you should water it, once a week or so, using up to a gallon of water each time. During the next years, water the tree somewhat less frequently, but you may have to increase the amount of water at each dose. This sounds like a large amount of water, but in reality it will barely dampen the soil in a planter of the size needed for a tree.

Water the plant slowly, so that the water does not penetrate too quickly to the bottom of the planter, beyond reach of the roots. The tree absolutely must not be watered daily, as an affliction called root rot may result. On the other hand, the soil must never be allowed to become completely dry.

When you are watering the tree, it is important that the leaves be carefully bathed by wiping. Like all evergreens, the lemon tree breathes through the pores in its leaves, so these must never be allowed to become clogged with soot or dust.

Keep the humidity as high as possible. The tree may refuse to blossom if the air is too dry, and will certainly drop its fruit under arid conditions.

Nutrition A steady supply of nitrogen is essential to the good health of a lemon tree. If you supply this in the form of well-rotted manure or manure water, trace minerals, potassium, and phosphorus will be added at the same time. The tree annually needs about ⅔ pound of nitrogen for each year of its age, which may be administered fractionally throughout the year. You can also use a 6-percent nitrogen carrier, raking it into the soil prior to watering, or you can feed the tree monthly with a 20-20-20 water-soluble plant food.

Temperature Lemon trees are injured by temperatures below 26 degrees, and fruit will drop if you expose the tree to temperatures anywhere around the freezing mark. At the other end of the scale, the fruit is easily burned by hot sun. Optimum growth occurs at exactly 70 degrees, but worthwhile production can be had at room temperature—65 to 68 degrees.

Light The light requirements of lemon trees are among the lowest of all fruit trees. Nearly normal growth results when the trees receive 1000 to 1500 foot-candles of light. They will, of course, accept much brighter light, but if you move trees outside during the summer

Lemon

months, they must be gradually shifted from shade to full sun, allowing them to adapt.

The duration of light should be twelve hours daily.

Pollination The lemon tree will produce only lightly during its first year in the planter. The waxy white blossoms are perfect flowers—capable of producing fruit without help at pollination. But you can stimulate production by hand pollination, merely touching a cotton swab to the center of each flower. Never spray these blossoms with a hormone compound, for, according to the Citrus Growers' Association, to do so will result in less fruit. After the first year production will be almost constant, and the tree will be beautiful with blossoms and fruit at all times—and potted lemon trees may live for as long as a hundred years.

Special Culture Lemon trees need more pruning than most other citrus varieties. When the tree is very young, succulent sprouts may appear on the trunk just below the main branches. While these are still small and green, they should be pinched off with the fingers (pruning shears are not necessary). A vigorous tree will also produce shoots that tend to become tangled among the main branches. These can usually be pulled down and bent to the outside, improving the structure and appearance of the tree. About once a year, as the tree ages, you should also trim away the shoots which arise from the trunk and main branches on the inside, where they are denied light.

Harvest The lemons produced by the Meyer variety will be a light, bright yellow when they are ripe, of average size and with a very thin skin. Since the Meyer is a result of long-ago crossing with orange stock, its fruit is far sweeter and less acid than most lemons, making it incomparable when used in the most ordinary ways.

The Ponderosa, on the other hand, produces gigantic, thick-skinned fruit that is highly acid. The thick peels are ideal for marmalade, and the acid juice is among the best for making fresh lemonade.

In either case, allow the fruit to remain on the tree until it is fully ripe, then pick it with a gentle twist of the hand. A lemon can remain on the tree for several weeks after it has ripened, so there is no need to rush the harvest. Such tree-ripened fruit will be far tastier and far richer in vitamin C than fruit that is picked while it is green and then ripened—as are those in the marketplace. They are even tastier because you have grown them yourself.

Lime
(Citrus aurantifolia)

The lime appears to have originated in Southeast Asia and made its way to Europe through India and Asia in the hands of Arab traders. Columbus is said to have taken it to the New World, and now in the West Indies the trees often grow wild.

Standard trees may grow 12 feet tall. However, the dwarf varieties can easily be kept pruned to a height of only 3 or 4 feet. In appearance they are very much like the lemon trees, but the white flowers are smaller and often appear in clusters.

Stock and Soil Dwarf varieties include Bearss Seedless, which produces large fruit throughout the year; Mexican Dwarf, which bears a smaller and sweeter fruit; and Rangpur, which bears one crop annually of orange-colored fruit.

Limes are extremely tolerant of soils, so any

neutral (pH 7.0) potting soil is acceptable for growing them. The amount of soil needed is a little less than that required for lemons.

Culture   Limes require less pruning than lemons. They are also less resistant to cold. They must never be exposed to temperature lower than 40 degrees. In all other respects their needs are identical to those of the lemon (see p. 240).

Harvest   Lime trees seldom bear before their third year of life, but the size of the crop increases each year thereafter and peaks around the tenth year. Most are truly everbearing, providing one large and several small crops each year. In most varieties the fruit is lemon yellow and the flesh green when it is ripe. Most uses of lime juice are too familiar to need description, but you might be interested to know that rubbing a bit on the skin promotes tanning while reducing the risk of sunburn.

Loquat
(Eriobotrya japonica)

Despite the fact that it is a native of China rather than Japan, the loquat is frequently known as the Japanese plum. People have cultivated this attractive evergreen tree since antiquity for its fruit. The tree is very fast-growing and quite attractive, and has won wide acceptance as a houseplant, perhaps because it is so easy to grow.

Stock and Soil   Loquat trees can be started from seed, but the mature trees seldom bear fruit. If the tree is to be grown for its fruit, you should start by ordering young rootstock of a dwarfed, self-pollinating variety. Half a dozen varieties are available, including Tanaka, Oliver, and Champagne. Buds that have been grafted onto quince root produce the smallest trees.

The loquat grows best in a light sandy loam, with a pH that is about neutral. If the soil is too alkaline, the tree will absolutely refuse to grow. Ordinarily, young trees sold by nurseries are of a size that require only 2 or 3 gallons of soil, but since they grow very quickly, it is better to start them in a larger pot, one that holds at least 5 gallons of soil.

Planting Roots are usually bare when the trees are shipped. Any growth from the root-stock, which will be below the union, should be trimmed away before planting. If well-rotted manure or compost is available, a pound or two of it added to the soil in the bottom of the planter will help the young tree get off to a good start. Set the tree in the soil so it is covered to the swollen union where the graft was made. Set it in a warm spot with full light, and flood the soil with water. Keep the soil very moist for the first two weeks, then reduce the water slightly.

Water The goal is to keep the soil abundantly moist without waterlogging. Since slight acidity will do the tree no harm, a layer of peat moss may be spread over the soil to help prevent evaporation. If you increase the amount of water slightly while the fruit is still on the tree, larger fruit will be produced. Remember to bathe the evergreen leaves weekly. A humidifier near the tree is helpful but not absolutely necessary.

Nutrition The loquat tree is not a heavy feeder except when it is setting fruit. A monthly feeding of a complete plant food with a formula something like 10-10-10 will serve.

After the blossoms appear and fruit is set, the size of the fruit can be increased by bimonthly feeding or by switching to a 20-20-20 fertilizer. Nutrients should be drastically reduced after the fruit has ripened, when the plant will need a period of rest.

Temperature   The tree itself is very resistant to frost and can withstand temperatures as low as 12 degrees. However, if even the lightest frost touches it, it will produce no fruit during the year that follows. Exposure to frost is a major reason that many indoor-outdoor trees fail to bear.

Temperature plays a key role in the setting of loquat fruit. Maximum fruiting will occur if you keep the temperature at 65 degrees or higher while the tree is in flower, then lower it to about 50 degrees while the fruit sets and ripens. Some fruit will set and ripen, however, under ordinary room temperature.

Light   A favorite houseplant, the loquat will thrive and blossom under a wide range of lighting conditions. It will do well if you place it in any spot that receives a few hours of sunlight each day, or under fluorescents which produce 1000 or more foot-candles of light. Set greenhouse plants as far back from the glass as possible, to protect the leaves from burning.

The loquat is a day-neutral plant. However, as it normally produces its flowers in the period from October through February, when days are short, less than twelve hours of lighting daily should induce maximum flowering.

Pollination   The flowers are yellowish white, very fragrant, about ½ inch broad, and hermaphroditic. They are borne in woolly clusters as much as 8 inches long, which may contain

Loquat

as many as a hundred flowers each. A small number of loquats may appear without hand pollination, but hand transfer of pollen will increase fruit production. Because the individual flowers are so small and fragile, try using a tiny watercolor brush as your pollinating tool. Don't fret if a few blossoms are knocked loose; some thinning is desirable, and in any case, not more than a dozen loquats will develop from each cluster of flowers.

Special culture Cut back the branches from time to time in order to keep the tree about 3 feet tall and to allow light into its center. The best time to do this is a month or so after ripe fruit has been picked, when food and water should be reduced and the plant allowed to rest. You should also remove the dead branches from older trees. And at least every third year you should lift the tree from the planter, trim its roots back a few inches, and repot it. This, too, is best done when the tree is in semidormancy.

When the tree flowers and sets fruit, the fruit size can be increased by thinning either fruits or blossoms so that only six or eight loquats mature in each cluster.

Harvest The tree will produce a small crop in its second or third year. The crop should be very substantial by the fifth or sixth year, and it will peak when the tree is between fifteen and twenty years old. The fruit is borne in clusters, is 1 to 3 inches long, and according to variety, can be pale yellow, reddish yellow, golden yellow, or orange; sometimes the colors blend. The surface is somewhat downy, and the skin has about the same texture as a plum. The flesh is cream-colored and juicy. The flavor is sweet and mildly acid, but faintly reminiscent of apple. Each fruit contains two to four hard, brown oblong seeds, which are easily removed from the flesh.

Allow the fruit to ripen on the tree. If it falls before ripening, this is a sign of insufficient water. When the fruit is ripe, the entire cluster of fruit should be snipped from the tree. The ripe fruit is generally eaten fresh for dessert, but if you cook it, be sure to pit the fruit first or else it will become bitter. The pitted fruit may be used for making jelly, jam, or preserves, following any recipe for making the same from plums. Fruit that is not fully ripe can be used to make loquat pie, similar in many respects to pie made from sour cherries.

Monstera Deliciosa

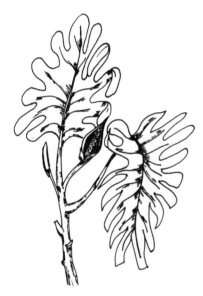

The genus *Monstera*, part of the *Arum* family, includes about thirty species of evergreen climbing vines, most of which come from the tropical jungles of South America. *M. deliciosa*, which comes from Mexico and Guatemala, is one of the most attractive of the species, and not the least of its attractions is the sweet fruit produced by the mature plant —shaped something like an ear of corn but far larger, and combining the flavors of banana and pineapple.

Probably you have seen this plant without realizing it is capable of bearing fruit. Chances are fair that you already have one in your home. It is an extremely popular houseplant, but usually under some other name. It is often sold, while it is young, as the Cut- or Split-Leaved Philodendron, Swiss Cheese Plant, or Hurricane Plant. It is an ornamental climber having large leaves that are broad with long lobes and which are curiously perforated. It is also an aroid—that is, it produces aerial roots— and it climbs by attaching these roots to any support within its reach. The vine can climb to a height of 8 feet or more if you provide proper support.

Stock and Soil Although the plant can be started from seed, seed is rarely available. Young plants, however, are frequently seen in the plant section of discount stores and you can also obtain them through any nursery that specializes in houseplants. Or if you happen to have a friend who owns one of these popular plants, you can propagate it at any time of year from stem cuttings which have two or more segments or buds. Insert the cutting in moist, sandy soil and keep the temperature at 68 degrees. The plant will root easily.

Use a slightly acid soil, with a pH around 5.5, that holds water well. Mixing equal parts of sand, peat moss, and neutral potting soil will meet these requirements very well. The plant has a relatively small root structure and does not require large amounts of soil.

Planting Although the plant will probably be potted when you buy it, you may find it necessary to transplant it after several years. The idea is to maintain a balance of 40 percent soil to 60 percent roots. The fibrous roots are easily lifted as a ball and are not easily damaged by transplanting. About 3 gallons of soil should be adequate for even the largest plant.

Water Never allow the soil to dry out completely. Like many tropical plants, *deliciosa* grows best in soil that is almost, but not quite, wet. A layer of peat moss over the soil is a good idea, since the plant can tolerate the slight acidity this will impart.

High humidity is essential to fruit production, so using a humidifier is a good idea. Mist-ing the leaves daily is also helpful. The leaves should also be bathed once a week.

Temperature   Like humidity, temperature is one of the keys to production of fruit. Fruit will set when temperatures fall as low as 65 degrees during the daytime and 55 degrees at night. You will have optimum results, however, when you keep daytime temperatures in the 70s or higher and nighttime temperatures no lower than 60 degrees. This means it should be set in the warmest spot in the home, and also means it is the ideal plant for growing in a winter-heated greenhouse or in a spot warmed by sunlight entering the home through glass. Never expose the plant to frost.

Light   Few plants have lower light requirements. It thrives under just a few hundred foot-candles of light, and it is one of the few plants that does well indoors in a north-facing window. Probably you will want to grow it in a naturally bright part of your home and reserve your light fixtures for other purposes, or beam a single incandescent growth lamp over it from a distance. If you move it outside during the summer months to take advantage of higher temperatures, or grow it in a greenhouse, set the plant in the shade or give it some protection from the direct rays of the sun. The plant blooms best when provided with short hours of light—nine hours out of each twenty-four-hour cycle.

Nutrition   The plant needs very little nutrition until it sets fruit. Feed it monthly prior to blossoming with a water-soluble plant food, the formula about 10-10-10. After the first fruit is on the vines, switch to a 20-20-20 formula and feed the plant once every other week.

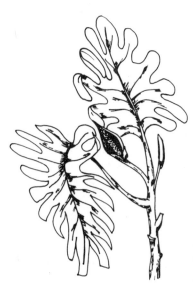

Monstera Deliciosa

Special Culture   Some of the aerial roots may attempt to enter the soil in the planter. If so, allow them to do as they wish, for they will help the plant feed. If the plant grows too tall to handle, its growing ends may be cut back. Remove any leaves that wilt immediately.

Harvest   After the plant is at least a year old, its first flowers will appear. The flowers are greenish-yellow and enclosed in a creamy white sheath that may be as much as 10 inches long. A spike rises from the çenter of this sheath. Without pollination this odd flower arrangement turns into a fruit that at first will be green and covered with scales. From the time of flowering to the maturity of the fruit takes about twelve months—a long time, admittedly, but a healthy vine may have several fruits in various stages, coming along at any time.

When it is fully mature, the green color of the fruit gives way to yellow and the scales covering the surface gradually drop off. Cut the fruit from the stem anytime after the lower half, which ripens first, has turned yellow. The fruit ripens gradually from the base upward and not all at the same time, but the ripe part can be cut away and used and the rest will ripen nicely in the refrigerator, covered with plastic food wrap. The sweetly delicious fruit is best when served cold.

Oranges
(Genus Citrus)

Most of our oranges are varieties of the species *Citrus sinensis,* the sweet or common orange. Often they are mixed in with strains of the Satsuma or Mandarin species. So many hybrids and special varieties have been involved in the development of modern orange varieties that it would be impossible to trace their lineages or to go back to their original parents.

The sweet orange probably originated somewhere in India, Thailand, or southern China. As early as the first century A.D., the Romans were wintering citrus trees inside buildings, and this method of cultivation slowly moved northward. Trees planted in English orangeries in 1526 lived more than two hundred years, finally expiring during the bitter winter of 1739. The orange remains an excellent tree for the small greenhouse. However, because of its temperature and light requirements, I don't suggest it as a plant for the indoor garden, although you can grow oranges by wintering the tree under lights and setting it outside during the summer.

If you are interested in having an indoor orange tree for its decorative value, however, you can easily grow an Otaheite orange tree. This is a true dwarf citrus fruit, seldom growing taller than 2 or 3 feet. Frequently sold as a potted plant around Christmastime, its fragrant pink and white flowers are followed by tiny oranges that hang on the tree for months. The oranges are perfectly edible but have a flavor that can only be described as insipid. Its culture is exactly the same as for growing kumquats (see pp. 232–235), except for the fact that it does not need such intense light.

Standard orange trees may grow 20 to 30 feet tall. They have waxy green leaves that are pale when they are new but which darken with age, the new leaves contrasting beautifully with the old, and pinkish-white blossoms that produce the familiar fruit. Dwarf trees offer the same beauty but grow no taller than 5 or 6 feet; with careful pruning they can be kept to 3 feet or so—suitable for even the smallest greenhouse.

Stock and Soil   It is possible to start an orange tree from seed, but for the following reason, I don't suggest it. Most orange varieties are created by grafting a cutting from one type onto rootstock from another. When seed from the resulting fruit is planted, the tree will revert to type, producing a full-size tree with blossoms that are likely to be self-sterile and incapable of producing fruit. For this reason the purchase of young rootstock is necessary.

Nearly every type of orange tree is now available in dwarf form. These include Valencia and Navel oranges, as well as the Mandarins and tangerine hybrids. They differ mainly in the type of orange they produce and the length of time required to ripen a crop. The dwarf Washington Navel ripens in only ten months, as compared to the fifteen months required by the Valencia and most of the others, so I suggest the former variety. The culture of all orange trees is so similar that they are here described as one.

The soil should be a slightly acid sandy loam. The ideal pH is around 5.5. The plant may die if the pH is higher than 7.5. Two parts potting soil, one part sand, and one part peat moss makes a good medium for growing.

Use the smallest pot that will handle the roots of the young tree. An 11-inch pot should serve for the first three years. You will need to make slight increases in the size of the pot as time goes by, but an 18-inch pot will do for a mature tree. Initial planting procedure is the same as for grapefruit (see pp. 229–230).

Water Do not allow the soil in the pot to become completely dry between waterings. Although the orange is an evergreen and does not go into true dormancy, you should reduce the water greatly for about three months each winter, allowing the soil to become almost dry before watering. Mist leaves daily and bathe them frequently. The orange will tolerate lower humidity than many other citrus trees, but high humidity is helpful for the setting and growth of fruit.

Nutrition   About once a year, remove a few inches of soil from the top of the planter and replace it with well-rotted manure or compost. The tree can also use a monthly feeding of plant food, but the nitrogen content should be low; a formula around 5-10-10 is good. Adding bone meal to the top dressing will provide much-needed calcium.

Temperature   It is temperature more than any other factor that makes the orange more suitable for a greenhouse than a light room. While the tree itself is fairly resistant to cold weather, growth is greatly retarded at temperatures lower than 50 degrees. More important to the home gardener, the orange tree needs very warm surroundings to develop its fruit properly—temperatures that are not easily provided inside most homes.

The time fruit requires to mature and ripen is determined largely by temperature. When temperatures are too low, the fruit will be small, watery, and insipid in taste. Tests by citrus growers have established that, if the *mean* temperature is lower than 65 degrees during the period of active growth, the fruit is apt to be small and bitter. When fruit is on the tree, a minimum temperature of 70 degrees and a maximum of 80 degrees is suggested, though brief spells of higher temperatures will do no harm.

A constant room temperature of 68 degrees will probably produce some oranges if all the other requirements are met, but remember that the fruit is likely to lack quality. If you live in an area where winters are short, however, and the temperature seldom drops below 50 degrees in autumn and spring, you may be able to grow reasonably good fruit by cultivating this as an indoor-outdoor tree, wintering it under lights at high room temperature. Such treatment should not destroy the quality of the fruit, nor would bringing the tree inside for a brief period of display beneath your lights.

Light Prior to blossoming the orange needs nine to twelve hours of light each day. After the blossoms open it can be given longer hours of light, but the duration should not exceed sixteen hours daily.

The fruit needs very bright light for growth and ripening. A tree can be kept alive for a few months and even made to flower by placing it beneath fluorescents that provide 1000 to 1500 foot-candles of light at the level of the upper branches, but much stronger illumination is needed for development of full-size fruit. Most experts agree that the orange needs brighter light than any other citrus to ripen its fruit. Exactly how much it needs is debatable, but probably you should not attempt to grow the fruit indoors without lights capable of producing 2000 to 4000 foot-candles. A week or two of display under less intense light will do the tree no harm, however.

Pollination The orange tree is, of course, noted for its fragrance when it is in blossom. Unlike the lemon tree, which may blossom almost continuously when conditions are favorable, the orange tree only flowers once a year, usually in the spring. The flowers form on shoots in the axils of leaves that the plant produces during the previous year. They are bisexual and may produce some fruit parthenocarpically (without hand pollination).

Orange

Never spray these blossoms with a hormone compound, as it may damage the pollen. Hand pollination will greatly increase the crop, but do not do this until the tree is two years old, as younger trees are not yet ready to bear.

Special Culture   Replace the soil around the roots annually, or at least every second year. The best time to do this is during the winter, when the tree, though it is not entirely dormant, will be resting. Giving new soil is the best way to assure this tree's nutrition.

Just remove some of the soil around the rim of the pot, then tilt the pot gently to the side. You can then easily remove the tree with a ball of soil around its roots. Any roots that are exposed and bent up against the inside of the pot should be loosened free of the soil. Prune any very long root back to two-thirds of its length. Wash and dry the inside of the pot. Fill the pot with fresh soil and pack it down firmly. When you replace the tree in the pot, put it at such a height that its topmost roots are just covered with soil when the planter is filled to within an inch or two of the top. Soil should be put in around the sides, an inch or two at a time, and rammed down with a piece of wood. When the potting is completed, loosen the top of the soil to prevents its hardening. Other citrus trees may benefit from this treatment, but they need it less frequently than the orange.

Orange trees need very little pruning. If they are left to themselves, however, they will not grow as a single stem, as most fruit trees do, but will start branching close to the union, and sprawling. Low shoots, therefore, should be removed as they appear. Branches that prevent light from reaching the fruit may be removed during the winter, when the growing tips may also be cut back to control upward and outward growth.

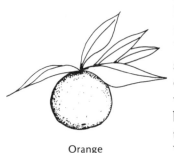

Orange

Harvest An orange tree may bear its first crop when it is three years old, but usually the first crop will be limited to a few oranges on the lower branches. Most varieties require nine months or more for fruit to mature and ripen. Thinning the fruit does not affect the size of the remaining fruit. The size of the crop should increase annually until about the tenth year, then level off.

Color is not always a sign of maturity in oranges. Their skins contain green, yellow, and orange pigments. The green usually fades out as the fruit ripens, but if fruit is left on the tree for a long period of time, the green color may reappear in fruit that is perfectly ripe. Testing by taste is the only sure way to determine ripeness.

Oranges with tight skins, such as navels and Valencias, are picked by freeing them from the stem with a slight twist of the hand. Those with loose skins, such as Mandarins, Temples, and tangerines, should be picked by using clippers to cut the stem near its juncture with the fruit; pulling these free may damage the branch and cause it to be attacked by fungus.

Passion Fruit
(Passiflora edulis)

Also known as purple granadilla and as water lemon, this plant is an evergreen climber native to Brazil. Its most popular common name, passion fruit, was given to it by early Spanish explorers because its flowers, which have a multitude of raylike filaments, suggested to them the symbolic rays used by medieval and Renaissance artists to represent the passion of Christ.

The vine has dark green leaves, each with three lobes, and it climbs by means of tendrils. Flowers are about 2 inches wide, white, and topped by a crown of purple and white. A vine is capable of growing as high as 20 or 30 feet

but is easily kept to 5 or 6 feet by careful pruning. A single vine has been known to bear in a
single year more than 40 pounds of fruit—considered a delicacy because of its unique flavor—and the plant is very easy to grow.

Seeds and Soil Seed dealers offer seed for
starting several members of this large genus,
which includes four hundred species. All are
sold as Passion Fruit or Passion Flower, and,
indeed, may species other than *edulis* do produce edible fruit. The species *edulis,* however,
is considered superior.

Passion-fruit vines grow well in any rich
loam with a pH between 6.0 and 8.0. A good
growing medium consists of two parts loam,
one part peat moss, and one part fine sand.
Manure, if it is available and well-rotted, can
be mixed into the soil prior to planting. A
young plant needs only a 7- or 8-inch pot, but
later the entire root system should be lifted
and set in a deep pot with a diameter of 18
inches or so, where it can stay for years if you
replace the top soil each year.

Planting Germination is poor, especially if
the seeds are old, so start several seeds. Sow
them ½ inch deep, and then place the pot in a
warm spot. Germination occurs in two to
three weeks. Seedlings should be given twelve
hours of light daily, but not light that is too
intense—about 1000 foot-candles will do. If
you want more than one vine, extra seedlings
are easily transplanted when they are about 2
inches tall. However, after the first vine has
grown, more may be propagated by vegetative
means. Make cuttings in early summer after
the vine has flowered. Just select a pencil-
thick branch with at least three buds, cut it
below the lowest joint, and then insert the cut-

ting in moist, sandy soil. A rooted plant will be available for transplanting in about three months.

Water Water plants only lightly during the first few months of life, and keep the soil a little on the dry side. After that keep the soil evenly moist and never allow it to dry out completely. Mist the plant daily. After the plant flowers, gradually reduce the water, keeping the soil almost completely dry while the plant is dormant for about three months, then increasing it again as new growth starts.

Nutrition Feed the plant weekly while it is actively growing, usually from April through September, using a fairly mild plant food of the formula 10-10-10. Following fruiting, give the plant no food at all until new growth starts, about four months later.

Temperature Room temperature—68 degrees by day and 55 degrees by night—is nearly ideal. High temperatures cause the vines to grow very luxuriously but then they produce very little fruit, so if you grow passion fruit in a greenhouse, it must be kept cool. Outside plants are killed if the temperature dips to 25 degrees.

Light Like many jungle plants, the passion-fruit vine does not need exceedingly bright light. If you set it outside it will grow in the shade. In the greenhouse it should go against the back wall. Inside plants will grow, blossom, and bear fruit if you provide them with about 1000 to 1500 foot-candles of light. Light should not exceed twelve hours daily.

The biggest problem is getting light to all parts of the plant. Because of its height, artificial lights placed overhead will not provide for the lower parts of the plant. Probably the most workable solution is to let the plant grow up a support placed close beside a vertical light fixture, or allow it to vine like a living curtain in front of a sunny window, using artificial lights for increased brightness and greater day length.

Pollination   Stamens and pistils are contained in the same flower. They are so arranged that pollination may occur at the slightest movement, or when the plant is sprayed with a hormone compound (see pp. 77–79). Several horticulturists have suggested that using such a compound increases fruiting.

In some instances, however, the plant produces pollen while the pistils are not receptive. The reasons for this are far from understood. The flowers remain open for several days, however, so the problem is easily overcome by repeating the process of hand pollination daily, until they close and drop from the vine.

Special Culture   Pruning should be done in the winter, while the plant is dormant. To prune, completely remove any weak growth and cut the strong vines by about one third. Since the fruit is borne on new shoots which arise from the older vines, this increases fruiting by encouraging new growth while removing old wood. Even with such heavy pruning the vines need some support to climb, but this is no problem since they will cling to anything that you provide, even a taut wire.

Harvest   From blossom to fruit requires about three months. When it is ripe and ready to be picked, the fruit is deep purple in color, about the size of a very small egg, and has a somewhat leathery rind. Largest fruit may weigh about 2 ounces.

The fruits are round to oval in shape. They contain numerous edible seeds that are surrounded with juicy orange pulp that is slightly acid but extremely fragrant and flavorful. The rind, which is also edible, is high in pectin and makes a good jelling agent. The fruit itself is generally served like strawberries, with sugar and cream, but is also excellent in jelly or preserves. The juice is frequently added to punch.

The plant will produce only lightly, if at all, during the first year. However, it will fruit abundantly by the second year of life and each year thereafter until about its eighth year of life, when production will start to diminish and the plant will need to be replaced.

Peach
(Amygdalus persica)

Peaches originated somewhere in the Orient, probably in China or Persia, and were introduced to the West around the beginning of the Christian era. Their cultivation spread rapidly, and they were not only among the first fruit trees brought to the New World but were also among the first fruit trees to be grown in greenhouses. Only a few varieties need cross-pollination, and all the dwarf varieties now offered by plant suppliers are self-fruitful, so the peach is the very best of the deciduous fruit trees for the apartment gardener. However, like most deciduous fruit trees, it requires an environment that is hard to provide inside the home, so I suggest it here as a plant for growing outdoors or in the home greenhouse, though it is possible to bring it inside for periods of display beneath artificial light.

Your peach tree may also bear nectarines. The two fruits are botanically the same, except that nectarines lack the fuzz that covers peach skin. Nectarines have been known to grow from peach pits, and peaches from nectarine pits, without cross-pollination. The two have even been known to grow on the same tree. The scientific community has not offered any explanation for this phenomenon. Culture of the two is nearly identical.

While standard peach trees may grow as tall as 20 feet, the dwarf varieties seldom grow taller than 6 feet, and with judicious pruning they may be kept much smaller. They are easily trained to grow in a variety of shapes, and their fragrant pinkish-white flowers, appearing singly or in small clusters, are followed by fruit that is popular throughout the world.

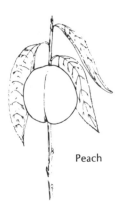

Peach

Stock and Soil It is extremely important to select a variety of peach suited to the section of the country in which you live—even if you plan to grow the tree in a greenhouse. Climate is the single most important factor in growing peaches. Hundreds of peach varieties have been developed and new ones are constantly coming on the market, each one suited to a special part of the country. By ordering a variety with known requirements, you can more easily provide for the needs of the plant and grow it successfully. The information beneath the temperature heading will make the reasons for this clear. The peach is hence best not started from a pit, since it is unlikely that you could know the temperature requirements of the parent tree and you might not be able to make it bear fruit. A tree grown from a peach pit might also not come true to the parent of the fruit from which the pit was obtained, and the flowers may be self-sterile, requiring the presence of a pollinator.

Dealers always sell stock according to the

temperature zone in which the buyer lives. By
ordering a tree suited to your part of the country and exposing it to ordinary winter conditions—which, as you will see, are essential to
fruiting—you can be sure you are providing
the temperatures required for the production
of fruit. After you have some experience, you
may want to try growing varieties that are native to other areas, but choosing a type developed for your own region is the best way to
get started. Since the peach is a tree you
should grow with the seasons, order stock in
time for planting in the spring.

Soil should be neutral, so commercial potting soil is a good medium. However, adding
some sand to the soil for better drainage is a
good idea, and so is putting the soil over a few
inches of gravel or broken crockery, as no
peach tree will tolerate water standing around
its roots. The planter should be about 18
inches deep, and a pot of that same diameter
will accommodate a tree until it is five or six
years old. Enriching the soil with a pound or
two of well-rotted manure prior to planting is
also a good idea. Stirring in a few ounces of
bone meal will provide further nutrition for
the young tree.

Planting Trim away any damaged roots, cutting them back until living tissue is exposed.
Fill the pot with soil, then dig out a hole large
enough to accept the roots without crowding.
Set the tree so that the bud union will be at or
near the surface of the soil. Cut the tree back
to about 24 inches if it is taller, making the cut
just above the branch. All branches should
be trimmed back to about 1-inch stubs. Do
not cut them back flush with the trunk, for
that will damage the buds from which new
branches grow. Start training the tree during

the first summer, as described under Special Culture. If you grow the tree outside, set it where it will receive all the sunlight possible.

Water The soil should always be moist to a good depth. To induce growth, spray water on the leaves of the tree and even the leafless shoots frequently during the spring and summer months, but never on cold days or when the tree is in blossom. Never syringe the tree while fruit is ripening. If the soil becomes completely dry and you then water the plant while fruit is on the tree, the fruit may split or drop from the branches. The tree will need more water while fruit is swelling than at any other time. A mulch of manure or compost will help retain moisture while providing nutrients each time the plant is watered. After the fruit ripens, gradually reduce water to almost none as the plant slips into its winter dormancy.

Nutrition Peaches do not require large amounts of phosphorus or potassium, though their potassium needs are the higher of the two. A yearly light application of rock phosphate and granite dust over the top of the soil will provide all that is needed. Nitrogen, however, is another matter, and when it is given is of extreme importance.

Supply nitrogen at the rate of 1 ounce of pure nitrogen for each year of the tree's age, up until the tree is receiving a pound of pure nitrogen each year. An ounce of nitrogen is found in 8 ounces of blood meal or 16 ounces of bone meal, but as the tree grows older, using a concentrated nitrogen carrier is preferable because working the blood meal or bone meal into the limited amount of soil in a pot becomes nearly impossible.

The idea is to encourage maximum growth

during spring and summer; therefore, begin heavy feeding as soon as the plant awakens from its winter dormancy and shows signs of new growth, and continue it until the fruit sets and ripens. Then, as fall and winter approach, reduce the feeding so that the plant lives during dormancy on the nutrients that are already in the soil. If the soil is topped with manure, even that should be removed during dormancy. If you feed the plant during the winter months, you will absolutely destroy any chance of having fruit during the following year, and most likely you will kill the tree. For this reason time-release plant foods must never be used to feed a peach tree. Resume feeding in early March.

Peach

Temperature One reason the peach tree is not really suited for growing indoors is that it needs winter chilling before fruit can be set. Unless the trees have a certain number of hours of winter cold—750 to 1150 hours below 45 degrees, according to variety—their winter rest period is not complete and they refuse to set fruit. Within certain limits, trees will accept a shorter chilling period with the temperatures going below 45 degrees and staying there, than when they drop below that at night and rise during the day. If you grow the tree in a greenhouse, you must provide this chilling by turning off the heat or by setting the tree outside during the winter dormancy period.

There are very few areas in the country that do not have a suitable winter climate for growing some variety of peaches. In areas where there are fewer than 750 hours below 45 degrees, as in Hawaii and a few parts of Florida, Texas, and California, peaches cannot be grown at all. On the other hand, outside peach trees will not survive where winter temperatures regularly fall to 15 degrees below zero during the winter months. Alaska, northern New England, and the upper fringes of the Plains States are too cold for outside peach trees. But in all other parts of the country, you can grow the fruit by ordering a tree suited to your region and exposing it to the normal conditions of winter.

After the winter dormancy is complete and flowering occurs, the tree must once again be protected from cold. Blossoms on the tree may be damaged by temperatures of 25 to 30 degrees. If a sudden cold spell is predicted after the blossoms are on, some provision must be made for protecting outside trees.

Summer temperatures are less important to peaches. Fruit ripens best at about 75 degrees, but lower temperatures only slow the ripening process; they will not stop it altogether. After fruit sets on the tree, it will ripen quite nicely at room temperature or slightly lower—which explains those peaches you may have seen growing on trees displayed under lights at shopping malls and in other commercial buildings.

Light   Light is another reason why it is best not to attempt to grow this as a completely indoor tree, since at this point very little is known about the light needs of the deciduous trees, including the peach. We lack information especially in the area of photoperiodism.

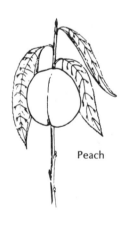

Peach

Many plant scientists suspect that the deciduous trees begin to measure the total hours of light and darkness only after the winter chilling requirement has been fulfilled, and that the hours of each are accumulated as if the tree were banking them. The tree then blossoms, according to this theory, only after a sufficient total of each has accumulated.

The fact that most peach trees blossom very

early in the year, while days remain short, strongly indicates that the plant would show a preference for less than twelve hours of light during each twenty-four-hour cycle, as would the fact that peach trees grown in greenhouses regularly blossom without the help of artificial light to extend the day length. Solid data is lacking, however.

Even in the popular gardening literature, there are no accounts of peach trees being grown entirely under artificial light; at least not any that I have been able to locate. The noted British horticulturist Alan Simmons, in his book *Growing Unusual Fruit,* does state that the nectarine has been grown in sun rooms with supplemental artificial lighting Since the culture of the two fruits is identical, this would indicate that the same is possible with the peach. However, Simmons provides no information regarding the intensity or duration of light, so any attempt to grow the peach under artificial light alone must be regarded as experimental at best, and dangerous to the tree in all probability.

That the tree can be maintained at least for a few days under artificial light, however, is well known. If it is bathed in light of 1000 to 1500 foot-candles, the tree will stay healthy for quite some time and fruit will continue to ripen. The trees you see in those commercial buildings are greenhouse trees brought in for display, and you may choose to do the same with your containerized peach tree. However, you should not attempt it for more than two or three weeks at a time, and at the first sign of leaf drop, return the tree to a healthier environment.

Pollination The flowers are perfect, which means that, even in the greenhouse, some fruit may set without hand pollination. All trees—

even those grown outside and especially in the city, where few bees are likely to be present—will benefit from hand pollination. It must be done with care, however, for the blossoms are easily dislodged.

Special Culture   Be certain to remember that the peach needs a period of winter dormancy. When fall comes, after the fruit has ripened and the leaves fall from the tree, reduce food and water and arrange for the tree to receive its winter chill. This is absolutely essential.

Thinning is important to fruit production, and young trees, especially, should not be allowed to overbear. Most young trees will drop some fruit during June or early July; however, more thinning may be required. The best rule is to leave one peach for each 4 inches of branch. Or you may also calculate the proper crop by leaf growth, leaving one peach for every 50 to 75 leaves.

Peach trees need little pruning after the first year; what pruning is done would be mainly for shaping the tree. After bearing starts, terminal growth should be about 6 inches per year. If growth is greater than that, the nutrients should be reduced; if less, they may need to be increased.

Harvest   Bearing starts in the third year after planting and peaks when the tree is about twelve years old. The tree may live much longer, but is really ready to be replaced after this peak has been reached. A dwarf tree may produce 2 or even 3 bushels of fruit each year if conditions are ideal.

The length of time required for fruit to set and ripen varies not only according to variety, but also according to the temperature of the air. Fruit is fully ripe when the green color in the skin changes to yellow and when the flesh yields to a light pressure of the thumb. Peaches that ripen on the tree are far sweeter and less acid than those that are picked while they are green.

Remove the peach from the tree with a slight twisting motion. A direct pull will bruise the fruit and cause it to spoil quickly. Unbruised fruit may be stored for several days in a cool spot.

Pineapple
(Ananas comosus)

The pineapple is one of the most beautiful of the fruit-bearing plants, its fruit one of the most delicious, and under the right conditions it is one of the easiest to grow. However, because it requires about fourteen months from planting until harvest, the pineapple is a plant you will want to grow for its tropical beauty rather than its food value—with the aromatic fruit a tasty reward for your care and attention.

The pineapple is a member of the Bromelia family, which includes many air plants. Pineapple, however, is strictly a terrestial member of the family, a perennial herb that sends up a beautiful rosette of stiff, spiny leaves with prickly edges.

Native to South America, the early Spanish explorers who discovered the pineapple were so impressed by the fragrant fruit that they took samples of it around the globe with them and left shoots of it to be planted in many lands. By 1555 it was known in Europe; by 1605 the Portuguese had taken it to India; and by 1789 it was so popular in England as a greenhouse plant that several booklets had been published describing its cultivation. It may be grown under artificial light alone, as an indoor-outdoor plant, or, of course, in the

Pineapple

home greenhouse. The size of the fruit depends on intensity of light, temperature, and the proper induction of flowering, described here under Special Culture.

Cuttings and Soil   Select a pineapple from the store, then cut off its tops and remove all bits of white or yellow pulp. Set this in a warm place for about a week; allow it to dry thoroughly before planting. Later, when your plant has grown to maturity, it will send up a sucker from its lower leaf axils, which you may remove and use for starting another plant. A cutting from the top of the fruit, however, remains the best way for home gardeners to start the plant.

Pineapples need an acid soil with a pH between 5.5 and 6.0. Ideally, the soil should be sandy and enriched with as much rotted organic matter as it will readily hold. Since the pineapple roots will eventually penetrate about 14 inches downward into this soil, the soil should be a little deeper than that, placed over a little gravel or broken crockery so that water will never be allowed to stand around the tips of the roots. Give each plant an individual pot at least 12 inches in diameter.

Planting   Do not place the planting piece too deeply in the soil. The tip must be raised sufficiently so that sand cannot sift into the bud, which will injure or kill it. To prevent this, after removing the pulp, the tip—the hollow part of the top—may be filled with a bulky organic matter such as cottonseed meal or fertilizer that has a base of tobacco stems.

During the first few months of its life, the pineapple plant has only a few roots. Thus, at this time, the plant food, which ideally should have a base of cottonseed meal or tobacco stems, should be applied sparingly near the main stem or sprinkled lightly in the lower leaf axils. As the plant grows larger, the roots will fill the spaces between them and the plant can be fed like any other, spreading the nutrients over the entire planter surface.

Water   The moisture requirements of pineapples are among the most flexible of all plants. When grown in a pot, they are best watered with frequency, keeping the soil moist but never soggy. Bathing the leaves with water once a week will be beneficial, as will an automatic mister set close beside the plant to provide high humidity. Water should be greatly reduced so that the soil is allowed to become nearly dry when fruit is on the plant and starting to ripen.

Nutrition   The pineapple needs relatively little food. If a layer of tobacco stems, cottonseed meal, or well-rotted manure can be kept over the soil, the plant will receive plenty of nutrition as you water it. If not, give it a monthly feeding of liquid manure or any water-soluble food that is not extremely high in nitrogen.

Temperature   The pineapple plant can survive exposure to temperatures as low as 28 degrees. But if it is exposed to temperature of less than 55 degrees, its growth will stop and it will never bear fruit. Fruit can be grown at the normal room temperature of 68 degrees, but fruit size increases when the temperature is 70 degrees or higher. This means it is to your advantage to move the plant outside during the hottest months of summer, unless the plant is growing in a greenhouse, where the high temperatures will be ideal. Be sure to have the plant inside before the approach of cool weather.

Light   There are reports of pineapples having been grown and made to bear fruit under 1000 foot-candles of light. However, as I have noted earlier, fruit produced under such conditions will be small and the plant will be weak and spindly. The size of the fruit is directly related to the development of the foliage, and the foliage needs brighter light for proper development. At 4000 foot-candles the growth will be entirely normal and the fruit as large as any grown on a tropical plantation. Worthwhile fruit can probably be grown under light half that intense.

If you have no greenhouse or elaborate light arrangement capable of producing those high intensities, you can partially compensate for the lack by providing long hours of light—sixteen hours or so each—since this will stimulate foliage growth and will not prevent flowering. When the time comes to induce flowering, reduce light to twelve hours daily, which is the photoperiod under which the pineapple flowers best. Setting the plant outside in full sun during the summer is another way to stimulate growth.

Special Culture   As the plant grows, it will send up a beautiful rosette of leaves, and from the center of these will rise a stem that may grow as high as 4 feet. In about the sixth month of life, a spike of flowers should develop near the tip of this stem, surmounted by yet another tuft of leaves. These blossoms are intended by nature to coalesce into one mass with the stem and form the fleshy fruit we savor as the pineapple. It follows, then, that the fruit cannot be produced unless these blossoms open, and that the greater the mass of these blossoms, the larger the fruit they will form. Blossom production, and thus fruit production, can be stimulated by a method long used by growers of pineapples and other bromelias.

After the plant sends up its flower stalk, slice a large apple in half and place the halves, cut side up, close beside the plant. Cover the entire plant with a large plastic bag and leave the bag in place for about two weeks. Gases given off by the apple slices will stimulate flowering. Remove the bag as soon as the flower cluster is red-violet in color. Failure to flower is the major difficulty those who try to grow the pineapple encounter, and this technique almost always does away with the problem.

Harvest The first pineapple should be ready to cut twelve to fourteen months after planting, but may be left on the stem as long as sixteen months. When you are harvesting it, use a sharp knife to cut through the stem just under the fruit, being careful not to damage the rest of the plant. If you leave it in place and give it proper care on a continuing basis, the plant will produce fruit for another two years, perhaps longer.

The first crop will be a single pineapple. During the second year, however, the plant may send up more than one stem, each capable of becoming a pineapple. Multiple crops, however, are rare.

After the first pineapple has been cut, a new shoot will appear and produce the next crop in a period varying from six to twelve months. Cut this exactly like the first.

A pineapple ripens from the bottom up, and the lower part of the fruit is always sweeter than the top. Its sweetness increases greatly if it ripens on the plant, so never be too quick about cutting it. If a harvested pineapple

Pineapple

tastes unripe or too acid, it can be quickly ripened by cutting off the crown, but it will not keep as well after this is done.

Pineapple Guava

(Psidium guajava)

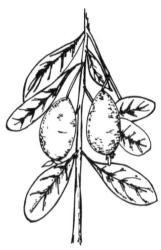

Known also as the feijoa, this small tree or evergreen shrub is not really one of the guavas, though it is closely related to them. Actually a member of the myrtle family and native to South America, the pineapple guava was known to the Aztecs as the sand plum and was among the first plants the Spanish conquistadores transported back to the Old World. It can grow under a wide variety of conditions but is very fast-growing and needs frequent pruning to keep it small enough for the home garden.

Seeds and Soil   The named varieties include Andre, Coolidge, and Choice. Seed is usually obtainable from suppliers in Florida and California, where the pineapple guava is grown commercially. Seed taken from the fresh fruit may also be used to start the plant and should be used as soon as possible, for it does not keep very well.

Soil should be neutral and slightly sandy. An ideal mix is four parts commercial potting soil, one part sand, and one part well-rotted manure or compost. Enriching the soil lightly with fish emulsion or bone meal prior to planting will cause faster growth and cause the tree to bear at a younger age. The tree needs only a pot with a diameter of 10 inches or so during the first year, but by its fourth year it will need to be transplanted into a large pot or tub with a diameter of no less than 18 inches and soil about that deep.

Planting   Plant the seed ¼ inch deep, preferably in the pot where it will grow for the first year. Set the pot in the brightest spot in the warmest room. Keep the soil moist until germination occurs—about two to three weeks—then reduce the water and let the soil become a little dryer while the plant passes through the tender seedling stage. Chances of growing the pineapple guava are always improved if the seed is started in the spring, for the seed may resist germination at other times of the year.

Water The pineapple guava needs more water than most other fruits. After the tree passes the seedling stage, keep the soil moist at all times, reducing the water only during the winter months. When the plant is actively growing, it will probably require water at least once a week. Humidity should be kept very high, and the leaves, which are light green with reddish veins, should be sprayed with water frequently.

Nutrition During the period of active growth, which begins late in February and continues into late autumn, feed the tree every six to eight weeks. The nutrient formula may be as high as 20-20-20. A scattering of rotted manure, fish emulsion, cottonseed meal, or bone meal, scratched into the soil above the roots, will provide further nutrition but should not be given too frequently. Discontinue all feeding from November through February.

Temperature The pineapple guava will grow and bear well as long as the average temperature is above 60 degrees; if the average falls below that for any length of time, the tree may go into a sudden decline and die. It will produce more and larger fruit when summer temperatures are very high, however—as in a greenhouse or on a patio—and winter temperatures should not drop below 45 degrees.

Light   The tree will not only grow under relatively low light—1000 to 1500 foot-candles —but will also flower and produce fruit. However, fruit size and overall growth is greatly stimulated by a brighter situation, especially during the period when the fruit is on the branches and swelling to size. If you grow the tree indoors, then, it is a good idea to move it outside when temperatures are high and the summer sun is at its brightest. The plant flowers best when it receives twelve hours of light daily but will benefit from longer hours of light after the blossoms drop and the fruit sets.

Pollination   The flowers will appear from spring to midsummer. They are white, thick, about 1½ inches in diameter, and borne singly or in clusters. These thick petals, by the way, are perfectly edible; many growers consider them a gourmet treat. Sweet in taste, they are most frequently used to add color and flavor to salads. The flowers are hermaphroditic and will set some fruit without hand pollination, but some growers report that fruiting increases if the flowers are sprayed with a hormone compound (see pp. 77–79). Do not use such a compound on flowers that are to go into salads. Hand pollination, simply by touching a cotton swab to the center of each blossom, is suggested.

Special Culture   The tree has a tendency to produce suckers near the base of the trunk, and these should always be removed as soon as they appear. Pruning should be done in January or February. The tree accepts pruning readily, so it can easily be kept to the size of a

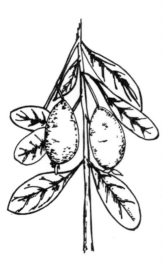

Pineapple Guava

small shrub. Every third year or so, remove the tree from the pot and trim back the roots to about two thirds of their length, to prevent overcrowding.

Harvest If light is adequate and temperatures high, the first fruit should be ready three to four months after the opening of the flowers. The tree will be at peak production by its fourth year and should bear for many years thereafter.

The fruit varies considerably in its form. Some trees produce fruit that is nearly round, while others bear fruit that is oblong. Fruit ranges in size from 1 to 4 inches in length. The skin surface may be smooth or ridged, but it is always waxy. The color of the flesh may be white, pink, yellow, or red. Most fruit has a sweet but mildly tangy flavor, which is often described as a cross between strawberry and pineapple.

The fruit is best when slightly soft to the touch, and it should not be plucked from the tree until it is in this state. The entire fruit is edible—the papery skin and the numerous seeds as well as the pulp. It may be eaten out of hand, sliced and served with cream, stewed, preserved, or made into pies, and it is frequently used to make a jelly that is delicious when served with lamb, pork, or venison.

Strawberries

(Fragaria chiloenisis)
(everbearing)

The origin of the name of our most popular small fruit is a matter of debate among those who concern themselves with such things. Some say it derives from the Old English for strew—"strewberry"—because of its habit of spreading over the ground. For the same reason others insist that the name was originally "strayberry." Still others attribute the popular name to the fact that straw has long served as

Strawberry

mulch for protecting the plants in outdoor gardens.

No matter what the origin of the popular name, the Latin name for strawberry, *Fragaria*, has an uncontested meaning. It signifies a pleasant odor, calling attention to one of the strawberry's most cherished attributes and one of many reasons for adding it to the apartment garden.

Not too long ago such cultivation would have been impractical. Although strawberries were known to the Romans, who eagerly picked them from the wild, strawberry cultivation has been practiced for less than two centuries, with the first hybrids appearing near Boston in 1830. It was not until this century that plants with hermaphroditic flowers—nearly essential to indoor cultivation—were developed, and until about twenty years ago such plants could be difficult to obtain. Today there are hundreds of strawberry varieties, almost all of which produce perfect, or self-pollinating, blossoms, and strawberry cultivation is easier than ever before.

Plants and Soil   Your success with strawberries will depend on selecting the right variety. Most strawberries are borne on plants that grow at the end of long runners sent forth by older plants. Because of the limited amount of space available to the indoor gardener, however, the runnerless varieties are preferable.

The plants must also be of an everbearing variety, because of the problem of photoperiodism. Not only are the everbearing varieties capable of producing three or even four crops each year and are thus more worthwhile to grow, but they are also day-neutral plants and will bloom with any reasonable day length. Many of the standard strawberry varieties are short-day plants, but with many others the photoperiod has not been established. Garden centers offer dozens of everbearing runnerless varieties, but Twentieth Century and Rich Red are two of the most popular.

Plants should be one-year stock. Look for healthy tops with a few green leaves, moderately strong crowns, and vigorous tassels of straw-colored or white roots arising directly below the crowns. Blackened crowns or wiry roots indicate older plants or some kind of injury.

Any soil except that which is very sandy may be used for growing strawberries. The very best soil is that which is loose, fertile, and slightly acid, with a pH between 5.0 and 7.0. Add a little lime to the soil if the pH is lower than 5.0. Humus may be added to the soil in the form of sawdust, wood shavings, or leaves, and the soil should also be well enriched with nitrogen prior to planting.

For growing strawberries you do not need deep soil. The plants, however, do need some space between them (about 6 inches from crown to crown), so only a few plants may be grown in a window box or other standard planter. Plants grown in ordinary planters should be set exactly as deep as they grew in the nursery. All the roots, right up to the shoulder, should be covered, but the crown of leaves should be above the soil. Give each plant a thorough soaking as soon as it is set, and keep the soil very moist until the plants are well started.

If you want to keep yourself well supplied with fresh strawberries, however, you should consider building an old-fashioned strawberry barrel. Such a barrel serves as a vertical garden, one that is not only useful and ornamental but that also provides an interesting conversation piece. Some years ago the Federal Cooperative Extension Service at Corvallis, Oregon, published these instructions for making one:

"Use a barrel made of oak or any other solid material. Bore two or three 1½- to 2-inch holes in the bottom for drainage. With the same auger, bore a series of holes spaced 10 to 12 inches apart in a circle 6 to 8 inches above the bottom of the barrel. Six to 8 inches above these, make another series of holes staggered at least 3 inches to one side of the first holes. Repeat this process up the side of the barrel, making the last series 6 to 8 inches below the top. Paint the inside of the barrel with a wood preservative.

It is best to install some mechanism by which you may easily revolve the barrel. You may then turn it frequently so that all the plants receive light that is more nearly equal. This may be accomplished by mounting the barrel on a large set of coasters or rollers, a turntable, or a similar device. Strawberry barrels with such devices built in are sometimes available at garden centers.

At the bottom of the barrel, place a layer of gravel, broken crockery, or brick. Fill the bottom of the barrel to the level of the first holes with soil. Pat this layer of soil firm, and you are ready to proceed with the planting.

Place a young strawberry plant on this layer of soil, so the crown of the plant protrudes from one of the holes. Carefully spread the roots and press them into the soil inside the barrel. Repeat this procedure until each of the holes in the lower circle is filled by a plant. Add soil to the level of the next circle of holes. This process will be followed until the soil is built to the top of the barrel, when four or five plants will be set in a circle at the top of the barrel. But before the barrel is filled, you should install the automatic watering system, which is one of the most important features of the strawberry barrel.

After the first third of the barrel has been filled with soil and plants, place a pipe, tile, or wooden tube up the center. This pipe or tube should be 3 or 4 inches in diameter and well perforated with a series of small holes. Its upper end should be flush with the top of the barrel. The small holes will admit life-giving air and water to the soil into the barrel and will carry nutrients to the plants.

When the barrel has been filled, thoroughly moisten the soil by pouring water into the central pipe. Soil should be wet to the touch without being waterlogged. After this first watering fill the central pipe with a loose mixture of straw and high-nitrogen plant food. The water will wash through these nutrients each time the barrel is irrigated, carrying some of the food to the roots of the plants."

Water It is difficult to provide strawberries with too much water, especially when they are young or setting fruit. Keep the soil damp enough so that it will form a ball when squeezed. Soil that crumbles between the fingers needs more water. The water should be reduced during the winter months, when, as a part of the natural cycle, the plants will be resting.

Strawberry

Nutrition Strawberries require fair amounts of nitrogen. If the barrel planter is used, you can provide this by filling the central pipe with fish emulsion, blood meal, cottonseed meal, or water-soluble fertilizer mixed with straw. If they are raised in a standard planter, the plants should be fed biweekly with plant food that contains 15 or 20 percent nitrogen.

Reduce feeding for three or four months each winter.

Temperature Strawberries will grow quite well at ordinary room temperatures—65 to 68 degrees—though optimum growth occurs when temperatures are a few degrees higher. Greenhouse temperatures should never be allowed to exceed 90 degrees. Berry production is stimulated by cooler nighttime temperatures—50 to 55 degrees. If you grow plants outdoors, do not expose them to severely cold weather.

Light The plants need about 1500 foot-candles of light in order to grow, blossom, set, and ripen fruit. Simply because of its shape, there can be problems in providing this much light to all the plants in a strawberry barrel, so it is best to use it in a light room, a home greenhouse, a sunny spot on the patio, or, perhaps, in a bay window with supplemental lighting. If you use overhead lighting that is bright enough to provide 1000 foot-candles to the lowermost plants, these may produce some berries, but the size and number will be greatly reduced.

If there is any doubt about the intensity of the light, you can compensate, at least in part, by providing long hours of light—twelve or sixteen hours daily—since the plants will bloom on any day length. However, even though the everbearing strawberries are day neutral, maximum flowering occurs when the plants receive adequate light that is less than twelve hours in duration. After the berries are on the plants, flavor may be improved by providing longer hours of light.

Strawberry

Pollination The first blossoms will appear about thirty days after planting. These should be pinched off and not allowed to set fruit. About four or five weeks later the next blossoms will appear and will be truly perfect, capable of setting fruit without hand pollination. However, you may increase the size and number of the berries by hand pollination, or by two applications of hormone compound (see pp. 77–79), applying this first to the open blossoms and then, later, to the developing berries.

Harvest The berries mature about thirty days after the blossoms open. The first crop will be smaller and less sweet than those produced in the second crop, three or four months later. After this first cycle the plants should produce two crops of large, juicy berries each year, with a smaller crop of somewhat inferior berries appearing between these two. It will no longer be necessary to pinch away any of the blossoms.

Peak production occurs during the first year and drops by about half during the second year; plants need to be replaced by the third year. A large strawberry barrel can hold as many as fifty plants, and these, under ideal circumstances, can produce 3 quarts of berries a day over a span of three weeks, so the strawberry barrel is certainly a worthwhile addition to your indoor garden.

Allow berries to ripen on the plants. When you pick them, grasp them by the stem and pull them away with a gentle twisting motion. Do not pull them off the stems. If you remove the stems before the berries are washed, a much higher loss of vitamins, nutrients, and flavor occurs than if you remove the stems after washing.

The many delicious ways of using strawberries need little description. However, the leaves of the plant provide a second crop that is almost always overlooked by gardeners. A fragrant and bracing tea can be made by covering a cupful of the leaves with 4 cups of boiling water, then allowing them to steep for five minutes; and the fresh leaves also provide a delicious, if unusual, salad green, which is particularly tasty when topped with a thick and creamy dressing. Such bonuses make the strawberry one of the most welcome additions to your apartment garden.

Building Your Own Greenhouse

Deck (or balcony) Greenhouse

Materials needed:

FOR WALL AND ROOF PANELS

14 pcs. 1″ X 2″ X 72″
16 pcs. 1″ X 2″ X 22½″
4 pcs. 1″ X 2″ X 34½″
6 pcs. 1″ X 2″ X 48″
8 pcs. 2″ X 2″ X 22½″
2 pcs. 2″ X 2″ X 34½″

2 pcs. 2″ X 2″ X 24″
1 pc. 2″ X 2″ X 36″
2 pcs. 2″ X 2″ X 24″
1 pc. 2″ X 2″ X 36″
1 pc. 1″ X 1″ X 87″

FOR FOUNDATION

2 pcs. 2″ X 4″ X 87″
2 pcs. 2″ X 4″ X 80½″

2 pcs. 2″ X 4″ X 46″

FOR DOOR (OPTIONAL)

2 pcs. 1″ X 3″ X 70″
3 pcs. 1″ X 3″ X 17″

4 pcs. ¼″ X 6″ X 6″ plywood for triangular corner braces

HARDWARE

1 pc. 1″ X 1″ X 87″ aluminum "angle-iron"
48   1½″ #8 wood screws
9   3″ #12 wood screws
6   2″ X 2″ metal "L" brackets with screws
24   3″ metal mending plates with screws
2 pcs. 8′ long vinyl baseboard
40   3″ X 3″ metal "L" mending plates (optional, for corner reinforcement)
52   ¾″ #6 wood screws
2 lbs. galvanized 6d box nails
1 pr. 3″ butt hinges (optional, for door)
1 screen door hook (optional, for door)

PLASTIC COVERING AND HARDWARE

Clear, rigid plastic storm window material or plexiglas is the covering material best suited for most climates. Filon or corrugated fiberglass may also be used, but it is translucent and does not allow your neighbors to see into the garden. The putty or caulking compound is needed to seal the edges and allow for some expansion and contraction of the plastic.

Materials needed for covering:

> 2 pcs. 36″ X 36″ plastic (for side panels)
> 10 pcs. 24″ X 36″ plastic (for side panels; 12 pcs. will be needed if door is omitted.)
> 1 pc. 36″ X 48″ plastic (for roof panel)
> 2 pcs. 24″ X 48″ plastic (for roof panel)
> 2 pcs. 34″ X 34″ plastic (for door)
> 1 pc. 15″ X 48″ plastic (see Drawing E)
> putty or caulking compound
> 2 gross galvanized ¾″ #6 round head screws with washers
> 1 pc. 15″ X 50″ aluminum screen

This greenhouse consists of ten wooden frame panels, covered with rigid plastic, and screwed together on a wood foundation. Construction of all panels is exactly the same, only the size changing according to where they are to be used; the roof panels, for example, have an extra 2″ X 2″ on one end for added length. The door panel is optional, since this greenhouse is designed to sit up against, and be entered through, the sliding glass doors leading to your deck or balcony. The door is nice to have, however, as it provides easier access to your plants.

These are the panels you will need to build, as shown in drawing A:

> 5 24″ X 72″ wall panels
> 1 24″ X 72″ door panel
> 1 36″ X 72″ wall panel
> 2 24″ X 48″ roof panels
> 1 36″ X 48″ roof panel

Panels

Optional metal "L" plates strengthen corners
Note: An additional 2″ X 2″ must be nailed to
one end of each of the three roof panels.

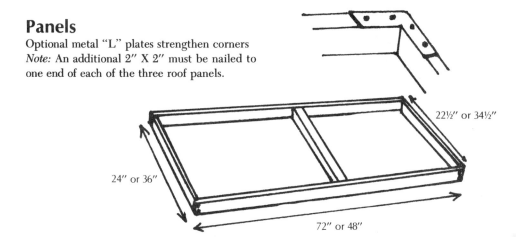

22½″ or 34½″

24″ or 36″

72″ or 48″

Door

Assemble door of 1″ X 3″s laid flat with ¼″ X
6″ plywood corner braces. Use ¾″ #6 wood
screws to hold corner braces. Fit door into
panel; attach hinges and hook.

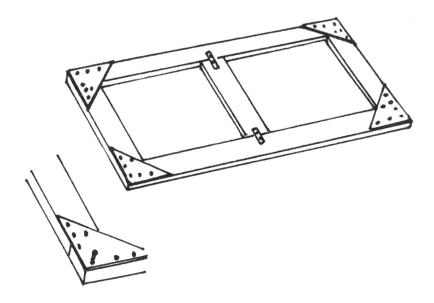

Step Two

Covering the Panels

Drill holes as indicated and screw the plastic sheets gently, not too tight, to each panel. Seal the edges with putty or caulking compound.

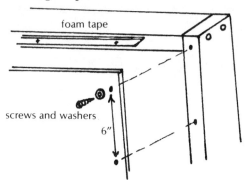

Step Three

The Foundation

The foundation should be built after the panels are assembled. It is simply an 84″ X 51″ frame of 2″ X 4″s, built as it looks in the drawing below. Use a level and framing square to be sure all the joints are square and the upright panels will fit snugly.

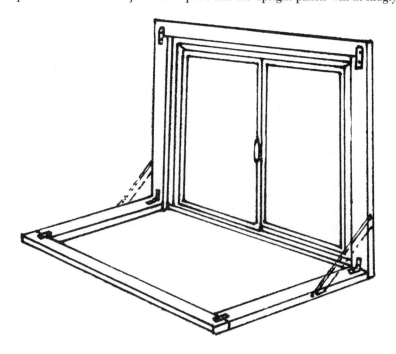

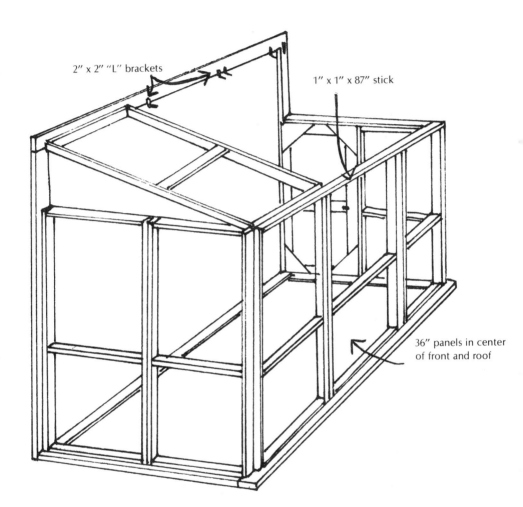

2″ x 2″ "L" brackets

1″ x 1″ x 87″ stick

36″ panels in center
of front and roof

Step Four

Assembly

Next come the wall panels. Set them in place and attach them to the foundation and each other with the 1½″ #8 wood screws as shown. A 3/16″ guide hole and a little wax or soap on the screws will make this job much easier.

Now nail the 1″ X 1″ X 87″ stick to the front edge of the front wall, attach the six 2″ x 2″ "L" brackets to the 2 X 4 above the sliding door, and set the roof panels in place. Secure them above the sliding door with the nine 3″ #12 wood screws.

The panels are shown here without their covering, to give you a better idea of their relative positions.

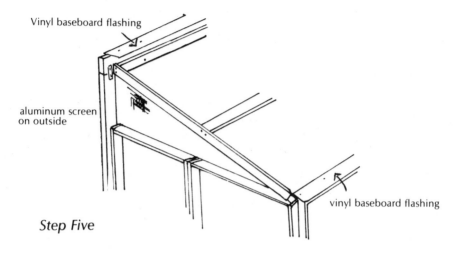

Step Five

Finishing Touches

Add flashing of vinyl base board pieces to back and front of roof.

Cut aluminum screen diagonally to cover the triangular spaces between the roof and walls, and tack or staple it in place.

Cut the 15″ X 48″ piece of plastic diagonally and shape the pieces to fit these same triangular spaces. Attach them to the inside with wooden turnbuttons and screws so you can remove them easily for ventilation (see drawing).

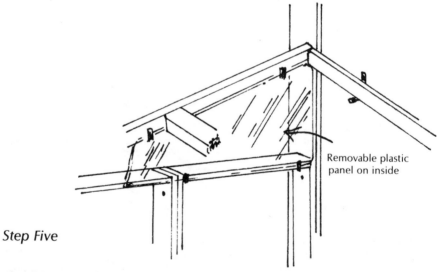

Step Five

Finishing Touches

(inside view)

This inside view of the corner ventilation system shows the plastic strip in place, as described with drawing E. The strip can be removed for ventilation during the summer, replaced for protection from the cold in winter.

Window Greenhouse

The window greenhouse shown here is designed to fit a standard double-hung sash-type or sliding-type window. It is not designed for use with windows which open outward, since these will interfere with the plants. Ventilation at the top is essential; bottom ventilation is optional but highly desirable. Shelves are also optional. Exact dimensions can only be determined by measuring your window.

The window greenhouse is essentially a glass box designed to fit outside your window. The framework of this box may be of metal or of wood, but the framework must be structurally rigid and capable of supporting a great deal of weight. Glass shelves are surprisingly strong and will admit more light to plants in the lower part of the greenhouse. Most glass dealers will cut the glass and set it into framework according to your specifications, or components may be obtained from the greenhouse suppliers listed in the appendix.

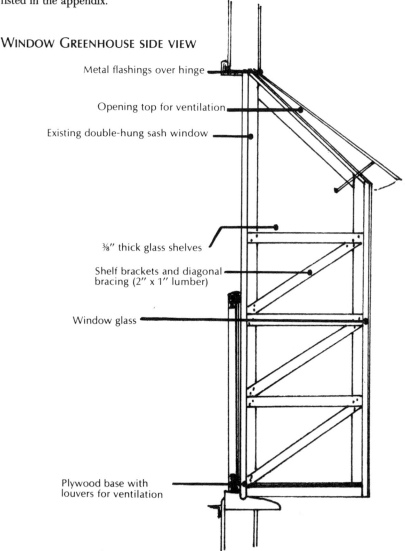

WINDOW GREENHOUSE SIDE VIEW

Metal flashings over hinge

Opening top for ventilation

Existing double-hung sash window

⅜″ thick glass shelves

Shelf brackets and diagonal bracing (2″ x 1″ lumber)

Window glass

Plywood base with louvers for ventilation

WINDOW GREENHOUSE FRONT VIEW

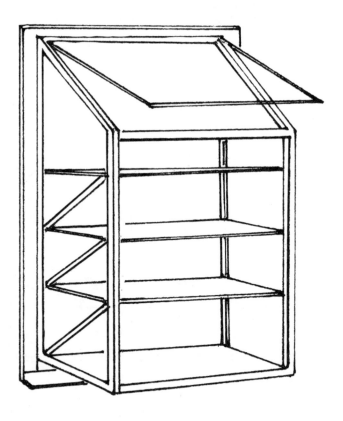

Mail-Order Sources for Gardening Supplies

Companies listed in the appendix supply items needed by the home gardener, and will fill orders by mail. Their catalogs are free.

GREENHOUSE SUPPLIERS

Prefabricated units or components for building according to your own design are available from these suppliers:

Aladdin Industries
P.O. Box 10666
Nashville, TN 37210

Aluminum Greenhouses, Inc.
14615 Lorain Avenue
Cleveland, OH 44111

Feather Hill Industries
Box 41
Zenda, WI 53195

Lord and Burnham
Irvington, NY 10533

National Greenhouse Company
P.O. Box 100
Pana, IL 62557

Texas Greenhouse Company
2717 St. Louis Avenue
Fort Worth, TX 76110

Verandel Company
Box 1568
Worcester, MA 01601

The government offers a free booklet that includes plans for the construction of a variety of home greenhouses. Write to the Consumer Information Center, Dept. 23, Pueblo, Colo., 81008. Request Booklet #569-H, Year-Round Gardening with A Greenhouse.

HORMONE COMPOUNDS AND OTHER GARDEN CHEMICALS; SOIL TESTING KITS

Science Products Company, Inc.
5801 N. Tripp Avenue
Chicago, IL 60646

HYDROPONIC GARDEN UNITS

B & C West Co.
350 Paul Avenue
San Francisco, CA. 94124

LIGHT GARDENING SUPPLIERS

Aladdin Industries, Inc.
P.O. Box 10666
Nashville, TN 37210

Environmental cases for light gardens; bulbs and equipment.

W. Atlee Burpee Company
Westminster, PA 18974

Bulbs and equipment for light gardens.

Craft-House Manufacturing
Company
Wilson, NY 10706

Lighted plant stands.

Environment One
2773 Balltown Road
Schenectady, NY 12309

Fluorescent lighted growth chambers.

Floralite Co.
4124 E. Oakwood Road
Oak Creek, WI 53154

Fluorescent plant stands, fixtures and "plant growth" bulbs.

Garcy Corporation
Spacemaster Home Products Division
2501 N. Elson Avenue
Chicago, IL 60647

Adjustable plant display trays and fluorescent fixtures.

The Green House
9515 Flower Street
Bellflower, CA 90706

Bulbs, stands and fixtures.

Grower's Supply Co.
Box 1132
Ann Arbor, MI 48106

Lighting stands, trays, timers and tubes.

H.L. Hubbell Inc.
Zeeland, MI 49464

"Furniture that grows" in traditional and contemporary styles.

Lifelite
1036 Ashby Avenue
Berkeley, CA 94710

Decorative fluorescent units and light garden supplies.

George W. Park Seed Co. Inc.
Greenwood, SC 29646

Lamps and other equipment.

H. P. Supplies
16337 Wayne Road
Livonia, MI 48154

Fluorescent fixtures, bulbs and tubes.

PLANTS AND SEEDS

Burgess Seed and Plant Company
Box 2000
Galesburg, MI 49053

Offers dwarf fruit trees; vegetables; some herbs; few citrus.

W. Atlee Burpee Company
Clinton, IA 52733 and Riverside, CA 92502

Complete line of vegetables including dwarf, miniature and bush varieties; some herbs; dwarf fruit trees include fig, peach, and all deciduous varieties, but not citrus. Offers coffee, passion fruit, and a few other exotics.

Farmer Seed and Nursery Company
Faribault, MN 55021

Specializes in dwarf citrus trees.

Hilltop Herb Farm
Route 3, Box 216
Cleveland, TX 77327
Complete line of herbs.

George W. Park Seed Company
Greenwood, SC 29647
*Complete line of vegetables including dwarf,
miniature and bush varieties; some herbs; plant
nutrients, growing mediums, etc.; some fruit
trees, but no citrus.*

Four Winds Growers
P.O. Box 3538
Fremont, Ca 94538
*Offers complete line of dwarf citrus trees, plus
kumquats and many other tropical and exotic
plants of interest.*

Sunnybrook Farms
9448 Mayfield Rd.
Chesterland, OH 44026
Herbs and house plants.

PLANTERS

The following associations will, upon request, send plans for constructing your own planters:

The American Plywood Assocation
P.O. Box 2277
Tacoma, WA 98401

The California Redwood Association
1 Lombard Street
San Francisco, CA 94111

INDEX